Women in Storytelling

Proceedings of the University College of Cape Breton's

Third Annual Storytelling Symposium, 1999

Edited by
Afra Kavanagh

University College of Cape Breton Press, Inc.
P.O. Box 5300
Sydney, Nova Scotia
B1P 6L2

The University College of Cape Breton Press acknowledges the support received for its publishing program from the Canada Council's Block Grants Program.

Cover and book design by Gail Jones
Cover painting by Basma Kavanagh, Sydney, Nova Scotia
Printed and bound in Canada by Atlantic Nova / McCurdy Printing, Dartmouth, Nova Scotia.
Edited by Afra Kavanagh

Canadian Cataloguing in Publication data
University College of Cape Breton Storytelling Symposium
(3rd: 1999)
Women in storytelling: proceedings of the University College of Cape Breton Third Annual Storytelling Symposium, 1999

Main entry under title

Women in Storytelling
Includes bibliographical references.
ISBN 0-920336-87-6

1. Storytelling–Congresses. 2. Women and literature–Congresses. I. Kavanagh, Afra, 1945 - II. Title.

LB1042.U67 1999 8093 C00-900582-X

University College of Cape Breton Press, Inc.
P.O. Box 5300
Sydney, Nova Scotia
CANADA, B1P 6L2

Table of Contents

Storytelling within Texts

Preface

Women In/And Storytelling at University College of Cape Breton

The year 1999 seemed like a good time to dedicate the University College of Cape Breton's Third Annual Storytelling Symposium to women in/and storytelling. The call for papers was aimed at folklorists, literary scholars, historians and to those involved in women's studies. The responses came from Spain, England, the United States, and Canada.

Linking women and storytelling seemed natural since there is a historic and traditional connection between them. As mothers, elementary school teachers, or librarians, they have kept stories and the love of stories alive. By lending an ear, women have encouraged storytelling by the young and the old, and their role has expanded so that besides being collectors and scholars, they are now editors and publishers. Also, as festival-organizers, some of us bring together tellers and enthusiasts.

Women then may be said to encourage and control the story to some extent. But the story may also be said to have, at worst, controlled women and, at best, to have encouraged them. We are only now beginning to realize that the portrayal of females in tales and stories has been sometimes limiting, especially when they have been portrayed as victims and sorceresses. But women have also been presented as queens and goddesses, and therefore as having a great deal of power and potential. Wise or foolish, complex or simple, women have not lacked a presence in traditional stories.

At the symposium we collectively wondered about the extent to which women have been manipulators of the stories they told, and it seemed reasonable to look for a parallel between women's ability to control stories, and particularly their story, and an increase in their political power.

The Symposium

Gorgeous weather helped make our gathering memorable. The sun and river, all shine and shimmer, filled our meeting room at the Delta Hotel in downtown Sydney. On Friday evening, we listened to Diane Wolkstein and to Nina Jaffe tell stories about glass mountains and the way meat loves salt; to Justin Lewis describe the sayings of a holy woman, and to Dan Yashinsky tell about a worldly but wise woman. We listened to Eleanor Johnson, professor of Mi'kmaq Studies, tell how the Mi'kmaq got medicine. On Saturday, in addition to the papers in this book, we heard from two Cape Breton writers. Beatrice MacNeil read her short story, "Sancastles," and local broadcaster, Ian MacNeil (no relation to Beatrice) read "A Ferry Tale." After dinner, we were all entertained by Ellouise Shoettler who used handmade quilts as her focal point to tell stories about the lives of some of her women ancestors. Then we heard Father Dan Doucette of Sydney read from his *Parables of Big Pond.*

I am grateful to UCCB's Research Evaluation Committee for a grant that paid for a student assistant, and I thank Melissa Grant for her perseverance and for a job well done. I also thank those who continue to come to the symposium and to support it.

Afra Kavanagh
Editor and Symposium Co-ordinator
February 7, 2000

Introduction

Women and Storytelling

In the introduction to *The Power of the Story*,[1] I treated all manner of stories —myths, folk and fairy tales, fiction, and oral storytelling—as one form, because my thesis was that stories affect us. But of course, despite their similarities, these narratives are different in their origins, their appeal, and their uses. They are also told differently according to a variety of traditions and paradigms, and *by different tellers*. This book is about this last difference.

It is relevant to discuss how we, the tellers, affect the story, and how in our hands the story changes its shape or form, and therefore its impact; also, how we manage to make the story serve our ends, while fully aware that the story sometimes imprisons listeners by its portraiture of our world, and by its pinning down of our roles. This dynamic relationship of reciprocal influence between humans and narrative may be observed in the way different cultures and different eras valorize different stories, or the same stories differently. Our relationship to a story is ever changing as we retell, rewrite or reinterpret it—in other words, assign it personal, historical or mythical truth. And while as different tellers from different societies or times may retain an element from a story they are reworking, such as the plot or the characters, they may also alter another element, such as the setting, the sentiment or the theme, and consequently create a different story, one that they infuse with a context and an energy, and make it their own. This form of appropriation of stories has been identified as part of the maturation process of individuals, groups and nations. As such, storytelling is an act of identity formation and self-definition for tellers who may represent both themselves and their society, race, or gender.

The telling of stories is a performance that calls for personal input, a particular vision or point of view that is an outcome of the teller's history and colours the progress of the narrative. Thus we would assume that a woman telling a story may inhabit it, and populate it differently than would a man, for example. Based on this understanding of the role of the teller, the call for papers for the Third Annual University College of Cape Breton Storytelling Symposium sought papers and presentations that dealt with the role of women in preserving or resurrecting oral storytelling, and which reflected upon the point of view or vision they bring to storytelling. The call for papers also solicited papers that examined the representation of women in oral traditions, especially as tellers or listeners. Ultimately at issue were considerations of whether there is a special relationship between women and storytelling; whether there is a difference between stories told about women and those told about men; whether the effect of these stories on people is benign or malignant; and finally, how women have managed, despite a variety of factors, to make a record of their stories—in journals, diaries, letters, and other types of self-writing that Domna Stanton[2] calls auto-graph, to assert their need to be the heroes in their own story in travel records, autobiographies, and fictionalized autobiographies, and ultimately to get these manuscripts discovered and championed by specialist and mainstream publishers or to create their own vehicles, such as this book.

These were questions that needed to be discussed. That's because, among other reasons, there has been an acknowledgment by scholars of a historical shortage of stories and histories by women even in the canons of many disciplines in which women have been consistently active and productive. Feminist critics have long lamented this, even in the Fourteenth Century, when Chaucer's fictional Wife of Bath complained:

> By God, if women had but written stories
> Like those the clergy keep in oratories,
> More had been written of man's wickedness
> Than all the sons of Adam could redress.
>
> *Canterbury Tales*[3]

She was tired of hearing clerics and others blame women for the fall of man. She hoped that by telling a story that attributes some of the wickedness and blame to the men and that presents the women as saviours, she might distribute the blame differently, and correct that error in attribution. She knew that stories have a historical and sociological function. She desired more stories by women because, obviously, they might create a balance in the way the world and its people were represented, and thus their acts of telling might redress the suppression of women's stories by the patriarchy and its agents who have kept women from literacy and publishing.

This view expressed by the Wife that women should tell and write their own stories is a result of her realization that women are themselves best able to deal with the complexity of their subjectivity and experience. Many today would agree with that assumption, and further suggest that stories chart a scenario of potentiality for both listeners and readers. In a story anything can happen, and people can do anything—fly or travel through time—and once that action has been imagined or "told" it is that much closer to being realized. I cite as an example of this the way science fiction has fuelled the imagination and inventiveness of some practitioners of science. Stories also create an opportunity for people of any gender to imagine themselves in any role. Feminists have been aware of this action-starting and role-modelling value of stories, and that is why some, such as Judith Fetterly,[4] have criticized stereotypical portrayals of women in literary works which do not deal with the complexity of female subjectivity or provide a variety of models. It is also why others, such as Carolyn Heilbrun,[5] have insisted on the need for women to be portrayed as the heroes in stories. Also, women have to tell the stories themselves because then they shape the way it represents them, and thus can use the story as a way to inspire many ways of being a woman.

Women, despite being latecomers to publishing, have always told stories. Within the family and the community and in their traditional professions, they have kept stories alive. Their cultural contribution in that role is immeasurable, and their connection to storytelling remains strong as contemporary women writers explore in a variety of ways—as writers of fiction, as poets and autobiographers, and as narratologists—the role of narrative in our lives, and the impact on our culture of stories and myths, especially as they evolve and change.

This Volume

The papers presented at The Third Annual University College of Cape Breton Storytelling Symposium and contained in this volume are about, among other things, storytelling as an art or a business, about identity formation in young students or in recapturing aboriginality, and about maintaining an Acadian culture beyond La Grande Derangement.

Wendy Welch takes a look in her paper at perceptions of women in storytelling- oral telling by professional storytellers at festivals and other gatherings, and suggests that there are ongoing debates among storytellers about who is telling what. She gathers from her qualitative research that there are ongoing misconceptions about how men and women tell, and how they view their personal input, and their telling performance.

Ona Siporin contributes a goosebump-raising rendition of the tale of Reno's attack on the native Indian settlement at Little Big Horn, and puts a personal and female face on this much told tragic event. Her tale is the more amazing because of its invocation of uncertainty, or the doubtful nature of the facts -"they may tell you..."—and her sensitive introduction of the consciousness of Tashnamani into the retelling of this incident in the history of the formation of American nationhood.

Elizabeth Mood chronicles one young girl's growing awareness of the art of narrating, as well as her growing mastery of it as she tells and retells in the classroom the story of her "grandad." Professor Mood's young narrator also seems to experience an awakening empathy for the subject in her narrative.

Nina Jaffe offers a comprehensive discussion of the use of storytelling as an educational tool. She reviews its importance in teacher education, and focuses on the role of the teacher as teller. She offers the view that experienced teachers can use stories and folktales to open up worlds of expression and literacy for younger children, and can deepen or extend the curriculum for older children.

Moving into a cultural context, we read that Diane Wolkstein sometimes feels a need to change the details in the traditional tales she likes to tell because of her belief that stories reflect us and our changing attitudes. Wolkstein, a respected teller and scholar, sees the princess as a changing metaphor, who, like the rest of us, is always becoming.

Cheryl Bartlett's paper is about the importance of metaphor in a different area—the conceptualization and understanding of science. Professor Bartlett tries to impress on readers how practitioners of science have for too long denied the role of the subjective, of creativity and original thinking in the teaching of science. She finds it useful to speak of humans as "pattern recognition and storytelling" creatures, and insists that we should be mindful of metaphor because it is a cognitive tool in scientific discovery and can influence the configuration of the questions, intuitions and understandings that characterize particular world views.

Mary Flanagan explores how we, in a society that is increasingly dependent on computers and the Internet for entertainment, personal relations, and shopping, have to use interactive narratives and Virtual Reality as a way to record, and participate in the creation of stories. This is particularly important to the sick or bedridden. Her navigable narratives are tools for expression, communication and entertainment.

Emma Zevik provides a new way of looking at fragmented personality. Her paper is revolutionary in introducing an appreciative view of multiple personalities. She calls them person-societies and wonders at the insights we might gain from studying them in the same way as we do world societies. Stories have in the past helped us understand and accept the 'other,' who may be outside us, but Zevik calls upon us to accept the sharding and multiplicity of selves within us.

The topics of the remaining twelve papers range from holy women to mermaids, from the middle ages to the Second World War, and from Canada to Japan and Australia. And for all the women and men who have contributed to this book, stories have a mainly salutary effect on both tellers and listeners, and their new tellings offer us new ways to see and new ways to be.

Endnotes

1. Afra Kavanagh. *The Power of the Story*. Sydney, Nova Scotia: UCCB Press, 1998.
2. Domna Stanton, ed. *The Female Autograph: Theory and Practice of Autobiography from the Tenth to the Twentieth Century*. Chicago: University of Chicago Press, 1987.
3. Geoffrey Chaucer. *The Canterbury Tales*. Trans. Neville Goghill. Middlesex: Penguin Books, 1977. P. 295.
4. Judith Fetterly. "Introduction: on the Politics of Literature," *Feminisms: An Anthology of Literary Theory and Criticism.* Eds. Robyn R. Warhol and Diane P. Herndl. New Brunswick, New Jersey: Rutgers University Press, 1991. 492-501.
5. Carolyn Heilbrun. "The Woman as Hero." *Towards a Recognition of Androgyny*. New York: Harper and Row-Colophon, 1973.

Perceptions of Inequality: Women in the Art and Business of Storytelling

Wendy Welch

Women in storytelling make up between a third and two thirds of the telling force in any given Western country. In North America, female tellers are commonly held to outnumber males, while in the United Kingdom the reverse is generally considered true, but a quick perusal of the various national directories shows this is not necessarily the case. When you actually count the number of male and female tellers in these countries, you wind up with the figures shown in Table 1. While the storytellers who choose to advertise in these directories are certainly not all the tellers to be found in these countries, they are likely to be the majority of those who have chosen to market themselves as professionals.

TABLE 1

DIRECTORY	MALE	FEMALE
USA (purchase)	295	176
CANADA (purchase)	26	60
AUSTRALIA (free on-line)	40	83
ENGLAND (purchase)	101	69
SCOTLAND (invitation only)	25	21

Women tellers are not the majority in the National Storytelling Membership Association's directory, the dominant American publication. Why, then, are they thought to be in the majority? Communicating through email, a storytelling chat group to be introduced later, and face-to-face interviews, many storytellers responded to my questions about this. Most thought this discrepancy stemmed from the educational roots and uses of American storytelling, the legacy of the National Story League, and the continuing association of storytelling with teachers and librarians. In fact, many women felt that modern storytellers in the United States were trying to "outrun" the librarian legacy. Canada, however, is a different story and will be discussed shortly.

Outrunning the Librarians

Storytelling's current renaissance owes much to the turn-of-the-century revival among educators, most of them women. The National Story League began in 1903 as the National Storyteller's League, founded by a teacher in Knoxville, Tennessee. According to Anne Pellowski in The World of Storytelling:

> Its purposes were to encourage the art of storytelling and the use of classic and folklore stories in schools and education centers; to foster creative work in the arranging and re-writing of stories from various classic and historic sources; to serve as a medium of exchange of stories and experiences in the use of story; to discover in the world's literature, in history and in life the best stories for education and to tell them with love and sympathy for the children and to bring together in story circles those who love to hear and tell a good story. (Story Hour 1, 1908, 38)

Members were "not only educators but also librarians, kindergarten teachers, playground workers, and ordinary interested people." The name changed in 1923 to National Story League "to encourage appreciation of the good and the beautiful in literature through the art of storytelling." Meanwhile, French-born educator Marie Shedlock entered the world of storytelling around 1904. Anne Carroll Moore, director of the New York Public Library Children's Services, heard Shedlock telling Hans Christian Anderson stories in the city and brought her to the library in 1906. This initial storytime program developed and thrived, becoming a regular rather than a special event. Moore's successor Anna Cogswell Tyler became the first supervisor of storytelling in the New York Public Library. As this program made its influence felt, storytelling schools opened across the country, most notably the Training School for Children's Librarians in Pittsburgh, which opened in the 1930s. The New York Library women had a strong impact on the world of storytelling, one that continues unbroken from the 1930s to today. Respected modern tellers such as Ellin

Greene, Augusta Baker, and Diane Wolkstein are associated with the tradition of excellence expected from this New York program.

But the important point here is that the National Story League and the New York Public Library were gyno-staffed organizations. American storyteller Laura Simms commented:

> I do think in the '30s the bulk of librarian storytellers were women in the States. In fact, I don't ever recall hearing of a single male. The tradition of the library storytelling was based on the idea of increasing reading and the story being told in a way of bringing the text alive, rather than our view now of bringing story off the page into the life of the listener. It had little to do with the storytelling that was occurring in the South. (private email)

Throughout the 1940s and 1950s storytelling continued institutionally through efforts of women like Mary Gould Davis (who succeeded Anna Tyler) and Frances Clarke Sayers, an academic who published the renowned work *Summoned By Books*. The future patron saint of modern storytelling, Ruth Sawyer, began what was to become the defining work of her life. One could refer to these librarians and upper-middle-class women as the monks (or would that be nuns?) who kept storytelling alive as television hit the mainstream in the post-war culture. Ruth Sawyer in North America and Eileen Colwell, 20 years later in the United Kingdom, lamented and warned against the effects of television on children's imaginative capacities. They begged for storytelling to continue in time-honoured tradition at home and in the newer tradition at the library. And as television's crippling effect hit the libraries, participation plummeted. Yet the storytime sessions continued, infused with very little new blood and beginning to suffer the side effects of the '60s pendulum swings into feminism, equality, and the fierce new doctrine of individualism, as well as the beginnings of what would become known as multiculturalism. While the impact of these philosophies on traditional storytime programs is beyond this paper's subject matter, the thinking reader can quickly see how certain effects would manifest themselves. Still, the librarians kept telling and reading as the times, they kept a'changing. A new breed of storyteller was coming. In Jonesboro, Tennessee the National Association for the Preservation and Perpetuation of Storytelling was born in 1972. For about ten years it clipped along at its own pace, putting respectably on stage a house-bound and institutional art form–in an increasingly effective festival. In fact, NAPPS did its work so well that the annual festival it organized, known in the United States as "the National," became a drawing point for people who, until its organization, had not known what to call themselves. Professional teller Heather Forest said, "Until I heard about Jonesboro, I didn't know what to call myself.... When I got there, there were people like me. And they had a name: professional tellers. I felt I had come home" (personal interview).

By 1982, storytelling was experiencing The Great Boom years as participants came from every possible background—theatre, education, no prior experience, television, to name a few—to join the ranks of professional tellers. Things became so crowded that the 1985 National Storytelling Conference earned the sardonic nickname "blood on the porch," referring to the hordes of storytellers attempting to tell a story on the traditionally low-key swapping ground stage (Storyteller Dan Keding, personal interview). Ironically, as storytelling boomed, it also attempted to change its image. Storytellers who had been on the scene since the 1970s were now recognized as both pioneers and stars, and their performances before largely adult crowds in Jonesboro sparked new ambitions in practitioners of the art form; the war cry became "it isn't just for kids anymore." As the pendulum swung, librarians became something of a target for the type of storytelling associated with stale, dry, talentless performances in institutions. Nationally-known teller Milbre Burch, writing in *Storytelling World* in 1996, said:

> Some Not-So-Popular Realities
>
> 1. Storytelling has a bad rap in the modern world....
>
> This news just in: The word storytelling has a bad rap in America, except when invoked with poetic license to describe the craft of a filmmaker or novelist. Otherwise, it seems to call to mind the image of a musty librarian reading from a book to a group of two-year-olds. Storytelling is popularly associated with babysitting. This PR problem can get you coming and going. If your work as a storyteller is aimed at adults, no one will believe you. And if you are dedicated to your work as a children's performer, some people may wonder why you can't make it in the real world (18-19).

By the time of Burch's writing, NAPPS had already changed its name to the National Storytelling Association, distancing itself from images of bedtime tellings and sleepy stories. Storytelling, as it surged forward in its renaissance form, was definitely not for children anymore. But within the United States, many tellers disagree with this pendulum swing away from storytelling's library past. They remind tellers that it is not the roll call of those who performed at Jonesboro between 1972 and 1982 who are the pioneers, but the librarians who nursed the flickering flame of oral narrative from 1906 to 1972. Ironically, in many cases, those who told at Jonesboro in its inception were librarians.

Veteran storytellers Elizabeth Ellis and Gayle Ross were librarians; Jackie Torrence was a librarian; Connie Regan-Blake and Barbara Freeman, known as the Folktellers, were librarians.

And about 100 of the 500 members of the Internet chat group STORYTELL are librarians or educators. Suzie Schaeffer, STORYTELL member, has some definite opinions on this subject:

> Having come to storytelling as a librarian and being a teller who works with children more than adults, and very young children most of the time—there are times when I feel as if what I'm doing isn't considered 'real' storytelling by some (much? Most?) of the current storytelling world. Yet without those librarian tellers and other tellers to children, there wouldn't have been enough left of telling to have a renaissance when it came.

Susanna Holstein, a STORYTELL member researching library storytelling for a grant application, agrees:

> I am still working on this, and still waiting for a few interlibrary loans to come in. I'd be glad to send you the list of resources I'm using and a copy of my article too when I'm finished. What I have learned so far is that storytelling has a long history in US libraries, dating back to the very first children's departments. In fact, in many of the books/articles I'm reading, they say that libraries kept storytelling alive during a time when storytelling was dying out in communities and homes, replaced by radio, TV, and movies.

Perceptions of Inequality

Schaeffer is just one of the many members of STORYTELL who had strong thoughts on the subject of male and female tellers. STORYTELL is a chat group of about 500 storytelling enthusiasts and practitioners; its subject matter ranges from jokes to advice, technique, and everyday life concerns. Although the list is international, the great majority of members (perhaps 90 percent) are American. Thus, their perceptions as a group were of interest to me in attempting to find out, not so much what was the reality of American and Canadian storytelling, but what was the perception of reality.

Members of STORYTELL were eager to share their thoughts. One opinion held by the majority was the afore-mentioned, that there were more female tellers than male in the United States. When I posted the actual tally of tellers in the national directory showing a male-female ratio of 3:2 and asked why this belied the perception, STORYTELLers had definite thoughts. Many women on the list agreed with list member and internationally-renowned teller Heather Forest that it is because women choose not to market as aggressively: "Men seem to have glossier brochures and tend to ask for a higher fee. I like how (national teller) Elizabeth Ellis puts it... she says that 'I want to be paid the same as your highest paid male performer'." Priscilla Howe, a STORYTELL member and teller who works regionally in the United States, commented:

> Men will not hesitate to offer a workshop or seminar for a fee without ever having done it before, while women are more likely to offer it for free a couple of times to test it out.... Men do seem to hesitate less about their fees. When I look at the program for the NSF every year, I notice that there are usually quite a few men, despite the fact that there are more women storytellers than men in the country.

A white female storyteller from the American southwest took this one step farther:

> I believe there is a discrepancy in the hiring of males and females, but I suspect it has less to do with gender than with race, except in the festival venues. There is this PC perception that having a balanced program means having one of each race and an equal number of each gender. Consequently if you are young or old, male, Jewish, black, Hispanic, oriental, etc. regardless of gender, you have a better chance of being hired by festivals—As a white woman of a certain age I feel this very strongly—in fact when we were putting together the conference concert for NSA last year we were told as much re: representation—we did break some of the guidelines with three white women tellers out of a total of seven tellers. This was strictly artistic based on complementary styles and it was received as one of the best conference concerts ever. I find this trend a challenge as it limits my opportunities as a white woman teller, even though we make up the demographic majority, There is greater pressure on us to find additional things to do such as sing, dance, etc. to give us a niche. In addition, it dismisses the cultural value of our heritage—it being no less wrong to group all European-Americans together than all Africans (My background happens to be predominantly Swed-

> ish and Polish—both areas with rich storytelling traditions). These are the facts, and I'm not pleased by it. It might be easier for women to get hired into schools, but I've heard that men get paid more—maybe because they ask for it, maybe because it is assumed that they're supporting families. Because I came from a strong business background, I've never had trouble asking to be paid or quoting a price. My rates are a lot less than others, but it has more to do with regional economics than perceived self-worth or quality of programming. I am fortunate to have no competition in my market and have enjoyed the luxury of being booked well in advance (6 months or more). I figure I get booked into schools because that is my background—I speak the language and my programs are directly pertinent to the needs of the educators that sponsor me. With pressure on test scores, etc. this is more frequently true for school market bookings—could be that women are more easily booked into schools than men because more often school environments are where they came to storytelling—many female tellers are former teachers and school librarians.

This posting met with silence. STORYTELL members seemed decidedly uncomfortable discussing such topics; the "R" word stymies all honest talk. I have encountered similar resistance in private interviews with various tellers, with one notable exception. A female storyteller who had been offered a coveted booking at the National Storytelling Festival in Jonesboro, Tennessee, recalled how fellow storytellers told her she had been invited because she was black. "Don't they know how much that hurts?" she asked with anger evident in her voice. "I am a good storyteller; I am not somebody's quota."

"Papa Joe," a teller working nationally, ignored the comments on issues of race, and took issue with another idea: he thought the discrepancies had less to do with gender than personality:

"There are differences in the marketing strategies of tellers, whatever the gender. I probably do more work and get less money than just about any other pro teller in the USA. I seem to have strong appeal as a male. My contacts claim it is because there are so few men in the early childhood fields." However, although no one posted a direct response to Papa Joe's experience, no women supported his assertion that personality is more important than gender. Many who were teachers or librarians indicated that they used this fact to advantage in booking inservices or school performances, but found it embarrassing when dealing with festival coordinators. "Oh another one, you can almost hear them thinking it on the phone," said one white female who quit her teaching job to tell full-time.

Yet, although this was a common complaint among American tellers, it was not among Canadians. Tonya Coulter, a part-time teller who coordinated the Yukon Storytelling Festival in Whitehorse, said in an interview that about two-thirds of the eighty storytellers normally booked for this week-long event were female. In Canada's national storytelling directory, the predominant number of marketed tellers are women. Women are also the driving force behind Storytellers of Canada, holding most of the offices on its board and many of the offices associated with its publication, *Appleseed Quarterly*.

One reason for this difference along the 49th parallel was the association of storytelling with writer's groups in Toronto, an area which dominates much of Canada's storytelling movement. The Toronto School of Storytelling has long been appreciative of, even in some ways derived from, writing organizations which have been largely female in their population. Mumbi Jonson, a writer and publisher from Toronto, expressed this in a brief interview: "I think women in Canadian storytelling have felt comfortable because they have been so welcomed and supported in the writer's associations. We never had to move in; we were always there."

American women telling stories could envy their northern counterparts, for they definitely feel discriminated against in certain situations. However, this cuts both ways, as they also feel being female is an advantage to certain booking situations. This in itself is a double-edged sword, as the places where women book more quickly are those associated with children, libraries, and educational venues. The consensus was that women book more quickly in schools, but more slowly in festivals. Beyond this, women had little to say, although some of the men on STORYTELL began to send thoughtful posts.

This leads to another, rather unexpected, area of perceptual inequality among male and female storytellers: male-bashing. As various men posted comments, very quietly, often with bids for humor, they began to express that they felt battered, put down. Stephen Hollen, an Appalachian teller, said:

> I do believe there is open season on men often on television, especially. Perhaps as retribution for many years of men lording over women. However, we are not two-dimensional characters, always making a mistake to be corrected by the all-knowing wife. Being able to poke fun should be equally distributed.

But women on the list had little sympathy for perceptions of male-bashing. In particular, when the fictitious petition regarding women's rights in Afghanistan was posted, one male list member (who stayed home with his daughter while his wife worked) responded with a comment that quickly drew fire. He claimed it was actually imperialism couched as women's rights to sign such a petition. He also suggested that women entering the work force in America had ruined the family structure, and thus the future of the country, as staying home with the children had become denigrated as a profession for either parent. As a house husband, he felt he was discriminated against and the victim of male-bashing on a daily basis:

> The house husband thing was a direct effect of my wife finding work! It was re-enforced by interest in preserving the family. There is, at this time, substantial pressure upon me to work full time. I am resisting this negative force which comes from neighbors and family and friends to be a parent at home and available to my daughter. Most people look down upon a man who does not seek full time employment. Being a house husband has been interesting. Women in the neighborhood who are at home exclude you and do not stop in to talk. Let alone drop in for a beer! Being seen with a man who is not your husband is a big deal herein Simpsonized suburbia in Baltimore. It is what folks would call a blue collar neighborhood (I prefer to use the term Simpsonized as tee shirts with rude slogans do not have any collars). When they do talk, it is of women's issues and I feel I have to back away from these private discussions held in public. Women are reluctant to let a male take their children on an outing. Girl Scout leaders will not ask men to volunteer or become involved. This is what letting women go to work has done to the culture of men. I do not find being a house husband hard. Most of the jobs I have worked have been much more demanding. But...house wives have more actual practical rights and inclusion than house husbands—at least around here.

These comments did not go over well. Many women, while sympathetic to the feeling of isolation this person expressed, were unimpressed by his assertions about female and male culture. Likewise, another male teller's assertion that too many programs were geared specifically toward women using federal funding, met with sharp resistance. Illinois teller Janice Del Negro sent a terse email stating that these programs were "so much smoke and mirrors." And when a few other men went public with their thoughts on male-bashing, they found little sympathy for their perceptions. Priscilla Howe offered this personal experience:

> I once gave a performance which included a number of strong women stories, and heard in a roundabout way that one of the listeners felt I was disparaging men. I thought back on my story list for the night and didn't agree. I don't remember if it was a man or woman complaining. I wondered if maybe my appearance and attitude prompted the criticism—I have very short hair, dress fairly androgynously, and am not afraid to express liberal views, so people have sometimes mistakenly assumed I'm a lesbian...,There are times I want to say, "look, I just happen to like short hair and comfortable clothes—this has nothing to do with my sexuality." Last summer I was at a party for the anniversary of a couple of women, and a guy actually said to me and the friend I was talking to, "Oh, you're wearing Birkenstocks, you must be lesbians..."

Women as Story Rather than Storytellers?

The subject of male-bashing will be debated ad infinitum wherever women's rights are brought up as a topic of discussion; the reactions of the STORYTELL men to my research questions aimed specifically toward women made that clear. (One man offered to dress in drag so he could participate.) But when I left STORYTELL to wade through the Audio Library of East Tennessee State University and the holdings of the National Storytelling Association in Jonesboro, I found an interesting observation: men who feel bashed by strong women storytellers are quite cheerfully telling stories about women—in most cases, strong women.

Women are indisputably the protagonists in a surprising number of stories, as Table 2 demonstrates. I took my findings back to STORYTELL, where ironically, a rousing discussion of Tam Lin was in full swing. A number of women wrote about "passive heroines" not being real heroines, casting Janet (the ballad's female lead) as an "I just want to get married" victim of a rape; others saw her as an assertive woman who set out to get what she wanted. What became rapidly clear, as this thread flowed (with a bit of gentle urging) into a discussion of which gender of teller told stories of female heroes, was that storytellers are hypersensitive to the issue of feminism and femininity in stories. The awareness that a paid performer owes the audience something they are going to like ran high in comments people made about telling "women's stories." It is possible to divide the responses into three broad categories: ignore the issue; look for stories with strong women; and change stories of passive women into strong ones. In addition, there were a very limited

TABLE 2

Type of story	Male protagonist	Female protagonist
Ballads	20	13
Jewish f'tale	49	23
Japanese	15	9
French/Cajun	11	7
Celtic Old World	67	15
First Nations	37	16
African (O/N world)	31	20
Strong/Clever	13	35
Foolish/Stupid	16	—
Urban legends	10	5
US Regional	28	13
Ghost	93	63
Western	68	5
Literary	35	13
Original to teller	81	37
General fairytale	523	350
Personal	118	53
Holiday	12	2
Biblical	19	13

few who declared it was not an issue. These people avowed that they told what they wanted to tell, and if the woman were passive, so be it.

Here's what Rick Carson, a regional teller from Kentucky, had to say:

> I don't believe it is necessary to change weak women into strong women in old folktales, since there are numerous folktales with strong women already in them. Ideally what I think we should be doing is presenting balanced programs. If you do a story that shows the weakness of women follow it up with one that shows strength. Because truth be known just like the male of the species there are strong, weak, smart, dumb, evil, good, pretty, ugly, etc. etc...females. We need to show there is room for all of them as well.

However, this attitude was not prevalent. Most storytellers were extremely sensitive to the issue of female heroes. It was only how they dealt with them that differed. There were some whose definition of tradition made them uncomfortable with alterations of characters; they looked for ready-made heroes. Internationally-renowned teller and musician David Holt was one of these:

> I mainly just look for a good story. If it has a strong woman in it...great. That is not so easy to find in traditional tales. A lot of the urban legends have women in them as the main character. The Hairywoman [a character appearing on one of his tapes] is certainly one hell of a gal. Eva Hart and her mother are main characters in the Titanic story. In Why Rabbit Never Plays the Banjo...the fox is a very self-confident woman. In The Blood Drawing Ghost (from Mostly Ghostly tape) the main character is a very strong and brave young woman. In The Jealous Bones of Aaron Kelly, Lilly is a very clever protagonist. I like to see a story with a strong female character. I want young girls to have some feeling that they can take charge. It comes from having a daughter. (private email)

Heather Forest specifically asserted that she looked for stories with men who showed sensitivity to feelings, like the Peddler of Swaffham. American storyteller Doug Lipman's tape "Milk from the Bull's Horn" was another example of looking within existing tales to find male characters that belie stereotypes. Then there were those who reworked their stories. Both male and female tellers said they changed stories to make female characters more assertive, although women did this far more often than men. There was also an interesting sideline: while women changed stories because they wanted to promote the image of women as strong and self-governing, men changed them at least in part because of economics. One Midwest male teller—the same one who had denigrated federal funding for women's programs—said he had worked up a single mom story specifically for female audiences. This was an economic decision; in order to continue storytelling among female-dominated groups such as librarian conventions and educational functions, this teller felt he needed a story with a particularly feminine appeal. His economic savvy was echoed in the stories recorded for sale in the United States. Notice the strong/clever and the foolish/stupid section of Table 2. STORYTELLers agreed it was "very un-PC" to tell stories about stupid or weak women. In fact, except where the women were simply an accepted part of the traditional canon of folktales or revival circuit stories, there were no men who said they told stories that had "stupid or passive" women in them. The question itself started a rather heated discussion of Sleeping Beauty on STORYTELL. Several women complained that this was in essence not a story that could be salvaged, its heroine being so incredibly passive that she slept through her own rape. Hearing that in some of the older versions, the girl fled to the woods to protect her children from an ogress, Margaret Sheehan of Illinois posted this:

> Well, all I can say is that it's about time she did something. She's about the most passive character in fairyland. About the only thing she gets to do is cry tears onto the Prince's eyes. BIG DEAL! I've got a re-working where she does make something of herself, but I think I'll look up this version & save it for Mother's Day.

But others found reframing the story valuable, pointing out that she kept her family together in the face of opposition, and that her options were so limited in her situation that she had done the best she could. Janice Del Negro, a well-known storyteller from Illinois, commented, "Sometimes passivity is the path of least resistance and the right way to go—what do you do then?"

Reframing/Reworking

If you are a storyteller, you generally look for a way to reframe or rework your story. Reframing has become a powerful tool in the arsenal of many storytellers dealing with images of women. It allows the person to alter in their own minds the meanings and associations of the various actions involved in the story, so that what looks like passivity may, in the end, become heroic action. Kay Stone analysed her own response to her favorite folktale: Mother Holle. At a panel sponsored by the Storytelling section of the American Folklore Society, Stone said that she found herself drawn to this story because she felt she was the curious little girl. Her own parents had constantly warned her of the perils of too much desire to know, but Kay had spent her life pursuing knowledge. She justified making the story empowering when it had been considered cautionary with one casual sentence, spoken with a great smile, "Burning brightly is no bad thing." Leslie Snape, a journalist and storyteller from Oregon, commented: "In my own telling, I don't like to tamper with the characters, so I don't change things to make passive women stronger. I believe that there are many kinds of strengths, and being assertive is only one way of being strong. I've always believed that 'beauty' in these tales is not the glamour kind, but the kind that anyone who is good, kind, wise, patient, understanding, curious and filled with wonder possesses."

Reframing can also be seen in a feminist interpretation of male actions, as a STORYTELL member said during her thread discussing the Biblical story of Lot:

> It seems easy to pass this thread off as current-day feminists doing more male bashing. I cannot accept that. I believe it

> has a deeper meaning for storytellers to consider.... Storytellers need to climb inside the skins of the characters, walk around in the setting. What is human nature now? Men want sex. (generalization!) What was human nature then? Men wanted sex. Is it beyond credibility that Lot forced himself on his daughters? No. So, do we deny this in our assessment or factor it into our thinking? There is also the matter of Zoar, the city to which Lot fled from Sodom. It is stated that Lot was afraid to stay in Zoar and moved up to a cave. So be it. But they knew the people of Zoar were there. Now, why the statement that there were no other men available? Wrong religion? Wrong age? No husband material? Wrong politics? Things to ponder.

STORYTELL members had many things to ponder, in fact, including an underlying discomfort with overt feministic actions. Moira Cameron, a Yukon ballad singer, posted this: "I tend to sing ballads more than tell stories, but I have dealt with these same questions when learning and performing a ballad. Often times I will put existing lyrics into a feminist framework, without changing the lyrics overtly. I like singing about all aspects of female strength, from obvious accounts of heroism to less clear songs of the hidden strengths of women as victims." Underlying messages in many emails said, in essence, "We don't want to HAVE to change things to be feminists." That seems to be a prevalent concern for many women, and reframing tends to be their chosen method. Janice Del Negro, who said she often reframed traditional stories to find the hidden strengths of the women portrayed, also had scathing comments for feminist storybooks: "This is what drives me crazy about collections of 'feminist folk and fairy tales'—they are always retelling Disney and thinking that that is all folk and fairy tales are. It is *so* irritating. And it makes me very cranky." Yet, when confronted with ballad scholarship that supported the idea that Janet, in Tam Lin, had been a rape victim rather than an aggressive woman, Del Negro switched gears: "So here's where we depart from past tradition re: women and their roles and create a tradition of our own." Del Negro is not the only storyteller willing to move back and forth between reframing and reworking. Reworking was the more common approach overall. Priscilla Howe rewrote Beauty and the Beast to reflect her values and promote what she considered a healthier image of relationships (Beauty becomes a beast). Heather Forest presented another reworked version on her tape "The Eye of the Beholder," which involved stories concerned with perceptions of reality. Women tend to make these changes when they believe a story reflects perhaps unintentional but still unchallenged ideas of femininity

(Tam Lin, e.g.). Howe and Forest were reacting to the idea that the prince had to change into something handsome before the female ingenue could love him, an idea they considered unfavorable to women. An example of a conscious male reworking of a passive heroine is found in Pious Power, a local storyteller in Newfoundland. Power, who is not a STORYTELL member, was recorded by his daughter-in-law Anita Best in the early 1980s, changing Cinderella for his five-year-old granddaughter. When he asked his young audience of one what happened next after the glass slipper fitting, the girl said the Prince married her. He said, "No, he asked her but she said she had some things she wanted to do first." And she went off and had adventures and settled someplace else. Power's change, Best wrote in an unpublished paper, came as a result of wanting his granddaughter to have more to think about than the expected role of marriage. The STORYTELLers reworked from a variety of motives-increased acceptability, resulting in increased economic possibilities; a desire to offer a broader range of portrayals of stereotyped gender roles; a hope that by showing their own creative abilities with traditional material, they could stand out in their artistic field, to name a few.

Where will it Lead?

Whether the women are passive or not, storytellers are becoming increasingly hyper-aware of their stories' content in the context of a modern society (not just gender—marked and unmarked categories); rather than recreating the past, they are actively engaged in packaging them for present-day consumption. This is sometimes a marketing decision, sometimes a personal one. In fact, the place where images of women as storytellers and as objects of storytelling show up most is in personal tales. Table 3 contains some examples.

There are interesting conclusions to be drawn here. One is that more males than women are telling personal stories, and these men often tell about women who influenced them. When women appear in story tapes by male tellers, they can be almost deified. John McLaughlin and Dan Keding are but two examples of this. McLaughlin, on a tape entitled "First Kiss" tells a 25-minute story of his cousin, who died of cancer, and who was his closest childhood friend. Keding, on his tape "South Side Stories," tells a story of a neighbor woman who is so quiet, no one ever hears her, until the day she shouts at a policeman who has come to arrest her son. This deification could have many origins; the point of this paper is not to explore those, enticing though they may be, but rather to point out the perceptions of women that exist within them. And by far the prevailing perception of women in personal tales is deification.

TABLE 3

MALE AND FEMALE PROTAGONISTS IN 143 PERSONAL STORIES

RELATIVE TOLD ABOUT	MALE TELLER	FEMALE TELLER
Grandpa	3	7
Grandma	3	10
Self	25	19
Mom	1	8
Female Relative	2	4
Male Relative	10	3
Friends/Neighbours	21	4
Dad	2	3
Teachers	6	4
Children	4	1
Spouse/Lover	2	1
Pet	3	–

Turning from women as the objects of stories to women as storytellers, there is another interesting trend just hoving into view on the horizon. The two tales by male tellers involving spouses and lovers were deification stories. The single story told by a woman was a spurned lover tale. When I asked on STORYTELL why women told "he done me wrong" tales but men didn't, an interesting thread began. Stephen Hollen sent this response:

> Wendy, I would love to tell stories about the women in my life...and I do tell some about my two great aunts, and life in an old log cabin. However when it comes to disastrous love stories, I just don't want to sleep on the couch. My wife might not appreciate them. I have this sign I bought her..."when mamma ain't happy, AIN'T NOBODY HAPPY" I have had some crazy women in my life at times, mother, sister-in-law, my Grandma who believed President Reagan himself was going to take her monthly pension away. But discretion is the better part of being a husband. And besides, when a woman beats on a man in storytelling, we are just big lugs who can take it. I have a story about a man named Jimmer Gray, lived in Kentucky in the early 1900s. He called his wife

> "doughbeater," or "the old doughbeater" TRUE STORY. I mentioned that as I was telling and this countryboy just about got whupped by some very angry ladies afterward. It is a great story, but hard to tell when I can't quote Jimmer Gray saying, "Doughbeater, go git my shotgun" (he really did call her that. No one in my family knows her real name. When he was feeling nice he just called her "old woman") Anyway, I suspect we may be afraid of suffering the wrath of the women in our audience.

This response came quickly back from Catherine Conant:

> I offer the following observation: The way I read Wendy's request for stories, it was more a challenge to provide or share stories that offer the wisdom, pain and joy of loving and/or losing the love of someone special. I can't imagine too many people being so innocent as to think we are only allowed one relationship in life, that being with our current spouse. Frankly I think I'm hearing a faint echo of some "Well, I'd tell the truth, but the old battle-ax would clean my clock." (Heavens! Is that a rolling pin I see behind her back?) The image of a furious woman, angry because her faults/shortcomings or previous rivals have been revealed could almost be called a stereotype. The freight the story carries might be what evokes a bad reaction. Is the story's core to ridicule or humiliate? If there are thoughtful stories, constructed with some kind of insight, humor or balance, then that's what we need to hear. I for one believe there are loving, funny and marvelous stories about the person you almost married but didn't, the breakup that in hindsight was a blessing or the person you loved who didn't love you back. Be it male or female, nobody likes to be thought of as a vaudeville character.

Stephen's public response to Catherine, via STORYTELL, was:

> Hmmm. Something to think about, but I daresay if I ask my guy friends, they too would hesitate before they would talk freely about the bittersweet memories of an old love. I did exactly that once in a relationship. I told of the one woman who I never really dated, who I grew up with. Who I knew like the back of my hand....She once said as we drove through the country with friends, "you know, I think Steve is someone I could live with and be happy for the rest of my life." OK, so

> I was young and stupid. I didn't get the hint. I can look back over 23 years and still see the sun in her hair, blowing in the hot Kentucky summer. I made the mistake of telling a lady I cared about this vein of thought. We were sharing one of those deep moments. I really opened up and let it flow from my memory. It was an important moment for me. I thought I had really met someone who I could share everything with. Then she broke up with me, Catherine. Said she couldn't compete with the ghost of a summer in 1975. Now, I have told that to my best friend...he has a similar experience he shared with me. BUT, that's the kind of thing best told in sweat lodges or around a campfire with hunting buddies. Because we do tend to put our mammas and women we care about on a pedestal. My wife is loving and definitely not one to hold a rolling pin over me. (I do all the cooking, so it's my rolling pin) But I do know that she loves me dearly. I just plain old won't go into feelings that might make her think I have regrets, because I don't. Never have, never will. And when I tell a story, even when ornery, I tell it with love for the people choose to remember. Jimmer Gray's wife, who he called "doughbeater" was loved by him. They were real people and she cared for him till the day he died...and he still called her "old woman" as he told her he was gonna miss her.

Thanks, Catherine for making me cogitate.
(putting my soapbox back under my desk)
I am done now.

Stephen then sent this email to me, and I include it here because it refers back to the male-bashing discussion held earlier:

> Wendy, I hope you read the thoughts I sent to Catherine. It made me think and realize men do tell stories about women. Very personal deeply felt stories. Stories of conquest, of angry breakups, of the best sex ever (pardon me, but it is true). We do tell of the lost loves and how glad we are that we didn't marry the crazy one. We relive the fights with spouses and the goofy things our mamma did. BUT, we only tell these things to each other. It is a guy thing I guess, but as I thought about it, I realized that I did tell a lot to guys, but seldom to women. And not to just guys, but to those few who enter our inner circle. Men are so competitive, we don't let our guard down often to others and then to those we can trust with our

deepest stories. And the story I shared with Catherine is my favorite to share with a pal.

The genie is out of the bottle; storytelling as an organic movement is now doing the corrective pendulum swings social scientists love to talk about, vibrating between frigid political correctness, and loud protestations that to change a story is the anathema altering of tradition. Currently we are on the super-sensitive swing toward political correctness, honouring women when we portray them. But as women continue to grow comfortable with their status in society, and as men become increasingly uncomfortable with aggressive humour or the perception of agendas targeting them, the emergent patterns will continue to be interesting insights into societal psyches. The current movement of feminism among storytellers in Canada and the United States seems to be from "Women's Rights" to "Equal Rights," which is somewhat different. Equality includes depictions of the less-than-perfect aspects of women. Perhaps these stories will influence the deities currently recorded tales in the American and Canadian mainstream. Perhaps female storytellers will begin to receive the respect that women as objects of story already receive. One thing is certain: the issue will not go away. Be it economic issues, a desire to stand out in one's own work, or a sincere conviction that men or women are not being portrayed as they should be, there are no storytellers unaware of the issue of how women are characterized in their stories. The genie will not go back into his or her bottle.

Bibliography

Burch, Milbre. "A Storytelling Artist at Work," *Storytelling World* 10 (Summer/Fall 1996): 17-21.

Gardner, Richard. *Fairy Tales for Today's Children*. Creskill: Creative Therapy, 1974.

The Horn Book, Special issue, 1942.

Phelps, Ethel Johnston. *Tatterhood and Other Tales*. New York: Feminist Press, 1978.

Sawyer, Ruth. *The Way of the Storyteller*. Middlesex: Penguin Books, 1942.

Shedlock, Marie. *The Art of the Storyteller*. New York: Dover, 1915.

Sobol, Joseph. *The Storyteller's Journey*. Urbana: University of Illinois Press, 1999.

Welch, Wendy. "Cross Culture Cross Class Crossed Wires." *Traditional Storytelling Today*: Ed. Margaret Read McDonald. Seattle: Fitzroy-Dearborn, 1999.

Storytelling in Education

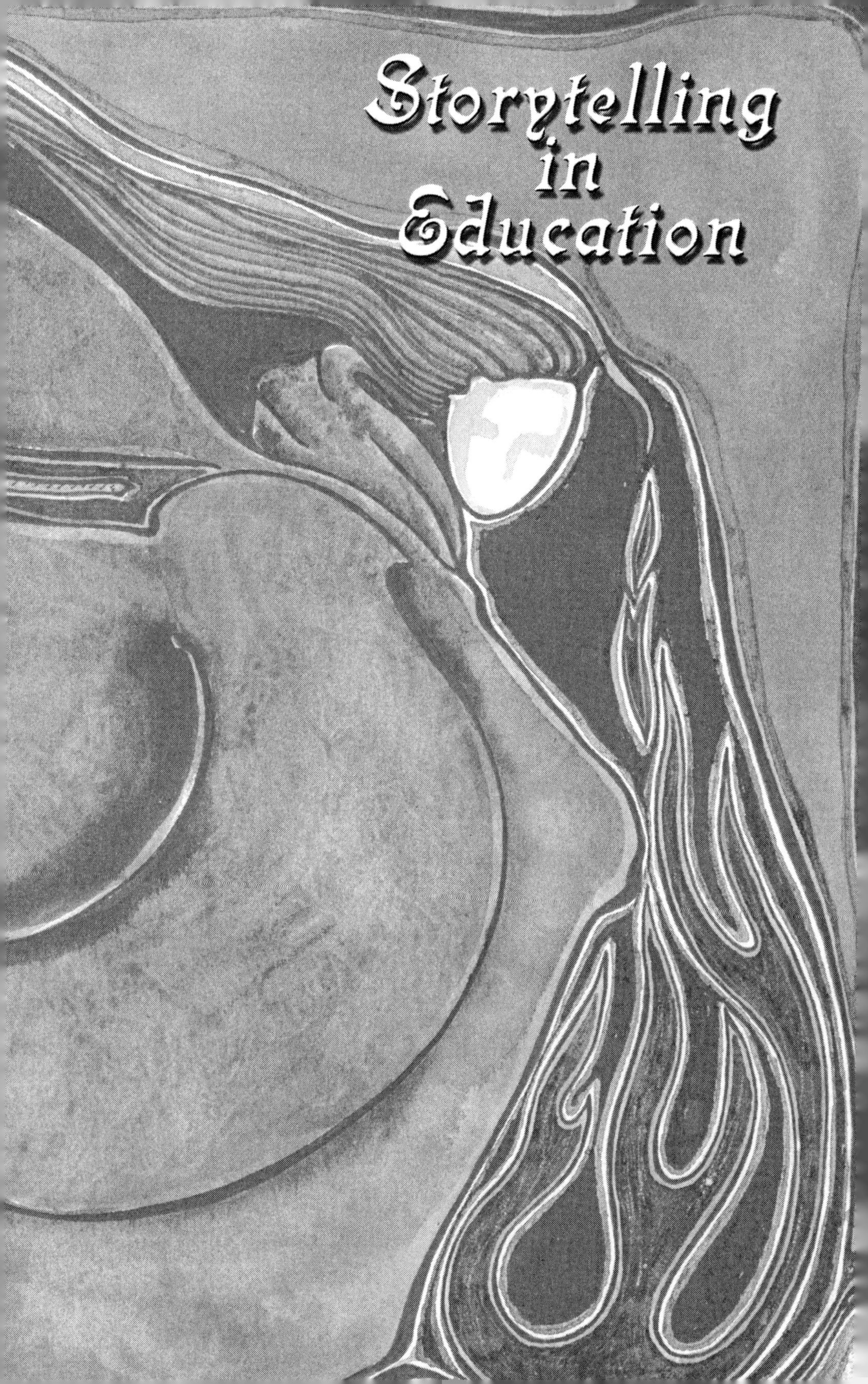

"Uncommon Common Women:" The Historian And The Storyteller

Ona Siporin and Anne Butler

The Historian:

I am not a storyteller. I am a historian. So, I come to this conference as one who is in "alien corn." You seem, however, to be a most welcoming group, and so I will plunge ahead. The only thing I can really do here is talk to you about what it is that Ona and I do and how our presentation, "Uncommon Common Women," came into existence.

Almost ten years ago, I received a call from the central office of the Girl Scouts of America, an inquiry about whether I could present a program about western women for the opening of a week-long scouting event in North Dakota. The audience, my caller explained, would consist of 250 scouts, between the ages of fourteen and seventeen. Organizers envisioned a lecture to prepare the girls, about to undertake a scouting wagon train across the western plains, to understand the social context of their nineteenth century counterparts.

Somewhat daunted by the thought of offering conventional academic fare to a group energized for an exhilarating week of horses, wagons, and campfires, I turned to my storytelling colleague, Ona Siporin, to ask if she thought we might design a joint presentation. Each of us had years of experience as speakers, presenters, performers, but each had always been a "solo act." Coworkers in our professional lives and friends in our community, we approached the notion of forming a "team" with trepidation. I was most comfortable in the lecture hall, behind a podium, or writing for scholarly publication. Ona enjoyed a wide reputation for her storytelling, poetry readings, and radio persona. Ours seemed an unlikely marriage, but we hoped to meld history and storytelling to illuminate the lives of ordinary women.

We went to North Dakota and simply did what we have learned we do best—we talked about women in the West. I established a historical context for the audience, drawing listeners in with slides of western environments and communities. Then I placed women in those scenes, showing groups and individuals who found identity and purpose in western challenges. Ona followed with stories that tied western women to the images. For example, a slide of a woman with chaps and a ten gallon hat, astride a horse and waiting for cattle provided entry into Ona's compelling tale of Little Jo Monaghan, who, for most of her adult life, dressed as a man and worked as an Idaho ranch hand. Our first venture with the Girl Scouts proved a great success. We returned to our homes in Utah, fired with enthusiasm for the possibilities of "Uncommon Common Women." Subsequently, with the support of the Utah Council for the Humanities, we took our presentation to every corner of the state and finally to a number of universities around the nation.

We are not entirely sure why "Uncommon Common Women" so touches our audiences, who have ranged from students to housewives to teachers to retirees. We are sure that the presentation of today has evolved far from the rigidly structured program we took to North Dakota. Our catalogue of slides is now several hundred and those presented change from show to show. The repertoire of stories has expanded to encompass more lives, more experiences, more diversity.

Before each event, we talk with the audience and try to identify what aspects of western women's lives would most appeal. We review possible slides and the general themes that I will use during the history "talk." We agree on the first and last slide, so that we both know the parameters of the opening segment. Ona decides on which stories seem most appropriate or which she feels inclined to tell. Then we set off with this amphoteric "thing" that has come to be very special to us.

Although I don't want to appear self-congratulatory, I do think Ona and I deserve credit for being willing to risk a great deal in this venture. We work in the same small office and we live in the same small town. I am the senior editor of a scholarly journal and Ona is the assistant editor for me. Our spouses are members of the same academic department at the university. We had a lot to lose if our efforts collapsed under the weight of disagreement. Understandably, we felt uneasy about crossing into uncharted territory, one that could be filled with the pitfalls of ego and artistic conflict. Once we navigated these waters successfully, we further tested ourselves by writing a book together, *Uncommon Common Women: Ordinary Lives of the West*. This took us into new areas of danger and yet the process proved amazingly smooth.

I comment on this, not to brag about our accomplishments or tempt the fates to twist our futures, but to indicate how much we each grew and learned from this process of joining two disciplines, of becoming part of a performing duet. Perhaps what that speaks to is the power of history and the beauty of storytelling, for each has enriched us, brought us closer, and engaged our listeners.

The Storyteller

This story, like the others in *Uncommon Common Women* (Logan: Utah State University Press, 1996), was created to be told aloud to a live audience. After a telling, people often ask me where I find my stories. I find them everywhere I turn, but speaking only of *Uncommon Common Women*, I have three sources: archives, general written material, and oral informants. My work on Tashnamani, who is a historical figure, came from archives and written material.

In the shapes of ink you see here on the page, this short narrative becomes static, a state unnatural to it. Though symbols are handy, they are not the living language and they cannot do what spoken language can. Given this, I ask you to consider this piece as only an introduction to Tashnamani. Like each of us, she too, is a paradox. Always the same, but always different, she holds a universe of secrets which surface only when I am researching and telling.

The story[1]

They will tell you that it is easy to diagram on a map: A B C D E F G H I. The Blackfeet. The Brule. The Cheyenne. The Minniconju. The Oglala. The Santee. The Sans Arc. The Two Kettle. The Unopapa.

They will tell you there were six Arapaha. Captured because the others thought they were in league with the whites, later proven to be merely a hunting party.

These are the Indians.

Easy, they will tell you: 1 2 3 4 5. Reno's advance. Reno's retreat to the trees. Reno's withdrawal across the river to the hilltop. Custer's stand above Deep Coulee. Custer's last stand against Crazy Horse, Gall, and Black Moon.

They will tell you that when Reno, a West Point graduate with Civil War experience, saw the enormity of the Indian encampment, he ordered his men to the cottonwood and the willow. They will tell you that the justification of that retreat has been disputed for over a century.

Maybe Reno was a coward. Maybe he was perfectly rational. Maybe he lost understanding or desire for any war when a Sioux bullet spattered the brains of his scout, Bloody Knife, across his face.

You will hear that Custer planned to strike from the north end of the camp at the same time Reno attacked from the south. You will hear that Reno did attack, fell back, retreated across the river to the hilltop. Custer was nowhere in sight.

Between five and six soldiers were killed running. The grey horses were mixed up with horses of different colors: the companies broke rank; they were confused and scattered. You will hear that the soldiers carried near-empty whiskey flasks. They will tell you about Lonesome Charley and about Lt. McIntosh, the mixed-blood. You will hear that Isaiah Dorman, the black interpreter, was tortured, shot in the legs, shot sixteen times with arrows through the chest and that a picket pin was rammed through his testicles. All this because he was beloved by the Sioux. He had married a Santee, spoke Sioux fluently—and had turned traitor.

You will hear facts and gossip jumbled together. They will tell you about the lascivious habits of Colonel Benteen. That Benteen and Reno did not get along, that Custer and Reno did not get along, that Benteen and Custer did not get along. They will tell you how Custer, thirty-fourth in his class of thirty-four at West Point held the record for demerits: he grew his hair long, he rested with his feet out the window, he adorned his uniform. He may remind you, when you hear this, of your teenage sons or nephews.

He wanted adventure. He exuded the egotistical spirit of his culture; his hubris was accepted, even awarded. He literally kept rising, literally. In the spring of 1863, on orders, he climbed into a hot air balloon to spy on Confederate forces near Richmond. Why didn't they pop his balloon? This vain man who later delighted in lashing his own men, this man who once dug a pit and is said to have ordered his own men into it for minor infractions of army regulations. They will tell you that Custer travelled with a sixteen piece band seated on white mounts, led by Felix Vinatiorri. They will tell you that Custer pretended to scalp his own men; that he lost 1200 men to desertion; that he witnessed an 8 percent suicide rate. There are so many things to tell. What shall I tell first? What shall I leave until later? On June 25, 1876, Tashnamani was digging wild turnips with her friends a few miles from camp. Tashnamani—it means "moving robe." (Was it for the way her skirts swayed when she danced?)

The morning was sultry. The cottonwood were in full leaf and the stands of willow held an intense red. Tashnamani was twenty-three years old, still unmarried, still a virgin. She and her friends were chatting—about the men they hoped to marry, about the meal they would fix with the turnips. They spoke with respect about Sitting Bull.

From time to time Tashnamani would stop digging and look around her. To the west she could see the nations' herds of horses. She remembered the song of Walking Elk greeting the rising sun. She could see the camp: hundreds of tipis. She sighed for the beauty of it.

When they had been digging a few hours, one of the women looked up to see a warrior riding toward them. The dust rising behind him brought to Tashnamani's mind a cloud of dust she had seen earlier rising behind a ridge in the east. The warrior was shouting. They waited for the breeze to carry the words to their ears.

Finally the sounds reached them: "Soldiers!! Soldiers!! Run to the hills with the children and the old ones!"

Tashnamani stood up, dropping her digging tool, an ash stick. It fell by the pile of gathered turnips. The others turned and ran; they called for her to come. The warrior was galloping back toward camp.

Tashnamani looked out at the land. This was one of her favourite valleys, thick with grass for the horses, covered with sunflowers. The river ran through deep clear pools. When the heat stifled her, the shadows of the trees were cool and dark. She looked at all of it. They had come here to rest, to regain spirit after last week's battle with these demons. They had come here to be a people on their own land.

She looked at her ash digging stick on the ground. The joy and hope she had felt earlier that morning were gone. She shook her head, as if to dispel a vision, and ran towards camp.

From her tipi, Tashnamani saw her father running toward the horses. In the next instant, she heard her mother keening, and turned to see her kneeling on the ground. She knew, at that moment, that the mourning song was for her brother, killed by the soldiers. Turning from her mother to the ridge, she saw the confusion on the rise just across Greasy Grass, the river the whites called Little Big Horn. She heard Hawk Man shout, "Hoke He! Hoke He!" And she watched the soldiers shooting and her father preparing for battle.

Tashnamani began to sing. The death song for her brother rose to the air in tangle of grief and fury. Later she said, "My heart was bad. Revenge. Revenge."

When she finished singing, she painted her face crimson and braided her black hair. She ran to the thicket to take her horse. "I was not afraid," she said, "even though I was a woman."

Reno's men had formed a battle line. She could hear the carbines. Bullets shattered the tipi poles. Women and children ran back and forth in a snare of fear and anger. The old ones continued to sing the death songs. (Didn't the soldiers think this terrible keening was a war cry? And weren't they terribly wrong? Terribly ignorant?) Tashnamani remembered how she felt, "the enchanting death songs made me brave, although I was a woman."

She turned to her horse. A warrior dropped beside her, dead from a soldier's bullet. She and her father mounted their black horses and rode together to the stand of cottonwood and willow. They were joined by many others. Rain-in-the-Face cried out, "Behold! There is among us a young woman! Let no man hide behind her garment!" Rain-in-the-Face said of her that she held her brother's war staff over her head and leaned forward on her horse. He said she looked, "as beautiful as a bird."

Red Horse shouted, "There is never a better day to die." Tashnamani rode with him and the others through the powder smoke, her heart full of revenge. For the first time she killed a human being. One she shot; the other she hacked to death with her sheath knife.

Tashnamani was not ignorant of battle. She had been on a raiding party, but this was different. This was destruction.

Much later, she would remember the beauty of the day before the attack. Like any of us would, she would remember that there had been beauty; and she would sift her memories of the knives and the guns and the screams of her kinsmen for visions of a glistening river, of fields of sunflowers, of myriad tents, and massive herds of horses.

But don't forget that the Battle of the Little Big Horn was carnage. Heads were found hanging from tent poles; bodies had been eviscerated, skin stripped, eyes gouged, skulls smashed. Soldiers who overran the deserted village in the days after the battle, cut the feet off Indian warriors or tore away their flesh to get at the beaded burial garments. Bodies lay naked in piles beside dead horses.

It is said that during the battle Tashnamani's friend, Tashnawambli (Eagle Robe) walked out from the village and pointed a revolver at one of Custer's interpreters who had fallen wounded from his horse. He pleaded, "Please do not kill me, as I shall be dead in a short while anyway." And Tashnawambli answered, "If you did not want to be killed, why didn't you stay home and not come to attack us?" And having said these, the wisest words about war that anyone could say, and standing on the land the beauty of which was obscured by powder smoke, she shot him through the head.

The Blackfeet. The Brule. The Cheyenne. The Minneconjou. The Oglalla. The Santee. The Sans Arc. The Two Kettle. The Uncpapa. Reno's advance. Reno's fall back to the trees. Reno's retreat. Custer's stand above Deep Coulee. Custer's last stand against Crazy Horse, Gall, Black Moon.

These things are easy to see on a map.

But who can show me on a map the spot where the young woman Tashnamani, dropped her digging tool of ash?

THIS ESSAY IS DEDICATED TO OUR MOTHERS
CAROL WHITE AND JEAN ATKINS POSEY.

Note

1. Reprinted by permission of the authors and Utah State University Press.

Voice, Narrative and Story in Oral Narrating Practices in an Educational Context

Elizabeth Mood

"I thought it was going to be funny
but then it turned serious."
(Class member's comment on Hazel's narrative)

When I flew from Manchester, England, to Sydney, Cape Breton Island, to give this paper to a conference of thinkers-about-story, conversations about our work became, for me, moments in a history of discourse around the narratives of family history on which I gave my paper. Together with me as speaker/ethnographer, those who listened to the paper or who read this written version are involved in constructing part of that history. This is not because the series of narratives by Hazel about her Grandfather's fall have any special significance in themselves; rather, they are part of an ongoing joint investigation by Hazel, as learner in education, her teacher as researcher and others to whom the research has been disseminated.

The Storyteller and Her Story

This paper comes out of my research on oral narrating in education. The purpose of the work is to explore the potential of storying in a social (educational) context to shed light on some issues in narrative theory. The paper is based on an analysis of transcribed data comprising a series of successive instances of narrating by one child, Hazel, working on a story of family history. I will discuss what the storyteller's task involves in bringing family history from a protected environment into the storytelling culture established in a particular classroom. I view narrating as process and as social practice.

The data is part of a transcribed oral narrative/non-narrative text, "Grandad," which itself is part of a collection of data from a class of ten year old pupils, collected over a period of about eighteen months. For twelve months of this time, I was also their teacher and during a further six months, I returned to record the same pupils in school as researcher. I refer in the following to extracts from "Grandad" comprising narrative and meta-narrative discourse (talk about the various versions of the story) by Hazel.

Hazel, and her mother and Grandfather before her, grew up in a former mining village in Northern England. "Grandad" is the story, told to Hazel by her mother, of her Grandfather's fall into a slag heap when out collecting coal dust to burn as fuel when fuel was short during the 1940s. Although only visible from the knuckles after falling, he was rescued by his friends who acted quickly and dug him out.

Story, Narrative, Narration

In his seminal work on narrative theory, Gerard Genette uses the word story for "the signified or narrative content" while narrative is "the signifier, statement, discourse or narrative text itself..." (27). More recently, within a movement towards a postmodern theory of narrative, the notion that it is possible to speak of story and narrative as separate is being challenged.[1]

The two issues in narrative theory I would like to explore a little, are these:

a) the question of what is story and whether this is separable from narrating, and

b) whether narrative can be said to be "voiced" linguistically and what we might mean by "narrative voice."[2]

I will argue that:

> i) there is no story separate from narrating and that
>
> ii) narrative voice is constituted by words spoken and unspoken about a story by others and teller during the storying process.

In other words, as I will show, narrative voice is informed by social interactions around story which shape future narration. I find the term "voice" useful for this purpose, in that it indicates both a period of time during which something is said and a social space in which a voicing might take place.

Social space implies a reading of words as they are spoken, as well as a writing between the lines and ahead of the words spoken.

In addition to space and time, voice suggests physical processes of speech and hearing, involving consciousness, thought and meaning making. The metaphor of voice in narrative is useful to identify the processual nature of the way in which we apprehend, produce and consume narrative text, whether written or spoken and whether as producer or consumer. So, I will use voice to represent the difference between the words in the head of the reader (including the teller, who reads her own text as she produces it) and the words of the text. Voice is therefore always multiple. Traces of social interaction in narrative with no necessary recourse to origin or source or to quotation is a kind of plagiarism that gives narrative its distinctive, eclectic, multiple nature.

If there is a voice in narrative with which we engage, it contains at least two voices of the listener or reader. These are both a reading voice which does the work of making meaning, structuring and classifying according to genre, and a writing voice, differentiating and deferring meaning.[3]

Below is a transcription of the first telling of her story about her Grandad by Hazel in school. I provide this as a reference point for the following discussion of changes Hazel made in later tellings and talk about the story:

HAZEL

em this is about my this is about my grandad that's dead
em it was in the middle of World War Two
me mam thinks
and em (.) they didn't used to have any coal
so they used to go to this place
where there was coal dust
and usually em like put their hand in
and see if they could get an
like there usually be (..)
the they usually found some
and em (.) my grandad em was putting his hand in to em like look around
and em he found the em coal dust
and e it was like quicksand
like it it dragged him in
and (..) he (.) e they had to em dig him out with their hands
em and they they went for help
and em on the (..) interview with me mum
I asked u if me grandad was in the war
and she said no

because em he was in a in he was in hospital for a very long time
and cause of this accident that he had
em his back was bent
and that's how he he wasn't able to be in the war
(Hazel "Grandad," First Telling to class in school).

In this first telling in school, Hazel brings an aspect of her mother's telling into current telling time. A reading of her mother's voice penetrates the narrative voice, validating it. This is the voice of a "writerly"[4] reader explicitly acknowledging a former text simultaneous with the constructing of a new text:

em this is about my this is about my grandad that's dead
em it was in the middle of World War Two
me mam thinks
(Hazel "Grandad," First Telling in school).

Just as each telling writes a new story with a different play of signifiers, each time I examine the research data, I bring it into a new synchronic time/space and process of reading/writing.

Below, in the first version, a narrator finds an explanation for phenomena said to have been manifested in actual time ("it was like quicksand...it dragged him in"). There is a relationship of difference between this text and the story Hazel's mother told. It is an aspect of the role of the teller in an educational context, the child, bringing her story from the family, to offer possible ways of making sense. Here she does so by using a comparison, a simile, "like quicksand," which may or may not have been drawn from her mother's telling:

and em (.) my grandad em was putting his hand in to em like look around
and em he found the em coal dust
and e it was like quicksand
like it it dragged him in
and (..) he (.) e they had to em dig him out with their hands
(Hazel "Grandad," First Telling to class in school).

Readers Engaging with a Text

While narrative may be chiefly told in a past tense, it is addressed to and negotiated in a present, and to a future writing/reading of it. The telling of a story at each point is momentarily prior to a developing reading of a text, which is interplayed by a listening reader with her/his internal writing between the lines. Both reading and writing anticipate a resolution and closure, towards which narrative, by its nature, promises to move.

The practice of questioning the storyteller after her telling was established early on in the year during which I made these recordings. A child wanted to ask the teller more about her story and this became an accepted practice, giving status to children's voices during the fifteen minutes of storying at the end of each day. As in the case below, the child's question or comment often probed the telling of the story, or what might have been omitted. Meta-narrative or the language being used to talk about story from outside a telling, often, simultaneously, offered potential new narrative material.

Holly's comment below is, perhaps, unanswerable in terms of expertise about the physical properties of the environment. Does she require an explanation for Grandad's survival; or is she pushing for something in the narrating which would indicate the near to death nature of the situation, and therefore the extraordinary nature of "Grandad's" survival?

> well you know like you you said
> that he had got pulled in
> well with him with all like the dust and that going over his face
> I would have thought
> he would have suffocated or something
> when he couldn't breathe
> *(Peer group comments/questions to Hazel after first telling of "Grandad").*

Holly is a reader invited to engage with the text, and this engagement can be traced in later instances of narrative voice. The extract below comes from a first person telling of the story, a task I gave the class following on their initial telling of stories brought from home:

> and when I was inside I just couldn't breathe properly
> and if I was and every time I was breathing I was breathing the coal dust in
> an I felt as if I was going to die
> and I just didn't know what was happening
> *(Hazel, "Grandad," Second Telling to class in school).*

A Child Reading Between the Lines of Her Own Narrative

Comment on a story by teller or audience can be seen in these storying sessions to address a future narrating and therefore narrator or voice. In a succession of oral "drafts," voices engaging with the text at various stages can be identified, showing how earlier and future voices shape text in the process of its construction. In the extract below, Hazel was listening to the recording of her own storytelling of a year previously. In the presence of teacher/researcher, and a tape recorder, she was thinking through how she could make a switch in perspectives, shifting the narrative point of view from the perspective of Grandad, to that of his friends. The realization that this was a possibility, came through the reading and rewriting of her own work of a year before:

well what could happen is
I could say he fell in
and then go over to what his friends were doing
(Hazel reflecting while listening to a tape recording of her telling a year previously).

The practice, well established in education, of evaluation of a previous draft as a basis for a new draft, written or spoken gives rise to a comment on how a new narrative might differ from a previous instance of narrating. This comment is addressed by the teller to a potential new narrator/narration by the use of modal auxiliaries expressing conditionality, "I could..." There is also a representation of a potential narrating voice, "he fell in."

A History of Discourse

Each successive draft is intertextual with previous and future text and forms a history of discourse. Hazel tells several versions of a story, the telling of each implying former versions, whether or not sources are acknowledged. The presence of an audience (here peer group, teacher in the classroom and the potential audience for the recording) implies a reading/internal writing and response. It implies an address to an audience now as well as an audience (for the recording) in the future.

A theoretical idea that I find helpful is the notion of a "natural history of discourse;"[5] natural history as a system of classification, a way of structuring our understanding of our environment by discovering relations between species, or in the case of discourse, between genres. To examine text for the purposes of research we may juxtapose textual traces of processes produced separately in time, thus bringing diachronic relationships (through time/history) into a synchronic relationship (of a given moment/natural history).

Questions about a Story Shaping Subsequent Narration

In examining her previous tellings, we could say that Hazel herself was involved in a process of doing research or working with her own text by activating it in a new context. When, as below, she examined a recording of her own narrating of a year before, she acted as researcher on her own discourse, bringing a text previously produced into a present moment and writing between its lines. The questions underlined below, then, have emerged out of this educational practice of interrogating the text. I will call this last the "latest" telling, to avoid the finality of closure suggested by "last" telling, though this was the last time Hazel worked on the story in my presence:

it one day me gran great grandmother told me grandad
to go to the coal dust
to go and get some coal for the fire
so he decided to go with his friends
cause they were going
(.) they were go
they went through some gates
and were crossing some rivers
just enjoying themselves on a normal summer's day
me granda was fourteen years old
and his friends were about fourteen and fifteen
and they were just enjoying theirself walking along
and they came to the starting of the coal site on the road
and they were looking around
they were looking around for the for some coal
and they decided and they all decided
to go off in different ways
to have a look
and then saw the biggest one
cause the biggest heap
because that normally had the most coal in
so they all decided to go over to it
and they were climbing up
seeing if they could get certain bits
and they were putting it in heaps at the bottom
and throwing it to each other to put on the heap
so they could all carry it home
and me grandad had seen a big lump of coal
and so he struggled round to get it
and sadfully he fell in
his friends didn't
his friends hadn't recognised
that he had fallen in yet
but he was finding it really difficult to breathe
cause there was no air to breathe

and he was just breathing the dust in
and the dust was really bad for your chest
and then his friends (.) could (.)
then his friends went round the
went round to where he had fallen in
and they could just see this knu these knukles
and they were thinking like
whose are they?
and then they saw that
me grandad Jack em he had fallen in
and so they all came rushing up
and they were digging digging
and digging with their hands
and they were really scared
like it was their friend
what what would happen to him
how
and they were digging
and digging
and (.) me grandad (.) he was he was just like hoping
he would get out
cause he didn't know what would happen
and how (.) how would he get out
because every second the dust was
(.) bringing him under even more
then finally they got him out
(Hazel "Grandad," Latest Telling with teacher/researcher in school).

In this latest telling, first person can be seen to have informed third person narrative. A reader might ask who says, "and the dust was really bad for your chest"? Does the use of the possessive pronoun, "your," meaning "one's," suggest closeness to a lived experience? Is this the kind of retrospection/memory that constructs a Grandad consciousness? Does Hazel as teller, remembering a former first person narrator role, shape this new narrative through it? Does the reader with access to them, catch a resonance here of Holly and Hazel's voices talking about the story? Whether or not earlier talk is accessible, it is inherent in current telling and addresses audience/readers:

but he was finding it really difficult to breathe
cause there was no air to breathe
and he was just breathing the dust in

> and the dust was really bad for your chest
> *(Hazel "Grandad," Latest Telling with teacher/researcher in school).*

Unattributed thought or words or "free indirect discourse," maintaining the past tense and third person of narration, suggests another layer to a multiple narrative voice, and constructs the thought of Grandad.

Shifts in Genre Occur Through Shifts in Social Context

If history and memory are socially negotiated, then neither is in the text, but in the difference between this sign and another sign as grasped by a reader or community of readers. For Hazel, as reader of her own first draft and the ensuing questions and first person narrative, what is unsaid in each draft is implied by another draft set beside it. This succession of drafts, brought into one moment for examination allows her to view text synchronically, in this one time.

These tellings could be said to have a history, moving from tentativeness in the narrating voice or explicit references to a source or former telling;

> like it it dragged him in
> and (..) he (.) e they had to em dig him out with their hands
> em and they they went for help
> and em on the (..) interview with me mum
> I asked u if me grandad was in the war
> and she said no
> because em he was in a in he was in hospital for a very long time
> *(Hazel "Grandad," First Telling to class in school).*

to a more implicit narration where other voices brought in from the social practice of storytelling within the social context of the classroom are written into the voice of narration. This complexity has come about through work on possible alternative ways of telling the story, and therefore is likely to produce a more knowing, conscious narrator.

> what what would happen to him
> how
> and they were digging
> and digging
> and (.) me grandad (.) he was he was just like hoping
> he would get out
> cause he didn't know what would happen
> and how (.) how would he get out
> because every second the dust was

(.) bringing him under even more
(Hazel, "Grandad," Latest Telling with teacher/researcher in school).

If, as discussed above, the words underlined are not attributed in the narration either to Grandad or to a narrator's voice, it could be said that they are directly connected with Hazel's work on the story or narrated world. In narrative voice, here, we can trace a relationship with previous interactions in the storying process. Questions and comments on the story, as well as Hazel's response to her questioners, having been taken in to "inner speech,"[6] and/or "writing," then act to probe the story as it is being told. This narrative voice seems conscious of its own telling process; "how how would he get out" can be read as a delay[7] while the narrative action is suspended to invite reflection/ prediction by the reader.

The more Hazel engaged in a process of working on narrative, the more the "story world" of a succeeding version became self-reflective and evaluative. This has an effect on genre, or a reader's learned cultural classifying system for text. In later versions of this story the modality, or relative certainty of and attitude to the story world by the narrated actors within it becomes more tentative and less sure. The uncertainty of the narrating voice about the process of narration that we saw in the first telling, is here transferred from narrator to characters. As the genre shifts, uncertainty, or low modality, comes to characterize the narrated world so that it implicitly interrogates the narrating of it ("how how would he get out?"). This differs from an initial narration, the motive force of which is the desire for validation from a "higher" or earlier authority:

em this is about my this is about my grandad that's dead 1
em it was in the middle of World War Two
me mam thinks
(Hazel "Grandad," First Telling to class in school).

Meaning Deferred

Another theoretical notion I find helpful in working with this storying data is from Derrida,[8] that of the internal "writing" or play of signifiers as difference; each signifier occupying a shifting unbounded space indicated by its difference from other signifiers (table is not chair/love is not hate) so that meaning is deferred. This gives me a theoretical means to see text as that which differs from what is almost and potentially said and what is unsaid. In other words, the research data is a reference made by what is written (internally) before, after, and between and with the text by its writer/readers. This allows me to think text as unbounded, and as remnants of the process by which it was constructed. Each telling is a selection of signifiers from those potential in the process of telling, differing from those unsaid words, those of a previous teller/ tellings and current words internal to the listener:

I could have started it
about how his mum had told him to go and get some
or I could have started it
like they were walking along
or I could have started it
when they had actually got to the coal dust

(Hazel comments while listening to tape recording of previous narratives and meta-narrative).

Hazel commenting on her previous recordings thinks through possible alternative starting points, thus recognizing that narrating is a set of choices at each moment. Each point at which she suggests starting would be subtly different in terms of a reader's experience and therefore a reader's meaning-making process. Each choice made suggests those alternative choices, equally possible, that are not made and thus the notion of difference between what is said and what remains implicit or is written by writerly readers.

History as a History of Narrating

History is experienced by tellers and narrators as a history of narrating or discourse constructing an event said to have occurred in once lived time. Each time a new history is written it calls into question, or brings into play other histories or narratives constructing lived events, setting them side by side.

History, then is a process of retelling, re-wording and deferring meaning or re-meaning. To make it meaningful for ourselves, as readers, we engage in rewriting as Hazel, the teller, has done. The more work Hazel does in the particular social contexts set up for her by her teacher/researcher, the less visible are the mechanisms of her story making and the closer the story comes to a rhetorical, literary genre constructed as fictional. I see the latest version as no better than the first, in terms of pedagogic value judgements, though it is evidently operating differently. The role of narrator contextualizing the past in order to explicate a habitual state existing in another time and place becomes less important for Hazel with the elaboration of this state through ongoing narrative action:

and they were climbing up
seeing if they could get certain bits
and they were putting it in heaps at the bottom
and throwing it to each other to put on the heap

so they could all carry it home
and me grandad had seen a big lump of coal
and so he struggled round to get it
and sadfully he fell in
(Hazel "Grandad," Latest Telling with teacher/researcher in school).

If history is a synchronic event of comparing stories, it focuses on the moment of comparison from which the retrospective look is made and therefore is not an instance of the past, but rather words about an instance of the past. We can identify a shift in genre in Hazel's work. The first version is more like history because it discusses its sources more directly and becomes less like history when it conceals its sources.

As we have seen, Hazel responded to Holly's comments by drawing on resources from her Mother, ideas and words not brought out before this point:

em me mam says
they could only see from like his knuckles
they cul they could only see the top of his fingers
(Hazel's response to Peer group comments/ questions after first telling of "Grandad").

After listening to the tape recording of this comment and question session, and in subsequent discussion with me as researcher she reached a key moment of realization.

then (.) he might he might have been in there in there
for a few seconds
before his friends had recognised
that he was actually missing
(Hazel comments while listening to tape recording of previous narratives and meta-narrative).

This is the key to the source material becoming hidden, a secret of the text,[9] and so indicating the work of a reader to negotiate in response to the multiple voice, responsive and provocative. Here, the narrative motivation or force, shifts; the reason for telling is not to explain the past, but to play with narrating time and space in an exploration of a past. This opens out a potential for a space in which narration is recognized as jointly negotiated by teller and readers. Audience/readers will be invited to respond to questions of narration through the mechanism of thought of a character, as the story is being told.

Reading Narratives

As my research is showing, readers make sense of narrative, as other text, in reading time, that is the synchronic present of telling and narrating. When the researcher comes to look at successive related tellings she places them, in the form of transcriptions physically laid out on paper, side by side. Thus the difference in time of telling, which is textually encoded (since at each telling the teller had an experience of more or fewer previous tellings) is now in reading time brought into the simultaneity of a reading for the purposes of research.

The questions in the final draft of Hazel's narrative recollect and speak to the words of the comments of her peer group and her first person telling as well as her own exploration or interrogation of her text. They also speak to their readers or to the future in which the text is read in telling time, or to this future in which I am now, and you as reader, will be making sense of this text:

and they were thinking like
whose are they
(Hazel "Grandad," Latest Telling with teacher/researcher in school).

Below is an example of Hazel reading between the lines of her previous telling and articulating an important structural aspect of story, that is that a status quo is generally established in story; after some kind of disruptive action some new state of affairs may be established:

it would just be like a normal day to go out
just like we come to school
it just be normal
and it's just an accident
that sadfully happened
(Hazel comments while listening to tape recording of previous narratives and meta-narrative).

Writing and reading are simultaneous and inseparable components of storytelling and can be referred to as separate only for the purposes of analysis, for example, as Bakhtin separates the components of the "double-directed" voice in narrating.[10] This "double-directedness" arises out of our ability as human beings to read the codes of our culture and simultaneously to respond or speak back to them.

Story and narrative are related to the concurrent and integral processes of reading and writing, narrating being an internal writing process, which can be expressed in either written or spoken mode. Story is what we grasp when we read and is therefore necessarily more structural, than the processual narrating. Yet story is activated by narration, is a reading process, a summarizing, or getting the gist. We read what we write or tell, as we tell or write it; and we write between the lines of what we read. Thus narrative voice is constituted by both reading or structuring (sense-making) and writing or differentiating (making new).

Story as Structured through Reading

So in reading her own work, Hazel is able to make new meanings. Story, then, is a structuration, a product of reading, while narrative is innovative, and unfinalized, and is a process of writing or breaking down structure. Story is impossible without narration and therefore every instance of narration produces a different story, differently evaluated, newly negotiated between reader and text. As researchers we can find traces of these earlier discussions shaping Hazel's final story, which produces two narrative perspectives, that of Grandad and that of his friends:

and sadfully he fell in
his friends didn't
his friends hadn't recognised
that he had fallen in yet
but he was finding it really difficult to breathe
cause there was no air to breathe
and he was just breathing the dust in
and the dust was really bad for your chest
and then his friends (.) could (.)
then his friends went round the
went round to where he had fallen in
and they could just see this knu these knuckles
and they were thinking like
whose are they
(Hazel "Grandad," Latest Telling with teacher/researcher in school).

Latest Wordstory, History and Narration

I began by saying that the two issues in narrative theory I would like to discuss are first, the question of what is story/ history and whether this is separable from narrating, and second, whether narrative can be said to be "voiced" linguistically and what we might mean by "narrative voice." I have argued that there is no story separate from narrating and that narrative voice is constituted by words spoken and unspoken about a story by others and teller during the storying process.

A story is shaped by a history of its narrating and talk surrounding its narrating, whether it is a history or not. Therefore it is always shaped by the future of telling and reading into which it is moving. If narrative is viewed as processual then it is always potential. There is, then, essentially no transcendental story, about which we can say, "that's the story." If an audience or readers make sense of narrative and engage in writing it, then the narrative is shaped by them in reading time. A history of discourse can be spread out in synchronic time and readers at a given time will work collectively on texts, negotiating meanings which will later be renegotiated. Narrative, addressed to reading time and constructed in reading time, comes to be shaped in reading time.

Notes

1. Toolan provides a useful introduction to structuralist and poststructuralist thinking 9-11. For a discussion towards a postmodern view see Gibson. 69-97.
2. See Gibson 143-177.
3. Compare Derrida 55-57.
4. From Barthes on the "readerly" text 5, 29-30; on the writerly reader rewriting the text as s/he reads 4-6, 10-11.
5. See Silverstein and Urban 21-2.
6. Vygotsky 19-20.
7. Compare Barthes' hermeneutic code or Voice of truth, the voice of the delays in disclosure of the secrets of the text, Barthes 84.
8. Derrida 56-7.
9. Compare Barthes 19.
10. Bakhtin 199.

Works Cited

Bakhtin, Mikhail. *Problems of Dostoevsky's Poetics.* 1984. Trans. and Ed. Caryl Emerson. Minneapolis, Minnesota: Minnesota UP, 1994.

Barthes, Roland. *S/Z.* 1973. Trans. Richard Miller. 2nd ed. Oxford: Blackwell, 1992.

Derrida, Jacques. *of Grammatology*. 1967. Trans. Gayatri C. Spivak. 2nd ed. Baltimore: Johns Hopkins UP, 1976.

Genette, Gerard. *Narrative Discourse: An Essay in Method.* 1972. Trans. Jane E. Lewin. Ithaca: Cornell UP, 1995.

Gibson, Andrew. *Towards a Postmodern Theory of Narrative.* Edinburgh: Edinburgh UP, 1996.

Silverstein, Michael and Greg Urban. *Natural Histories of Discourse.* London: Chicago UP, 1996.

Toolan, Michael J. *Narrative: A Critical Linguistic Introduction.* London: Routledge, 1988.

Vygotsky, Lev S. *Thought and Language.* 1962. Trans. Eugenia Hanfmann. Cambridge, Mass: MIT Press, 1967.

BRINGING STORYTELLING AND FOLK NARRATIVE INTO CLASSROOM LIFE[1]

NINA JAFFE

Bank Street's developmental-interaction approach provides opportunities for children to explore and experience the real world as their primary field of learning and study. Eschewing formalized modes of instruction that left individual children out of the process, as if they were only empty vessels ready to be filled, Lucy Sprague Mitchell and teachers in following generations brought the world into the classroom and both children and teachers into the world. Using neighborhood walks and field trips; building with blocks or other hands-on materials to recreate what was learned; recording questions or results of investigations on class charts are among the repertoire of practices that teachers in this approach implement in their work with pre-school to eighth grade children.

It seems strange then, to be talking about storytelling, a form of teaching that predates current approaches—Bank Street or otherwise, by at least two thousand years—as a dimension of the developmental-interaction approach. In its most familiar form, storytelling might be viewed as a highly adult-centered, teacher-directed activity. The teacher sits on a chair; the children gather around to listen; he or she tells the story. The children may respond verbally, or not. If the story is a folk or fairy tale, children are absorbing images that often have little to do with their immediate surroundings or environment. Birds that talk, skeletons that dance and speak to the living, horses that gallop up the sides of glass mountains, giants and trolls, or a boy who travels to the home of the North Wind to chide him for blowing his bowl of grain. Yet slowly and from different perspectives, teachers in the developmental-interaction framework are beginning to explore this age-old mode with renewed interest and commitment. What does storytelling have to do with the daily work of teaching and working with children in a progressive tradition?

Interest and involvement in childrens' literature has been part of the developmental-interaction approach from its very inception. Lucy Sprague Mitchell wrote many stories for children, such as *The Here and Now Storybooks*, as well as materials for teachers. She also encouraged writers, such as Margaret Wise Brown (*Good Night Moon*) and poet Claudia Lewis (*A Big Bite of the World*).

Storytelling as part of teacher education has been included in graduate studies at Bank Street College since the 1970s, taught both by librarians and professional tellers. A strong emphasis on narrative and folklore is included as well in courses in curriculum and childrens' literature (see Vascellaro and Genishi, 1994.)

Storytelling and narrative as a field of interest have been occupying a growing number of scholars in the world of education. Foremost among these is Vivian Gussin Paley, a MacArthur Foundation grantee, whose books on childrens' spontaneous storytelling, as well as their responses to folk and fairytales, have gained widespread readership in the teaching community. For Paley, listening to and discovering the need for children to tell and retell their own stories, and the way children's perceptions of self and others develop through exposure to the narrative symbols of folktales, have become a keystone to her current classroom practice. In an interview, Paley (1996) remarked: "The idea of the universality of childhood experience is the strongest multi-ethnic approach to any curriculum. Memories of childhood create a profound sense of family and community in any of us. If it's in a story, it's believable, it's an emotional truth. Storytelling is the most ancient of communal occupations." By following a child through his particular interest in story, teachers can understand a child's needs on a deeper, more comprehensive level. In so doing, they can create a learning environment that encompasses more fully the child's cognitive development and growth as a social being.

Kieran Egan (1986), educational psychologist and author of *Teaching as Storytelling*, sees other connections. In this book (see especially chapters 1 and 2), Egan suggests in various ways that the role of the imagination has been overlooked in much theory about learning, such as that of Piaget. The focus on a hierarchical model of cognitive development, in which children move from concrete to abstract levels of thought has driven teaching style and school policies for several decades. For Egan, the imagination is not just an "added attraction" or primitive dimension of cognitive growth—a sub-category to logico-mathematical thinking. Rather, he sees it as the very foundation of all symbolic and abstract thought: "Fantasy is the workshop of abstract thinking." Drawing on the work of structural anthropologists such as Levi-Strauss (1978) he posits an approach to curriculum that builds on the power of children to imagine and "see" what they can't necessarily feel and touch—a horse in flight, talking fish—and use the inner structure of narrative as the underpinning for building a curriculum for both early childhood as well as upper elementary age school children. Egan, like Paley, recognizes that storytelling offers teachers a way of building a sense of comradeship and group identity; and a deeper sense of both individual children and the life of the group as a whole. "The teacher in the classroom," says Egan, "is like the storyteller in the tribe."

Teacher as Teller

"Children are the victims of electronic advancement."

—*Pauline Cole, infant and toddler teacher.*

In our current world, children are exposed to narrative from a wide, almost exhaustive range of media. Some children, many of whom are in first-generation immigrant families from Latin America, Asia and the Caribbean, are still told stories within the context of their extended families (see Miller, Wiley, Fung, and Liang, 1997). A mother, father or grandparent may recount folk tales or family stories as part of the oral tradition from the community of origin (Olmedo, 1997). Many immigrant children, especially in public school settings, may not be aware of the value of the rich heritage of narrative which they bring to their new environments, but these family experiences inform their growth and perceptions of the world and people. However, in what we may call "mainstream American culture" most childrens' first experiences of story and narrative—from pre-school years or earlier—comes through exposure to books, film, radio, television, audio and computer technology. Children are exposed to narrative in ways that are sometimes selective, but more often random and driven by consumer trends and distribution patterns (Zipes, 1984). How does literature become meaningful, when there is such a plethora of narrative flow from sources other than the school, community, or even the immediate home and family? This presents a challenge for teachers today.

The resurgence of interest in storytelling is not only a phenomenon within the educational community. The National Storytelling Association, founded in Jonesboro, Tennessee in the early 1970s by former English teacher Jimmy Neil Smith (Zeitlin, 1990), is a central organizational point and information warehouse for hundreds of local storytelling chapters, school-based projects, community events, and festivals across the country. Clearly, despite our increased engagement with narrative at a distance via print and media, there is a corresponding need for people to find their own personal voices, to connect across the generations, and to hear and be heard within a more deeply interpersonal and communal context. This is both the background and foreground, in which teachers can use and bring storytelling into the lives and learning of their students and classroom life.

> The participation of the whole family in storytelling itself, in a sense brings each individual into the body of the story, bridging the gap between reality and fantasy. In our society, where people have trouble finding opportunities where they feel their voices can be heard, storytelling could represent a new/old opportunity to enrich communication *(Timothy Lightman; teacher of four and five year olds).*

Early childhood and elementary grade teachers are trained in and often most comfortable with the read-aloud mode for centering their children's attention and work on storyreading and writing. In his book *On Teaching*, Herbert Kohl (1978) wrote: "In every teacher, there is the voice of the ancient storyteller." Yet for many teachers, this voice may not be so easy to recognize and claim. Like any other skill or art form, teachers (or any adult learners) need guidance or scaffolding to internalize the skills and understandings required to communicate the structural forms of folktale and myth with their students. And, as in other forms of learning, "every journey begins with the first step." Consistent with the developmental-interaction perspective, these learnings are embedded whenever possible in the teacher's own history, experience, and personal understandings. Through games (Lipman, 1995), memories of times when story played a role in their own growing up, and use of family objects, adults can often discover or rediscover some of the key narratives in their own lives. Often, it can be a time for teachers brought up in the oral tradition to share and remember the richness of these experiences with peers and colleagues. For other teachers, a sense of "being told stories" may seem more remote. But when given the time to participate in dialogue, write, and remember, teachers can begin to re-visit times in their lives when a family member, visitor or friend, gave them a precious gift of a story well-told—at a special time, a special place.

> It was a Thursday afternoon. I was seven years old. One Thursday as I was returning home from school I smelled my mom's cooking from a distance. I opened the door and said to my mom, "You know, I could smell the porridge you are cooking at a far distance." She smiled and said, "That is exactly what Esau said to Jacob when he came back tired from hunting." In second grade we had already learned this story where Esau gives up his birthright over the porridge. He said to Jacob, "Give me this red porridge." My mom told me that Iraqui

> Jews believe that was the exact dish Jacob gave his brother Esau. I was shivering. I was eating the same porridge that was eaten at biblical times so long ago! It is a tradition in my family to cook this dish every Thursday. I keep it up and my daughter adds her part. Now when my children ask me the same question, I simply answer them by telling about Esau and Jacob *(Tikvah Halperin, teacher of four and five year olds)*.

Reclaiming these memories are often the first steps for teachers to see and to remember the power of told stories in their own lives and experiences. Only then can they begin to discover a rationale for building similar experiences into the formal environment of the school and classroom. In a recent graduate school class, teachers gave the following responses when asked their association to the word "story": history; fireplace; interaction; bedtime; fantastical; pictures in your mind; entertainment; explanation; communication. From a psycholinguistic perspective, story and storytelling seem to carry quite a specific function—for narrative is above all a structuring device, deeply tied to memory (Clark, 1977). Story is the way human beings sequence their multiple fields of experiences into a series of events—with both temporal and spatial referents—through language in its many forms (Brewer, 1985; Bruner, 1990). This structuring aspect of story can be seen in the various meanings and uses of the word in different languages: the English word story comes form the Latin "*historia*" or narrative. However, the word "story"—in medieval times—was also used to describe the levels of a cathedral—each panelled with a series of stained glass windows—each telling a "story" (Spiegelman, 1996). In Spanish and French "*cuento, les contes, raconteur*" refer to counting or numbering. In Hebrew the word for story, "*sipur*," is derived from the root "*saper*," to count. Among the Luba people of Central America, the storyteller uses a heavy piece of stone or wood studded with small raised objects, the proper set of narratives or genealogies is recalled for telling. When teachers begin to explore their own personal narratives within a structural, value-laden and multilingual context, their associations take on more purposeful dimensions as they seek to find connections between family stories and their students' learning and divergent interests and needs.

> New Year's Eve means much to Chinese people. In principle at least, all members of the family have to come home for a reunion. I still remember one of the stories told in one of the New Year's Eve celebrations by my father. This is the story: "A friend of mine, who is a merchant, went to a place far away from home for a business trip. He stayed in a small inn

> for a few nights and used up all his money. Not being able to proceed with his trip, he asked a favor of the worker in the inn to sell his overcoat for money. He told the worker the coat was worth two hundred dollars when he bought it, so that the worker had an idea of the price. The worker then took the coat to the street for sale. After a while, he sold it with a good price and came back with two hundred and thirty dollars in his pocket. He gave all the money to the merchant and declined the commission." Stories like this were told by my father on New Year's Eve when we were small. Some, we were told, happened in his hometown in Szechwan Province, China. Some were my grandparents' or relatives' stories. After more than twenty years, I realized that people in the stories were not necessarily his friends or relatives, and neither did they necessarily happen in my father's hometown. I think the reason my father told the stories that way was to draw our attention and to make us remember. In his way, he transferred the moral values he believed in to us, such as: "We should always be honest." Indeed, this is a good way to plant moral ideas in childrens' minds. I will also transfer these values to my children and students in the future *(Li Chi Ho, graduate student).*

Of course, use of personal narrative is often the trademark of a truly engaged teacher. In her doctoral study *Building American history: Meditating performances in classroom and community*, folklorist Lynne Hamer (1995) at the University of Toledo has documented the way teachers use, even unconsciously, their own fund of memories for clarifying or modifying information that is either purely text-based or far from their students' own experiences and understanding.

Different from personal narrative, however, is the vast repertoire of tales from myth and folklore that teachers find included in curriculum guides, literacy-based programs, libraries, and trade publications (Hearne, 1993). Discovering their connections to this core of narrative–in a form of performance or oral retelling–is often a most challenging, yet rewarding process. For it is in the transformation of these narratives "from text to tongue" that teachers can find their own true connections to peoples, times, and places from "far away and long ago." In so doing, they can model powerfully for their students their belief and confidence in the power and beauty of the singular, individual, human being to communicate a shared vision of symbol, imagination and metaphor. By looking at folktales as embodying not only written, but spoken language, teachers begin to uncover some of the elements that have sustained storytelling for so many generations in oral cultures.

> I found myself engaging with the story in ways that I did not when I read to the children directly from a book....I felt the power of my words on each child as I looked out into the children's faces and saw that they were completely engrossed in the story regardless of my shortcomings as a storyteller.... It was like I had discovered a secret way of communicating directly to the experience of each child in the room *(Ted Mockrish, assistant teacher)*.

Folktales offer a body of work that allows a teacher to explore, albeit through translation or the author's interpretation, ways of thinking and knowing that are unique to local cultures, yet resonant with themes that mark the human condition in all parts of the world.

> Apart from localized myths and legends, which have a specific character, most tales are readily accepted by one culture from another. So long has this mechanism of acceptance been going on that a vast number of folktale themes are found today throughout the world....Tales we have thought of as having European origins were told anciently in many other far off places *(Courlander, 1963)*.

Without a body of quantitative research to refer to, teachers' own experience seems, continually, to affirm the validity of tale-telling as a way to engage their children as learners on many levels. For teachers of middle school years and upper grades, the strong focus on reading comprehension and writing skills can sometimes obviate childrens' ongoing need to explore language for the sake of language itself. Practicing or modeling the retelling of folktales can often spark renewed interest for children of this age and grade level.

> In recent years, I have found myself speaking more and more with teachers in a variety of contexts about the theory and practice of creating literature-based reading and writing programs....It is then somewhat jarring, and at the same time exciting, to discover storytelling, accent on the telling, as yet another facet of the reading and writing process. I frankly admit that my first inclination was to quickly slot storytelling as a sub-category under either a) providing a rich repertoire of literature for children to respond to and inspire their own or b) offering another meaningful way for children to rehearse ideas for writing. Now while there are ways that storytelling

> can enhance the reading/writing process, my experience during the past several weeks has led me to realize that storytelling is not a sub-category, but a major component of not only reading and writing, but of developing and strengthening oral language *(Rob Caramella; staff developer and teacher of nine and ten year olds).*

Stories in the context of the oral tradition are not learned or memorized word by word but rather are internalized as an unfolding of linguistic sequences, embedded in rituals of beginnings, and endings, repetitions and closures that continue to be immensely satisfying to listeners and tellers of various ages and backgrounds (Brewer, 1985; Favat, 1977; Jaffe, 1995; Livo and Rietz, 1986). During a storytelling session with a kindergarten class in the Northwest Bronx section of New York City, one teacher noted that children who usually were reticent about approaching literature through print were among the most active in participating with imaginative responses and retellings of the folktale they were hearing. Could consistent experiences with oral narrative eventually lead to a fuller understanding with literacy, as children in early elementary grades begin to internalize the rules and conventions of written language? Again, through experience, teachers can begin to discover untapped resources by engaging students in modes of storytelling and oral literature (Gumperz and Hernàndez-Chavez, 1972; Heath, 1983).

> The idea of being "encumbered by print" really hit home recently. I began storytelling in the classroom late in the year, but I have already made several observations that raise interesting questions. On at least three occasions, children who have consistently demonstrated learning and social issues have enthusiastically volunteered to tell stories. On each occasion, I have taken a deep breath and let go. Something magic happens each time. A child who struggles gaining entrance into a social group sits and spins a story that so totally captures her peers that they break out in spontaneous applause when she is finished. A child who has consistently worked with a reading specialist since entering school, tells a story with intricate sequencing and rich dramatic gestures. Clearly this can't be attributed just to chance. Was it the safety of a story that allowed a child to feel the power of being celebrated by her peers? Was it the putting aside for a moment the mechanics of written text that allowed a child to have a feeling of success and vital communication *(Rob Caramella, staff developer and teacher of nine and ten year olds)*?

In contrast to the work of teachers in middle and upper grades, teachers of younger children can use folktale repertoire to open up new worlds of expression and emergent literacy. Children at this age absorb these stories on many levels, both emotionally and cognitively (Bettelheim, 1977; Favat, 1977). They are eager to retell traditional tales and express themselves to their classmates with their own narratives. The structures and patterns of folktales can support young children's language learning and investment in oral and written language; and provide teachers a successful way to convey ideas, information, and social values.

> My kindergarten class has been enjoying several of the stories I learned from the course. Now they all have become storytellers themselves. *Almost everyone wants to tell his or her own story*. I was able to find some books of all different kinds of stories. Some I remember from my own childhood. It is exciting to be the role model for a classroom full of young storytellers, ready to carry on the tradition! *(Jennifer Ruff, teacher of five and six year olds)*

> Storytelling is a gift complete with joy....The art of the storyteller is the most fluid of all arts...the story comes alive as we are sharing it with them...*(Valerie Machado, teacher of three and four year olds)*

> In telling stories to children, it is music to the ears of the teller when he/she hears "tell me another." *(Mary De Souza, Special Education student)*

Curriculum: A Context for Oral Traditions

From a developmental-interaction perspective, the child is learning continually (see also Dewey, 1938). It is in the experience of curriculum as a lived and lively unfolding of questions, investigations, and adaptations of new knowledge that story can have its most powerful effect in the learning process—for children as individuals and with their peers. For Lucy Sprague Mitchell, the real world is a stage on which children can work and rework their own perceptions and understandings. Reaching out to and grasping ideas, information, and experiences from the family, school, and larger community give children a solid ground from which to think, discuss, and problem-solve according to their age and developmental level.

Discussions by the children, sometimes called "group stories,"

> reveal and develop relationship-thinking. they may also become a kind of play with language. Images—which should be distinguished from logical thinking—can become active in the words of an artist and make the experience live again. Children are artists in their play and spontaneously use words for play (Mitchell, 1991 / 1934, 27).

For Kieran Egan (1986), the dichotomy of images versus logical thinking is resolved through consideration of the imagination itself as the mediating force between abstract concepts, fantasy and empirical study. From this point of view, the intrinsic imaginative powers of the child, nurtured by narratives from print and spoken word, can serve as the fuel to drive the engine of curriculum structure and content. "Childrens' imaginative capacities do not only find an outlet in fantasy stories: they find their real work and growth in being applied to history, mathematics and science as well...story-form is a dominant sense-making tool" (108). Teachers can work with both of these important perspectives as they strive to meet the needs of children through the interpretation and construction of curriculum goals and content.

The oral tradition can provide teachers with invaluable resources for deepening and extending their curriculum studies in form and content. When teachers take a story or myth from text and make it their own, they can often discover significant new pathways and learning connections for their students. Storytelling can become a key component for teachers as a focus of integration for many curriculum areas—for it is the teacher who knows best when to tell a story, and how it can best be worked into his or her ongoing themes of the year. By connecting with students through eye contact, voice, and gesture, stories can become a powerful vehicle for teaching—from word problems in math, to rhyming games in reading, to a folktale that ties in to a history lesson or community study.

Suzanne Fogarty, a head teacher at an independent school in Brooklyn, in New York City, provides a powerful example of integrating a curriculum with storytelling. Recently, she developed a study on endangered species with her class of second graders. The study was full of connections to the oral tradition—from trickster tales to creation myths, with many opportunities for art and writing projects as extensions.

Suzanne drew on Joseph Bruchac's collection *Keepers of the Animals*, for her story repertoire. A Zuni myth called "Eagle Boy" tells about the friendship between a boy and the eagle that he saved, and how he learned the ways of the eagles, including their ability to fly. As a reward for his kind act, he receives a gift from his new eagle family—a pair of wings. But in receiving the gift, the eagles warn him not to fly to the Southland. At first, he follows their warnings, but his curiosity gets the best of him, and he flies off on the forbidden journey. Finally, the eagles remove his wings and ask the boy to leave their world. The boy returns to his family. He has lost his wings, but has gained a new respect and knowledge of these great hunters of the sky.

Suzanne told this story to her children at a group meeting time designated for social studies. A lively discussion of what it would be like to fly followed. One child brought up the fact that this story reminded her of Daedalus and Icarus, who flew too close to the sun. Another child said, "What would everything look like from up there?" Suzanne decided to use the childrens' fascination with Eagle Boy's flight to introduce them to a study of maps and perspective. The children created a project in which they pretended that they too were eagles and imagined what a place would look like from above—from a bird's eye point of view. The variations in children's drawings and descriptions offered opportunities to observe and assess the range of conceptual development in the class.

> About half the children were able to depict what it would be like to see the tops of things—trees or a lake. The other half saw the places they selected from the side. It almost was split down the middle. It was fascinating to see where these kids were. Most of them chose places that had special meaning to them. One child chose a summer house; another child drew himself flying over the Brooklyn Bridge. One boy chose flying over a rabbit house he has in his backyard. Then there were a select few who wrote about fantasy places. One chose what flying over Southland would look like. Another chose flying over a mountain range. His quote was: "This is a place far away from civilization." Another child drew a picture of flying over Venice, as she had been there when she was very young.

This is just one example of how a story from world myth, told in the intimacy of the classroom setting, stimulated children to think, investigate, and imagine in new ways. Suzanne gave children the option of pulling what meant the most for them for their bird's eye picture. She also moved and shifted other parts of the schedule, to incorporate this project immediately after its telling. As a result, the children's ideas and feelings were fresh in their minds, and they were able to make the most of their responses for this study. Later in the curriculum, Suzanne used another story, "The Lake of Atagahi," a Cherokee legend, to serve as a catalyst for a final culminating project, in which children expressed their sense of moral vision by painting murals of a world where animals could live safe and unharmed. Through capitalizing on children's spontaneous responses to the spoken story—in this case of Native American myths—new and valuable learnings were built into the framework of an entire unit of curriculum.

Oral narrative, with its related repertoire in childrens' lore of songs, chants, and games can also be incorporated into the literacy program, giving teachers useful strategies to enhance skills in verbal language, memory, and a general love of reading (Roney, 1993). One activity, "Grandmother's Trunk" is a children's storytelling game. Much like other cumulative stories or songs (for example, "I Know an Old Lady Who Swallowed a Fly"), each child adds an item to grandmother's trunk by saying: "Today I'm going to grandmother's house, and in my trunk I'm putting a "——." Before they add their own object, they must first repeat what has been said before. Each child has a progressively longer list of what will go into the grandmother's trunk. A version of this game can be played for the teaching of reading. In small groups, children can take turns repeating the opening phrase and then adding an object. Children derive enjoyment from the group process, as well as the accomplishment of memorizing longer and longer sequences of words. Teachers can record the children's story on lined paper, or even as a graph for display. Activities like these can also be powerful tools for the teaching of English as a second language as the story form gives opportunities for repetition of grammar and phonemes in a playful, engaging medium. Children of any language background can delight in using these age-old narrative patterns to discover their own growing skills as readers, writers and storytellers (Boyle and Peregoy, 1990).

Storytelling is a medium of words, but, as stated earlier, myth and folktales have strong elements of space, time and number embedded in their form and structures (Burns, 1992; Kaye, 1996). For example, in the Chinese folktale *Two of Everything*, a man is given a gift, a pot that doubles anything that is placed in it. In the end, the man not only has doubles of many household objects, but he and his wife as well! (Hong, 1993). Sets, groupings, and multiplication are implied in this folk narrative which also has humorous and philosophical dimensions. Rather than conveying the mathematical problems as they appear in textbooks, teachers can work with story form as children learn skills of computation and multi-step word problems. Placing these mathematical concepts in narrative context helps children engage more imaginatively with the problems at hand, given them a sense of ownership of their own number learning and problem-solving styles (see Kaye, 1996, for many helpful examples).

In many schools, teachers are given mandated social studies curricula, using text books and pre-designed scope and sequences, which cannot always take into consideration childrens' development, social environment or unique funds of knowledge. The challenges presented in implementing these kinds of curricula for children in a meaningful way can often be quite daunting. In a search for alternative ways of making history come alive, many teachers use stories—folktales and oral accounts—to help students conceptualize more strongly the gaps between contemporary life and earlier times or to see the history and values they share with people in their own communities (Galt, 1992; Fitzgerald, 1993).

The Alhambra Academy, a small school in Oakland, California, founded in 1995 by the late Daahia Taha, serves children from first to eighth grade. The name of the school reflects the core theme of study: global studies and science. One of the key goals for the school staff is to bring the wider world into the lives of students who rarely have an opportunity to leave their own immediate neighborhood, an inner-city area. In 1996, Ms. Taha and staff developed a global studies curriculum based on storytelling and world drumming. The study began with a visit to a nearby college campus and Korean students' community house. There, children shared in a traditional Korean meal and listened to a performance of Korean music and drumming. The children were fascinated by the instruments and rhythmic styles. In her investigation of further resources, Ms. Taha came upon *Patakín: World Tales of Drums and Drummers* (Jaffe, 1994), and decided to use the book as a jumping off point for her curriculum. The book includes ten myths from different parts of the world in which a drum or drummer plays an important role. Children formed small groups to learn and retell a story—from India, Ireland, Korea, Mexico or Haiti—to present to their classmates. Teachers also used the stories as a focus point for studying world geography, as students located each country on the map, and read more about the cultural background for each tale. Other trips followed, including a visit to a master class with C.K. Ladzepko—a master drummer from Ghana teaching in the San Francisco area. In this setting, children were able to observe college students—young adults from many different cultural backgrounds—learning and playing West African music. As children become more engrossed with the study, they developed further projects including: drum-building and instrument-making, and writing and illustrating their own drumming myths. The study ended with a culminating activity—a community event in which children performed the stories they had created for families and friends.

In this way, teachers can work with the oral tradition—both for specific curriculum areas and across disciplines. Storytelling—an ancient yet contemporary art form—can serve as an important medium for effective communication of curriculum content, with long lasting repercussions for children as learners and participants in a complex and demanding world.

****

In North American education, oral narrative and storytelling have often been seen as activities best suited to library hours; transition moments between subject areas, or as mostly appropriate in working with pre-school children. By exploring some of the current theory and research on storytelling, as well as the perspectives and experiences of teachers in the field, it seems clear that a framework which takes into account the developmental needs and cultural contexts for teachers as well as students across the grades can serve as fruitful ground for both the perpetuation and transformation of storytelling and folk narrative in educational settings.

"Those who do not have power over the story that dominates their lives—power to retell it, rethink it, deconstruct it, joke about it, and change it as times change, truly are powerless, because they cannot think new thoughts." *Salman Rushdie, New York Times, 1992*

Note

1. This paper is a chapter in N. Nager and E. K. Shapiro, Eds. *Legacies and new directions for a progressive pedagogies.* Albany, N.Y.: State University of New York Press, copyright 2000, and is reprinted by permission of the author, and the publisher.

References

Bettelheim, B. *The uses of enchantment.* New York: Random House, 1977.

Boyle, F. & S.F. Peregoy. "Literacy scaffolds: Strategies for first- and second-language readers and writers." *The Reading Teacher.* 44 (1990) 194-198.

Brewer, W.F. "The story schema: Universal and culture-specific properties." in D.R. Olson, N. Torrance & A. Hildyard (Ed). *Literacy; language and learning: The nature and consequences of reading and writing.* London: Cambridge UP, 1985.

Bruchac, J. and M.C. Caduto. *Native American animal stories* (selected from *Keepers of the animals*). Golden, Colorado: Fulcrum Publications, 1992.

Burns, M. *Math and literature* (Book One). White Plains, New York: Cuisinaire, 1992.

Bruner, J. *Acts of meaning.* Cambridge: Harvard UP, 1990.

Cazden, C. *The functions of language in the classroom.* New York: Teachers College Press, 1972.

Clark, H.H. and V. Clark. *Psychology and language: An introduction to psycholinguistics.* New York: Harcourt, Brace, Jovanovich, 1977.

Cohen, D. *The learning child: Guidelines for parents and teachers.* New York: Schocken Books, 1972.

Courlander, H. *On recognizing the human species.* New York: Anti-Defamation League /One Nation Library, 1960.

Dewey, J. *Experience and education.* New York: Collier Books, 1938.

Egan, K. *Teaching as storytelling: An alternative approach to teaching and curriculum.* Chicago: University of Chicago Press, 1989.

Favat, A.F. *Child and tale: The origins of interest.* Urbana, Illinois: National Council of Teachers of English, 1977.

Fitzgerald, S. "Helping children find their personal and community folklore." In G.T. Blatt, (Ed) *Once upon a folktale: Capturing the folk process with children.* New York: Teachers College Press, 1993.

Galt, M.F. *The story in history: Writing your way into the American experience.* New York: Teacher and Writers Collaborative, 1992.

Gumperz, J. & E. Hernandez-Chavez. "Bilingualism, bidialectalism, and classroom interaction." In C. Cazden (Ed.) *The functions of language in the classroom.* New York: Teachers College Press, 1972.

Hamer, L. Building American history: Mediating performances in classroom and community. Unpublished dissertation, University of Indiana, 1995.

Hearne, B. "Cite the source: reducing cultural chaos in picture books, Part one." *School Library Journal. 39.* 1993, 22-37.

Heath, S.B. *Ways with words: Language, life and work in communities and classrooms.* New York: Cambridge University Press, 1983.

Hong, L.T. *Two of everything.* New York: Albert Whitman, 1993.

Jaffe, N. *Patakín: World tales of drums and drummers.* New York: Henry Holt, 1994.

----. "Storytelling at the crossroads." *Forkroads: A Journal of Ethnic-American Literature. 39,* 1995. 73-76.

Kaye, P. Afterwords: *Folk and fairy tales with mathematical ever afters.* White Plains, New York: Cuisinaire, 1996.

Kohl, H. *On teaching.* New York: Bantam Books, 1978.

Kroeber, K. *Retelling/rereading: The fate of storytelling in modern times.* New York: Columbia UP, 1992.

Lévi-Strauss, C. *Myth and meaning: Cracking the code of culture.* New York: Schocken Books 1995/1978.

Lewis, C. *A big bite of the world: Childrens' creative writing.* Englewood Cliffs, NJ: Prentice-Hall, 1979.

Livo, N.J. and S.S. Rietz. *Storytelling: Process and practice.* Littleton, CO: Libraries Unlimited, 1986.

Lipman, D. *Storytelling games.* Phoenix, Arizona: Oryx Press, 1995.

Mitchell, L.S. *Young geographers: How they explore the world and how they map the world.* New York: Basic Books, 1991 / 1934.

Miller, P.J., A. R. Wiley, H. Fung, and C. Liang. "Personal storytelling as a medium of socialization within Chinese and American Families." *Child Development. 68.* 1997. 557-68.

Olmedo, I.M. "Voices of our past: Using oral history to explore funds of knowledge within a Puerto Rican family." *Anthropology and Education Quarterly. 28* (1997) 550-73.

Paley, V.G. *Wally's stories.* Cambridge, MA: Harvard UP, 1981.

Roney, J. "Telling stories: A key to reading and writing." In G.T. Blatt (Ed.) *Once upon a folktale: Capturing the folk process with children*. New York: Teachers College Press, 1993.

Spiegelman, A. Keynote Address at the Atlanta Jewish Community Center Annual Book Fair. 1996.

Vascellaro, S. and C. Genishi. "'All the things that mattered': Stories written by teachers for children." In A.H. Dyson and C. Genishi (Eds.) *The need for story: Cultural diversity in classroom and continuity*. Urbana, Ill: National Council of Teachers of English, 1994.

Zeitlin, S. "The storytelling revolution." *The Jewish Storytelling Newsletter*, 5, 1990.

Zipes, J. *Breaking the magic spell: Radical theories of folk and fairy tales*. New York, Methuen, 1984.

Recommended Readings

Barton, B. and D. Booth. *Stories in the classroom: Storytelling, reading aloud and roleplaying with children*. New Hampshire: Heinemann Books, 1990.

Bruchac, J. *Tell me a tale: A book about storytelling*. New York: Harcourt Brace, 1977.

Cooper, P. *When stories come to school: Telling, writing, and performing stories in the early childhood classroom*. New York: Teachers and Writer's Collaborative, 1993.

Egan, K. *Primary understanding: Education for early childhood*. New York: Routledge, Chapman and Hall, 1991.

Jaffe, N. *A voice for the people: The life and work of Harold Courlander*. New York: Henry Holt, 1997.

Jaffe, N. and S. Zeitlin. *The cow of no color: Riddle stories and justice tales from around the world*. New York: Henry Holt, 1998.

Lane, M. *Picturing the rose: A way of looking at fairy tales*. New York: H.W. Wilson, 1994.

Maguire, J. *Creative storytelling handbook*. New York: MacMillan, 1987.

Pellowski, A. *The world of storytelling*. New York: H.W. Wilson, 1992/1977.

Metaphors in Science

Cheryl M. Bartlett

Introduction

A good story often contains transformations in consciousness achieved with the aid of metaphors. So, being a university teacher interested in helping science students attain new intellectual horizons, and also being a research scientist seeking new insights concerning Nature, I thought it appropriate to tackle "metaphors in science" as the topic for this paper.

Had I chosen a topic from my area of scholarly competence, I would have focused on parasitic roundworms in animals. "Metaphors in science" is, on the other hand, simply a topic that intrigues me. Most recently, metaphors have surfaced while I have wrestled with the vexing question of "what, exactly, is science?" during the design of new post-secondary science curricula intended to integrate Western science with Mi'kmaw Aboriginal world views. At other times metaphors and the subjective dimension have surfaced while I have reflected upon my experiences in the realms of the undergraduate science student, the science researcher, the reader of science books, and the science professor.

My paper is divided into four parts, the first three being "the good, the bad, and the ugly" (in reverse order). The Ugly provides anecdotes that illustrate denial of the subjective in science. The Bad outlines some strong negative views recently expressed by others concerning metaphors *per se* in science. The Good provides reasons why I view their use in a very positive light. Finally, "ghost stories" outlines reasons for a possible *metaphor phobia* in modern science.

"The Ugly": Denial of the Subjective in Science

In 1977, in my fourth year of an undergraduate zoology degree, I became captivated by the discipline of parasitology and decided to pursue the field in greater depth at the graduate level. Upon applying to graduate schools elsewhere, I was required to ask professors at my home university to write letters of reference and send them off on my behalf. Some time later, after I had settled upon the University of Guelph, another university returned all my application documents, including the letters. Of course I chose to read them! Overall, they were quite positive, but one mentioned that the applicant (i.e. me) had only average abilities in the area of *original or creative thinking*. I remember that at the time this caused me considerable puzzlement since, to the best of my recollection, such skills were never mentioned (let alone taught) in my undergraduate science courses and here, out of the blue, they were suddenly significant in determining the success of my application to graduate school.

Over the intervening 20 plus years, I have had ample opportunity to reflect upon that experience. The same deficiency in undergraduate science training is pointed out by Isaak and Hubert (1999) who discuss the challenge students face when making the transition from undergraduate to graduate studies in science. And now that I teach undergraduate science and try to include some creative thinking dimensions in the learning process, I know its omission would meet with the greater approval of one of my first year biology students who, in 1997, strongly protested that he "could not see what imagination had to do with science, anyhow" (an anecdote related at the First Storytelling Symposium, see Bartlett 1997).

I offer three sweeping conclusions about undergraduate science. First, the typical undergraduate science student is reared in an environment that does little to encourage original and creative thinking skills, and this generally continues in the highschool science experience. Information is conveyed in lecture (the classroom) by the professor (teacher) and the student is later asked to demonstrate mastery by returning it at exam time in a form that draws heavily upon memorization skills. Seldom will there be a call for the student to "enter into" the information, i.e. to personalize the understanding. Second, the information learned is invariably presented to the student as having been established by "objective scientific methodology," without reference to any creative or original thinking or other subjective dimensions that "discovery science" entails (versus "journeyman prospector science," to use Wilson's (1998) label). Third, if an undergraduate science student does develop some inkling of the involvement of the subjective element in science, this probably occurs within the context of either an independent research project, or a co-operative learning course. Unfortunately, the former are generally restricted to honours or elite students, and very few universities offer the latter within science programs (Herreid,1998, offers an excellent discussion of the "why not" of the latter). This is doubly unfortunate because, in my experience, project courses and co-operative learning courses tend to "turn on" more undergraduate students to science than any other approach.

My present understanding, namely that there is a major role for the subjective in science, evolved over the course of 20 years of conducting science research, and it contrasts sharply with my perception as an undergraduate. I agree with something my MSc and PhD supervisor at the University of Guelph (Dr. R.C. Anderson) used to say to all his graduate students: "you need to live, eat, breathe, and sleep your research...or you won't amount to a hill of beans in science." At the time that we were the recipients of this wisdom, I don't think many of us understood its depth, and he did not elaborate. We generally translated it into a requirement to be in the lab from morning til night, seven days a week, and thereby succeeded in keeping "the boss" happy.

Science research is a quest which, when conducted in areas of the real unknown (i.e. not problems that simply require redundant application of methodology or instrumentation), demands commitment at the deepest levels of the senses of self and transpersonal self, including metaphoric understandings that come through living, eating, breathing, and sleeping one's research – dimensions that are unquestionably iconoclastic to objective, scientific thinking. Root-Bernstein (1997) has written an enlightening article in this regard, and I think it is high time to deliver his message over and over throughout all undergraduate science courses. If subjective dimensions are good for the doers of science, then so should they be for the learners. Thus, I strongly advocate requiring students in undergraduate science courses to engage their own original and creative thinking dimensions in the learning of science, with metaphor as a key tool.

"The Bad": Other People's Negative Views Concerning Metaphors in Science

In 1994, Gross and Levitt (a biologist and a mathematician, respectively) wrote a book entitled *Higher superstition; the academic left and its quarrels with science*. It explores their perceptions of, and concerns about, "muddleheadedness, science bashing, and antiscience among postmodernists, feminists, radical environmentalists, multiculturalists, and AIDS activists." They wrote it as a clarion call for all intellectuals, especially scientists, who they felt should be concerned with attacks against objectivity, critical thought, and rationality. Among their concerns is that it is characteristic of modern scientists to carry on in blissful ignorance of such attacks and outside opinions, and shrink from the duty to speak out against their absurdity.

Thus summoned, I read their passionately worded arguments. They reproduce a statement from a preprint of an essay by the feminist critics of science Campbell and Campbell-Wright: "Metaphor plays a central role in the construction of mathematics." Gross and Levitt's response (p.116) is: "No! It does *not*—certainly not the kinds of metaphors this paper alludes to. One of us, speaking as a mathematician who has seen an awful lot of mathematics 'constructed' and has constructed some himself, can testify to the *uselessness* of metaphor in mathematical invention, although *analogy*—a rather different notion—can be of some help."

This response bothered me immensely. First, Gross and Levitt did not elaborate on the statement about analogy maybe being OK, but its close relative, metaphor, being useless, nor did they explain whether they viewed mathematics as similar or different in this regard to other areas in science. Second, metaphors are used abundantly in many areas of modern science research in publications aimed at peers (evolutionary biology and immunology are excellent examples), and in almost all books written by scientists who seek to communicate science to the broader public.

Having entered the game, compliments of Gross and Levitt's summons, I pursued further readings on metaphors in science. Donna Haraway is a well known feminist critic of science who has expressed severe reservations about metaphors in science. I do not share her specific concerns, but do believe they should be acknowledged and thus, provide an example with the quote below which is from her 1991 book *Simians, cyborgs, and women; the reinvention of Nature* (p. 185):

> So, the further I get with the description of the radical social constructionist program and a particular version of postmodernism, coupled to the acid tools of critical discourse in the human sciences, the more nervous I get. Like all neuroses, mine is rooted in the problem of metaphor, that is, the problem of the relation of bodies and language. For example, the force field imagery of moves in the fully textualized and coded world is the matrix for many arguments about socially negotiated reality for the postmodern subject. This world-as-code is, just for starters, a high-tech military field, a kind of automated academic battlefield, where blips of light called players disintegrate (what a metaphor!) each other in order to stay in the knowledge and power game.

Thus, to Haraway, metaphors become important, evil brokers in the power game of science. I would like to clearly state that in my research area, i.e. parasitology, I have never experienced research *per se* or metaphors in this negative way. I do readily acknowledge, however, that politics in a university science department can be altogether different. And, I do share her interest in the issue and nature of objectivity and subjectivity in science, as do many current scholars, male and female alike.

"The Good": My Positive Views Concerning Metaphors in Science

Over the years, it has become increasingly apparent to me, in my capacity as a university professor teaching undergraduate science (a career that began in 1989), that students desperately need to have good metaphors offered to them to facilitate understanding of new concepts, and they also need to be encouraged to create their own metaphors as aids to develop personal understanding. Therefore, my efforts in the remainder of this paper are directed towards the positive role of metaphors in the generation of scientific and other human knowledge, as well as the question of why some scientists may have *metaphor phobia* unrelated to viewpoints such as those expressed by Gross, Levitt, and Haraway.

Whose view, or definition, of metaphor?

In exploring the positive roles of metaphors in science, I will employ the view of metaphor as a *cognitive tool*. This differs dramatically from the traditionally assumed view that metaphor was a matter of language peripheral to concerns of meaning and mind–as an ornament in literature or in a style of presentation–and is associated with the work of Lakoff and Johnson (1980), Lakoff (1987), and Turner (1987). They view metaphor as a matter of conceptual structure central to meaning and have been part of the revival of classical rhetoric, aided by linguistics and cognitive science, which focuses on the mind and the thought underlying the surface forms of language, rather than focusing on the surface of language and being inattentive to mind (Lakoff, in Turner 1987). Indeed, Lakoff (1987) considers metaphor as one of four innate cognitive models that humans employ, the others being metonymy, image schematic, and propositional. Metaphors, of course, require pattern recognition and comparison, and Gardner (1983, 1999) has advanced an entire theory of multiple intelligences based on 7-9 innate pattern recognition abilities in humans. Along with many others, therefore, I find it useful to consider humans as basically pattern recognition and storytelling creatures.

Metaphors as a cognitive tool

Upon accepting that metaphors are an innate way that the mind starts to context sensory information and perception, i.e. to create story, it then seems reasonable to also view them as a tool for the purposes of creative thinking, one that can be intentionally used to move towards new understanding. I would like, therefore, to consider the positive use of metaphor as a cognitive tool and means of creative thinking, for the purpose of science, from three perspectives: in teaching, in research, and during a paradigm shift.

Metaphor as a cognitive tool in teaching

Metaphor can be used as a catalyst in the transformation of information and logic to personal understanding, by a new learner. As the professor in this exercise, I can provide the metaphor or ask the students to develop their own. A few *simple* examples of the former that I use in introductory biology include buffer system sponges in the living organism, Gretzky bonds in the sugar molecules that fuel our bodies, and humans as stardust (with thanks to Joni Mitchell) and fatheads with intracellular shuttlebuses that transport high energy electrons. My offerings are semi-acceptable to OK with most of the students, although some clearly manifest discomfort with such unconventional comparative thinking and I run into problems if I use a referent that they claim is unfamiliar (such as the different houses in *The Three Little Pigs*). However, if I ask the students to develop their own metaphors, I immediately face a mini-rebellion from great numbers of them, the rebellion ranging from outright refusal to even try, to attempts that could only be interpreted as intentional stupidity, to claims of having no imagination. But, as I persevere I also start to see, in some and then more with time, the first flickerings of *real* understanding (i.e. not memorization) of a topic, first realizations of the self-empowerment of this approach to learning, and significantly, the first *transformations of consciousness* that occur when the student has made a *personal entry* into knowledge itself. For those interested in further discussions along this line, I strongly suggest Geoffrey Kane's book (1999) *Education, information, and transformation; essays on learning and thinking.*

If one holds that education is the kindling of a fire, then one will ask the student to develop his or her own metaphors, acknowledging that this requires active participation and interaction with the material. I emphasize *active* because it involves recognition by the student of his or her own *creative* abilities and their use, i.e. of a sense of Self (cf. self)—a Self that conventional ways of teaching ignore but one that Cajete (1994) suggests lies at the heart of traditional modes of teaching in Aboriginal communities. He (1999) also states that the use of metaphor as a teaching tool is an ancient strategy used by all great teachers of human history and contends that its intimate use is especially evident in Native American mythologies and elsewhere when creative insight is essential.

On the other hand, if one holds that education is mere information conveyance, i.e. the filling of a pail, then metaphor and other creative thinking skills have little role to play. Earlier, I related an anecdote that, as a newly minted BSc looking to enter graduate school in the late 1970s, I was puzzled by the inclusion of and the significance accorded to original and creative thinking skills. Today, as I fill out many forms each year for recent BSc graduates also seeking entrance to graduate school, I note that the forms invariably ask that the applicant be rated on his or her original and creative thinking skills. And, I still find it extremely curious that we continue to omit any substantive efforts in teaching such skills in the conventional undergraduate science curriculum. Furthermore, I find it shocking that a proposal to explicitly include metaphor (among other things) has provoked strong opposition from some science colleagues to, and labels of pseudoscience for, a new science curriculum at the University College of Cape Breton that integrates Western science with an Aboriginal world view. And it is all the more shocking when one finds metaphor listed with other creative thinking tools as those things that constitute "the art of genius in science" (Michalko 1998).

METAPHOR AS A COGNITIVE TOOL IN SCIENTIFIC DISCOVERY

Metaphor can be used as an aid to explore what is at the intellectually liminal zone or threshold of understanding, for a researcher in frontier science most definitely requires the ability to let go, to loosen the moorings of analytical and logical thinking considered the hallmarks of scientific thinking. In fact, Harré (1986) contends that "metaphor and simile are the characteristic tropes of scientific thought, not formal validity of argument." He sets his theory of science firmly against logical essentialism, i.e. the giving of primacy to logical structures as the inner essence of scientific discourse, and argues instead that primacy belongs to semantic structures and relations of likeness and difference (i.e. pattern recognition and comparison). For him, logic certainly does have a place in the creation of scientific discourse but not at its core and often as a socially motivated addition, i.e. a contribution to persuasive power.

Metaphor is the cognitive tool that one can use to help "feel" the unknown, when words fail and knowledge of the thing in itself (pure objectivity) is impossible. Surely, few would deny that a research scientist's reach (i.e. sense of mystery, subjective knowledge of "something" out there) most definitely needs, at times, to exceed her grasp (i.e. intellectual and objective understanding of that something). It may be, however, that this need, this cognitive struggle, is not experienced by the "journeyman prospector" type of scientist that Wilson (1998) felt characterizes the vast majority of today's highly trained and narrowly focused scientists.

Metaphor as a Cognitive Tool When a Paradigm Shift Occurs

Metaphors can significantly influence configuration of the questions, intuitions, and understandings that characterize particular world views and thus, it is important to be mindful of them and their influence. To this point, there are many modern scientists, philosophers of science, and science commentators who suggest that science may be currently undergoing a paradigm shift, although this is also hotly denied by many others and a shift is probably best judged to have occurred (or not) only in retrospect. Regardless, metaphor figures prominently in the most frequently encountered outlines of the competing paradigms, as can be seen in the information below which is summarized from Capra (1975, 1996):

> The dominant paradigm in science today is the materialistic or reductionist world view, with its primary focus on entities (physical or material), exclusion or relegation to irrelevancy of mind (consciousness), root metaphor of the Universe or Nature as a machine, and root metaphor of education and knowledge as foundational. In contrast, the emerging paradigm is referred to as the systemic, organismic, or holistic paradigm. Its primary focus is relationship (connectedness and interconnectedness), it acknowledges mind (consciousness), and has root metaphors of the Universe or Nature as a web and of education and knowledge as a network.

"Ghost Stories" ... Or, Why Might Metaphors Spook Conventional Scientists?

Reflection has led me to suspect that there may be a strong subconscious undercurrent of *metaphor phobia* in much of the modern scientific community. The reasons, I believe, reside in the way science is generally portrayed, in the possibility that metaphoric thinking would represent deviance from this established and acceptable image, and in the strong peer pressure that most scientists experience. My thoughts as to how this resistance to metaphor is played out as arguments by some members of the scientific community are outlined below.

1) the portrayal of science knowledge as shared or common, i.e. having only a public face: If science only has a public face, is it not unacceptable, therefore, to claim a role for personal knowledge in science, i.e. to suggest that science could have a private face that complements its public face? Cromer (1993), who wrote a book entitled *Uncommon sense; the heretical nature of science,* considered the scientific way of thinking as completely divorced from "common sense" and by "heretical" meant the primacy of objective thinking. In contrast, Polanyi (1958) and Kane (1999) considered scientific thinking as a layering onto, and therefore additional or secondary to, personal knowledge–i.e. primacy belongs to the private face. Metaphors can be very private, reflecting personal backgrounds and levels of consciousness.

2) the portrayal of science as having the "right answers": If science has the right answers, is it not then silly to risk displaying inadequate knowledge of an area outside one's speciality, given that it is the referent in the metaphor that often resides in the area of lesser personal understanding? For example, Gould and Lewontin (1979) certainly have been taken to task by some (e.g. Mark, 1996) who claim they misunderstood "spandrels" in Gothic architecture when they used them as a metaphor in the debate over biological adaptation.

3) the portrayal of science as distinct from religion: If science is distinct from religion, is it not unorthodox, therefore, to suggest that science shares some intellectual overlap with religion? In many religions and spiritual traditions, for example, it is quite acceptable to speak of a liminal zone where one senses "something" but cannot begin to express it directly although metaphors often suffice. This is the "reaching but not grasping" I mentioned earlier.

4) the portrayal of science as distinct from alchemy: If science is not alchemy, is it not preposterous, therefore, to advocate the use of metaphors in science if one realizes that metaphoric awareness, or correspondences, are central in magical and alchemical ways of thinking, and that science prides itself in having long ago departed from such thinking?

5) the portrayal of science as dealing with one reality: If science deals with the one reality, is it not intellectually retrograde, therefore, to accept two dimensions of understanding, objective and subjective? Consciousness studies are the latest frontier for Western science, and our current scientific understandings in the field have been likened by some to that of the understanding of the world by Europeans at the time that Columbus arrived in the Americas. In spite of this, the so-called 17th Century Cartesian split between mind and body, i.e. between consciousness and physical reality, still presents an invaluable "escape clause" for many conventional thinkers in Western science.

6) the portrayal of science as logical and objective thinking: If science is logical and objective thinking, then does it not follow that it can not include subjective elements such as imagination, dreaming, and the aesthetic sensibility of pattern recognition that underpins metaphoric thinking?

Conclusion

As outlined herein, most undergraduate science students, science researchers, and science professors are not likely to be mindfully aware of the innate cognitive significance of metaphoric thinking or may subconsciously avoid its use. I hold out hope, however, that this may be beginning to change. My optimism is based on the paradigm shift that may be occurring in science, which brings with it a world view inclusive of mind and consciousness. My optimism is also based on research that points to metaphor as an innate cognitive model of how the brain works, and other findings in cognitive science that point to an associative or connectionist basis for how our brains process information and naturally context it into "story." After all, who would have believed a mere 70 years ago, what modern physics and cosmology have now established–that we really are stardust?

Note: In respect to Dr. Bartlett's science focus, we are retaining her format within the essay and in her references.

References

Bartlett, C.M. 1997. Where is the storytelling in science? Chapter 1. In: *The power of the story*. Edited by: A. Kavanagh, University College of Cape Breton Press, Sydney, NS, Canada.

Cajete, G.A. 1994. *Look to the mountain; an ecology of Indigenous education*. Kivakí Press, Durango, CO.

Cajete, G.A. 1999. *Igniting the sparkle; an Indigenous science education model.* Kivakí Press Inc., Skyland, NC.

Capra, F. 1975. *The Tao of physics.* Shambhala, Boston. [3rd updated ed., 1991].

Capra, F. 1996. *The web of life; a new scientific understanding of living systems.* Anchor Books/Doubleday, London.

Cromer, A. 1993. *Uncommon sense; the heretical nature of science.* Oxford University Press, New York.

Gardner, H. 1983. *Frames of mind; the theory of multiple intelligences.* [10th anniversary ed.] BasicBooks, New York.

Gardner, H. 1999. Are there additional intelligences? The case for naturalist, spiritual, and existential intelligences. Chapter 6. In *Education, information, and transformation; essays on learning and thinking.* Edited by: J. Kane. Merrill, Upper Saddle River, NJ.

Gould, S.J. and Lewontin, R.C. 1979. The spandrels of San Marco and the Panglossian paradigm: a critique of the adaptationist programme. *Proceedings of the Royal Society of London,* B205; 581-598.

Gross, P.R. and Levitt, N. 1994. *Higher superstition; the academic left and its quarrels with science.* The Johns Hopkins University Press, Baltimore

Haraway, D. 1991. *Simians, cyborgs, and women; the reinvention of Nature.* Routledge, NY.

Harré, R. 1986. *Varieties of realism, a rationale for the natural sciences.* Basil Blackwell Ltd., Oxford, UK.

Herreid, C. 1998. *Why isn't co-operative learning used to teach science?* BioScience July.

Isaak, D.J. and Hubert, W.A. 1999. Catalyzing the transition from student to scientist—a model for graduate research training. *BioScience* 49: 321-326.

Kane, J. 1999. *Education, information, and transformation; essays on learning and thinking.* Edited by: J. Kane. Merrill, Upper Saddle River, NJ.

Lakoff, G. 1987. *Women, fire, and dangerous things; what categories reveal about the mind.* The University of Chicago Press, Chicago.

Lakoff, G., and Johnson, M. 1980. *Metaphors we live by*: The University of Chicago Press, Chicago.

Mark, R. 1996. In the debate over adaptation, which view is best served by the metaphors of the "spandrels" of San Marco and the bosses of King's College? *American Scientist* 84: 383-389.

Michalko, M. 1998. The art of genius. *Utne Reader,* July-August, pp. 73-76.

Polanyi, M. 1958. *Personal knowledge; towards a post-critical philosophy*. The University of Chicago Press, Chicago.

Root-Bernstein, R. 1997. Art, imagination, and the scientist. *American Scientist* 85: 6-9.

Turner, M. 1987. *Death is the mother of beauty; mind, metaphor, criticism.* The University of Chicago Press, Chicago.

Wilson, E.O. 1998. *Consilience; the unity of knowledge.* Alfred A. Knopf, New York.

Storytelling in Culture

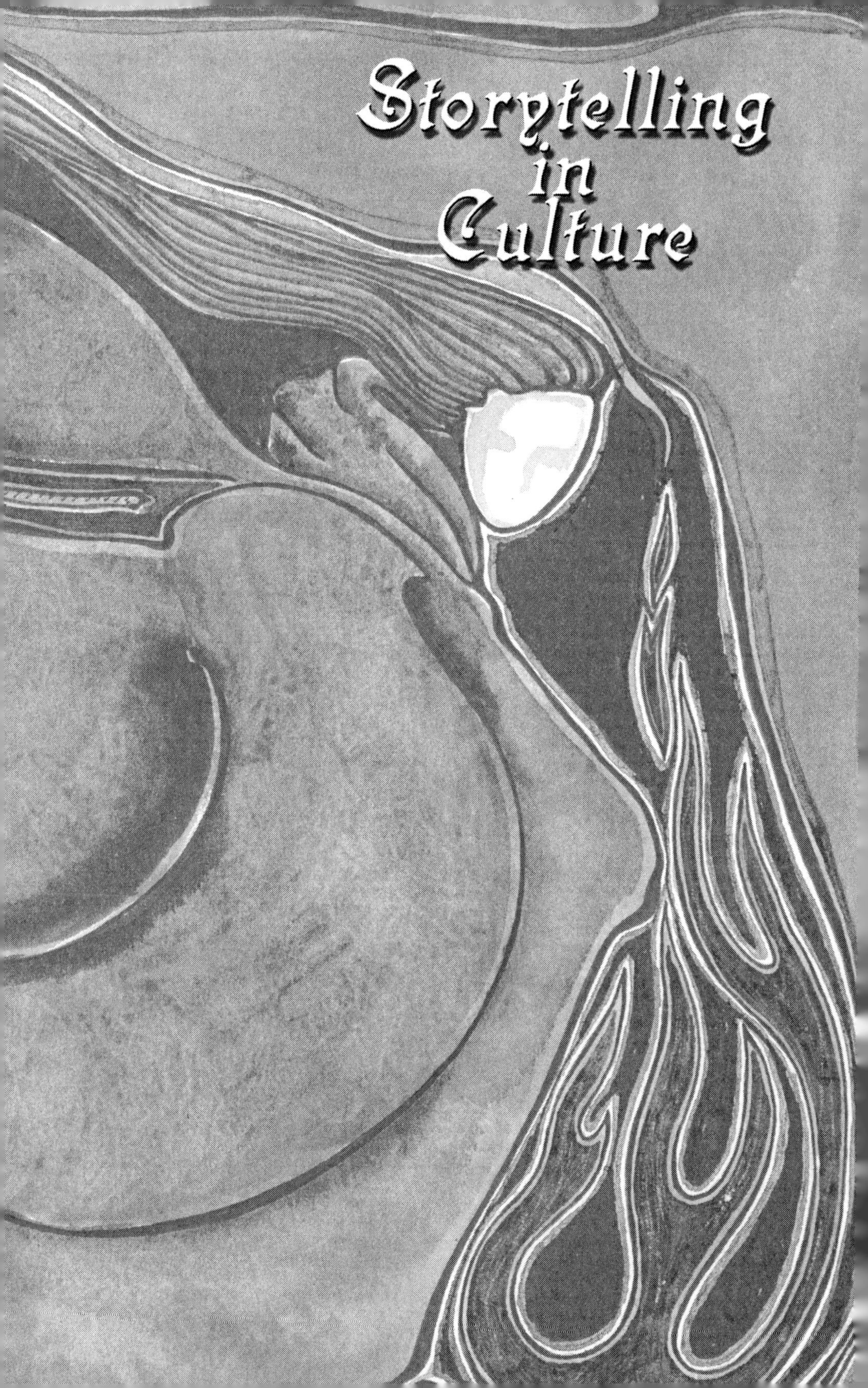

The Princess in Transition: A Changing Metaphor[1]

Diane Wolkstein

There was once a princess....These five words, despite our sophisticated technological advances, still conjure up worlds of wonder and possibility. As ancient as civilization and its first written record, the words "princess" and "story" have been linked together for more than three thousand years. Stories, both real and fanciful, of the lives of princesses circulated in the earliest kingdoms. These stories passed from one person to another until a certain few caught the soul of gifted storytellers who recounted them for their eager listeners. The word princess is as large as our imagination. She is us. Whatever it is that we might be wishing or needing to explore in ourselves she evokes. She is the young soul coming into being. As princess, she is not yet sovereign. She is not yet ruler of the kingdom. She is waking and her possible choices seem grand.

Until this century, with few exceptions, the fate of a living princess in the Judeo-Christian world was circumscribed. Her life was not her own. Her life belonged to her father and the kingdom. She was the king's daughter and property. She was a commodity to be traded and negotiated. Her value was in her face and her womb. Her task was to attract the sons of important kingdoms and thereby increase the power of the kingdom and with her womb's fertility to insure the kingdom's future. Increasing the borders of the kingdom and allowing for its furtherance, she was an asset to the kingdom in both space and time. What her soul or spirit wanted, needed, or cared about was not of importance.

Herein lies one of the many fascinations regarding "the princess." She carries the power of the kingdom, and, yet, she is powerless. Is she not all of us? We, men and women, could be so much, and yet, for either outer or inner reasons we are held back from that place of fullness. We are, as the princess has been all these centuries, sacrificed. What does it take for the princess to be more than her father's property? How can she claim her right to determine her future?

In the twentieth century, during the second World War, when men left their homes to fight, women took over their jobs. Wartime needs gave birth to a new technology and economy which offered women the possibility to become independent and choose their own destinies. Slowly, the concept emerged in the decades following the war years, that rather than increase their fathers' kingdoms, women might realize their own outer and inner kingdoms. They might write, fight, work in labs, teach, judge, doctor, play ball. A host of literary fairy tales, by such authors as Thurber, Munch, Paterson, McKinley, were written from the fifties onward about zany, eccentric princesses who wanted the moon and other seeming impossibilities.

From the fifties onward, "classic" fairy tales, such as Grimm, Perrault, Jacobs, and the Andrew Lang collections, continued to be published alongside the "modern" fairy tales. Children born in the forties and fifties grew up with contradictory versions of the princess. Was she to serve the kingdom? Or was she to become sovereign of her own kingdom?

In the person of Princess Diana of Wales we saw this paradox tragically acted out. Chosen to serve the British monarchy, once Diana bore the necessary children, she felt abandoned. Rather than accept an unauthentic, feudal relationship with the prince, she struggled to assert herself and to find a "needy" kingdom to serve outside their kingdom. Although she died before fully achieving her goals, her courage, vulnerability, openness, warmth, and concern for needy people forced the monarchy which had rejected her to change its impersonal, feudal style. Diana embodied the princess in transition. She wanted to serve the kingdom, and she wanted to be accepted on her own terms. She was a princess who had refused her appointed place and had not yet found a new place. She was struggling, caught "between stories."

During the time Diana was struggling with her identity, I was telling the nineteenth century Grimm fairy tale of Old Rinkrank. I loved the story for, although its princess suffers, she is feisty, resourceful, and ultimately successful. In the Grimm version, the King decides it is time for his daughter to marry. He sets a challenge for the suitors to climb a glass mountain, but the princess insists on choosing her own suitor. As she helps her chosen suitor, she falls through a crack in the mountain and is made into a slave by the mountain's underlord, Old Rinkrank. After a long imprisonment, she rescues herself and returns home. This spunky, resourceful princess pleased me. I had told this story for thirty years but it was not until I submitted it for publication and re-titled it The Glass Mountain that I began to question the story I loved.

My questioning began with my editor's request that I give a name to the King's daughter. "She's the princess," I said. "What's wrong with princess?" "She needs to be an individual," my editor replied. Having told the story for so many years, I had honed it so it flowed and its rhythms seemed to me to nearly embody the story. By giving the princess a name, the story's accustomed rhythm is broken and everything was then open to question: the beginning, the ending, the underlying power structure, the intentions. The story was no longer canon. The story became a story, a version, which had been told to one of the brothers Grimm by an informant. It was a powerful poetic story of a woman's liberation, but it had been told and re-told within a nineteenth century German cultural belief system. A princess with a name was no longer a princess who acted as the princess, she was a princess who could act as a princess with that name might act. The ability to change a part of the story may seem obvious to others. But just as I had been raised to believe that Bible stories were "carved in stone," over the years I had found so much comfort, sustenance, beauty, and truth in the "old" fairy tales that it had never occurred to me that I could radically change parts of stories and at the same time honor and hold on to their underlying truths. Myths and folk tales are cauldrons of collected wisdom which are clothed in whatever culture they take shape. Each story suggests a possible way of acting and so does the culture in which it is shaped. The tenth commandment in the story of Exodus states: "You shall not covet your neighbor's home, wife, or possessions." Three thousand years ago in middle eastern culture a woman's possibilities were limited. Today, since we know that women as well as men are capable of coveting and acting, by changing the assertion to read "You shall not covet your neighbor's home, *spouse* (ital. mine), or possessions," we help to make this early mountain story of ascent and liberation inclusive instead of exclusive. Our changing beliefs force us to carve new tablets. Once the story is retold it is already being re-shaped by the culture and beliefs of the new storyteller. The question is: is the storyteller aware of the implications of the story she is telling?

My first choice was a name for the princess. I chose the name Raina, symbolizing a ray of sunshine that would go into the darkness and be temporarily quenched. Once I had Raina's name I wondered: Whose story is it? In fairy tales, the beginning of the story sets the story's tone, and the first lines usually reveal the story's place and lineage. I considered the beginning which I had told for so many years: "There was once a King who had a daughter and he made a glass mountain and he said...." The story ends with the King killing Old Rinkrank and the King taking the gold and silver. Although the princess risks her life, nearly dying in the underworld, this version, told within the nineteenth century German patriarchal perspective, ultimately strengthens and re-enforces the power and riches of the father's kingdom.

My editor's second request was that the princess's suitor also be made more individual. If the princess was to be heavenly light, I wanted the suitor to have a complementary aspect, so I gave him the attribute of sound. I made him a whistler and chose the name Jared which contains within it the earthy word of passion, red. Once the two characters had names, I realized that this story was about more than the princess's liberation. It was about the relationship between the two. It was about the balance of masculine and feminine, love and power, and the creation of a realm.

Now I was also "between stories." I loved the nineteenth century resourceful princess. But I wanted her to emerge her own sovereign as well as support the realm she belonged to. I therefore decided to change the story's framework. I began the story of The Glass Mountain with these words: "Gold, crimson, rose, yellow, purple, orange, lime green—these were the colors the princess loved. She also loved to wander in the woods, listening to the songs of the birds. Her servants followed at a distance, and to please her, they caught the birds whose songs she enjoyed and brought them back to the palace and put them in cages." Instead of placing the foundation with the king, I let it encompass all the world. Initially, Raina imprisons the birds for she acts as she has been brought up, in a controlling, unfeeling way. When the young suitor Jared appears, whistling spontaneously, she waits for him the next day at the glass mountain and says, "I will go with you and help you. The mountain is slippery, so I have taken off my shoes." Raina attempts to free herself by standing on her own feet, but if the princess is to be a heroine, she must confront her nemesis so she falls into the underworld and is imprisoned by a second tyrannical male figure, Old Rinkrank.

In the Grimm version, the princess contrives her escape when enough time passes. I chose to let it be Raina's memory of her suitor that activates her desire, for it was her initial desire to be with him that led her on her quest. Once Raina escapes, instead of following the Grimm version in which the father appropriates the gold and silver, I sent the two lovers back to the mountain so that Raina might claim what is rightfully hers and her beloved might experience some of what she has undergone. When Raina says she will return, Jared says, "I will go with you and help you." As they are digging up the gold and silver in the underworld, Jared acknowledges that what she has accomplished is hers, by asking, "What will you do with all this gold and silver?" Raina answers, "I would like to make a beautiful garden filled with fruit trees and flowing streams where all living creatures can come and go." "If you wish," Jared replies, "we can build it together."

I ended the story with the princess freeing the birds after she escapes from Old Rinkrank. The last lines of the story are: "Raina toasted her bridegroom by whistling the song of the lark. Jared whistled a reply. And in the distance a flock of larks echoed their song." The princess, a symbol of light and color, learns to whistle, and her suitor, a musician, helps to create a place of visual beauty. They come into their fullness as they incorporate the other and then give to others. In response, all of nature celebrates.

The nineteenth century version allows the princess to free herself and increases the king's wealth and power. The twenty-first century version allows the princess to free herself and also to share the wealth and power with her spouse and all living creatures.

There was once a princess. She is in process. As we all are, she is becoming what she might be.

Note:

1. This essay appeared in the September, 1999 issue of the *School Library Journal.*

Navigable Narratives: Women's Use of Virtual Space

Mary Flanagan

I approach storytelling not from the oral tradition, but from a background in film, video, and multimedia production. My view of telling stories through visuals and audio and playing with the idea of linearity in narratives is that technology allows us an alternate space within which we can invent unique methods of telling stories, forming identities, and remembering. As a media maker, I value the ability to use digital tools and work comfortably within computer-generated spaces. I can combine tools, images, and multiple voices to create 3-dimensional computer worlds in order to "map" ideas in space like memories in the mind.

I am particularly interested in exploring online space in the third dimension to create "navigable narratives." Beyond a hypertext, where digital text is linked to other texts over the internet, these narratives—self-maneuvered stories—are created in a virtual space along X, Y, and Z planes and woven with both moving and stationary images, spatialized sounds, and coded messengers. Text, too, is spatialized, sculpted, and through motion and point of view, the user can interpret the story information in a different way with each telling, or be told the story a different way in each performance.

But the culture surrounding computer technology, as well as the shape of the technology itself, is infused with imagery, semantics, classification systems, and ordering structures which implicate computer experiences and products from the interior. These structures have great influence especially in the context of gender study. Ultimately, I wish to explore the possibility for using online space in the third dimension to create "alternate, spatialized narratives." My guiding questions concerns both the act of navigating—or performing—the 3D space, as well as the implications of spatial paradigms and their implicitly engendered aspects. In order to understand the construction of virtual bodies and space, I'll examine the connection between gender and these sites of manifestation. I will end the article by offering some possibilities, specifically in the arena of this navigable narrative form, to help address—perhaps overcome—virtual reality's (VR) political specificity.

Place and Space

Cyberspace has been described and referred to in a number of ways. Coined in 1986 by William Gibson from the 1948 term cybernetics (from kyberman, to steer),[1] the root of the word describes the acts of piloting and governing. There have been several feminist attempts to characterize cyberspace. Elizabeth Meese compares cyberspace to literary space: "the page of a book, like the computer screen, is a frontier through which we enter a nonspace space, the space that isn't "really" there. It is a safe space, which the actual, material spaces in which many people live is not."[2] However, Meese overlooks the agency inherent in virtual space. Unlike a book, a sealed, one-person space, actions taking place in networks can in fact be implemented—some in cyberspace and in some cases in realspace—and affect real (sometimes multiple) human beings through multi-user interaction, e-commerce, etc. Online, many people can lurk and/or interact; harassment is a frequent occurrence against any person describing themselves as female; a host of other violence is discussed or threatened. [3] Thus, the idea of cyberspace as a safe haven for women equal to that of the book has not been realized.[4] In online worlds, sites can be navigated in many directions and orders, breaking the prescripted order and scalable world of the book. These essential differences help define cyberspace apart from literature as a "nonspace space," and also go beyond hypertext in the multidirectional and multiuser aspects.

Other writers explore spatial concepts that are useful for defining the space of cyberspace. Liz Grosz, in her assessment of concepts of space in discourse and their possible relationship to architecture and other "texts," notes that texts could "be read, used, as modes of effectivity and action which, at their best, scatter thoughts and images into different linkages or new alignments without necessarily destroying their materiality."[5] To apply this line of thinking to cyberspace, one should think about digitally-rendered space in a different way than previous conceptions of space or place precisely because it does not function materially as geographic, as gravity-bound.

Even beyond these ways of considering the different models of interaction, one cannot seem to avoid using metaphors of space to describe computer activities. Even the term "cyberspace" renders an absolute connection, associating digital experiences with spatial descriptors. And more broadly, in daily life as well as in feminist discourse, there has been an adoption of such spatial metaphors in language[6] such as "working at the margins" at the "site" of one, singular point, and suggesting that "recentering" is a way to critique status quo tropes—these refer to space as a place for strategic and political action. Further, even programming languages suggest spatialization as an operating mode within code. For example, we ask in the Basic language for the computer to "run,"(not process) and commands such as "goto" and "get" or, in Lingo, "put" or "place" (rather than compute, display, or calculate input). Such descriptions using the language of geography[7] must be carefully considered given linguistic ties to a historic use of geography as a site of male power. Women in the sciences and in the arts investigate space in different ways using categories that may vary from the traditions in their fields. First, women haven't historically been privileged to define fields such as geography or architecture; and second, women have not been the primary designers of the computational architecture of virtual spaces.

But this discussion is not solely about metaphor. It is about the implications of spatialized thinking, both positive and negative, in virtual terms. In a sense, users of cyberspace have bought into the "spatialized" scenario, complete with its imperialist overtones, by utilizing "frontier" mentality when "colonizing" popular virtual worlds. Online spaces such as Alphaworld are examples of the colonization of cyberspace while highlighting and re-inscribing suburban values. Inside Alphaworld, one builds a virtual house, gets an address, chooses a color for the lawn, and acquires a mailbox as the worlds are gridded and parceled out to users in a system reminiscent of activities during a 19th Century land rush rather than what we would perhaps dream up in a contemporary virtual environment. Geographer Geraldine Pratt cautions that in articulating a feminist sense of self and self-location, the often-used metaphors of geography impart "areas of closure."[8]

Because of this metaphoric connection, we must be cautious—or at least aware—to adopt this specific use of spatialized metaphor for materiality in descriptions or depictions of virtual "space." Like images of the American West, cyberspace is described as wild, untamed, virgin, needing mastery and a manifest destiny to guide it. Essentially space is identified as female with all the attendant ideologies of subjugation carried along. Cyberspace, through its representation in popular cyberfiction by authors such as William Gibson, Bruce Sterling, et al, is likewise unearthed as female—albeit a Theweleitian female.

Navigating and Performing

This discussion of place and space is tied to the navigation within the space and the way in which a user relates to that space. First, I will show that navigation itself is a performance of the space; and second, I will argue that performance in virtual space has implications on the performance of gender both within virtual worlds and in realspace that have the danger of enmeshing users into conventional gendered subject positions.

How does the user of virtual space, especially the 3D space of a game or an online experience become a subject? Users navigate. They (or we) move. The more we maneuver in online spaces, the more we see that the 3D experience is distinct to computer interaction. Early visionaries of cyberspace spoke at length about control: control over the body, over thought, over representation of the wildest of fantasies. The architect Marcos Novak wanted cyberspace to fulfill fictive fantasies while having absolute control of the experience. He writes that the merging of cyberspace and the body compose an "embodied fiction," and that we are fascinated with cyberspace precisely because it is "the promise of control over the world by the power of the will."[9] This control fantasy approach damaged the potential of early cyberspace experiments, from which we may now just be recovering. One of the most exciting possibilities of cyberspace is the uncontrolled, the live, the dynamic, the fleeting, and surely there must evolve a place for stories and worlds that are not centered on the ideology of control. Perhaps we could design to give users control in an uncontrolled world as a way to break that paradigm.

At a fundamental level, how the user is able to interact with a virtual space constructs how that space is perceived. Most computer storyworlds offer an "interface" for the user that is the graphic base representation for the user. For example, we have Cosmo Player plug in for viewing VRML. The interface is the site for control or is the way to communicate desires during navigation. Often, consciously or unconsciously on the part of the designer, the interface takes the form of a control panel or a kind of dashboard. There are many implications in using a dashboard model as a vehicle for exploring a space. First of all, a dashboard-style graphic implies usefulness, information, status; point-to-point interaction; an end and a goal are instantly implied. In other words, linear interaction with a reward is fostered, rather than nonlinear, circular, or interrupted interaction. These of course could be seen as "gendered" interaction styles. This is because of the graphic style, the iconography associated with rows of controls, but also the information design and assumptions about navigation in realspace terms. Interface dashboards connote performance assessment; in physical vehicles, they communicate speed, fuel levels, and potential system problems. Finally, these types of tools imply absolute power over the experience. A single user/participant must enter and interact in the world through this predetermined interface which assumes a singular "driver" viewpoint. By creating a uniform interface that presents a story world from the first person, a single "subject location" is formed; participants in the story see the world from their point of view and are therefore constructed as a unified, individual subject. Via the interface, users can believe they have an omniscient relationship to the game world, when in fact this is not true. The designers and creators determine the amount of user-knowledge and participation in the experience.

In this model, then, the storyteller/performer/storyworld exist on one side, the audience/viewer/participant on the other. This binary opposition, however, oversimplifies and limits the construction of the participant's role in the space; movement can act as the link between the two. The idea of telling a story through movement has tremendous possibilities for repositioning the subject. Creating a story via movement could be equated with Deleuze's phantasm: the movement by which the ego opens itself up to surfaces and "liberates" the halted difference contained (such as point of view). This paradigm of teller/told or storyteller/listener relationship offers a gap in which new ways of identification in narrative, especially for feminists, can develop and which would allow for identification with disenfranchised groups.

Judith Butler has argued that in examining the implications of agency, rather than there be a "doer behind the deed," we should note that a "doer" is constructed "in and through the deed."[10] Beyond earlier text-based forms of interaction, where digital text is linked to other texts over the internet, these narratives—self-navigated stories—are actually created in a virtual space along X, Y, and Z planes, integrated with images and sounds, both moving and stationary. In effect, those who used to be "listeners" are not simply an audience any longer; they are, through their movement, creating the stage. Text can also be spatialized, sculpted, and through motion and point of view, the viewer can interpret the story information in a different way every telling, or be told the story a different way in each performance. Point of view is multiple, the body is nonexistent: the result is simply information.

But how does one get to experience such a position? Through the performance and navigation. I am referring to in fact two kinds of performance: performance as movement, going through spatialized worlds online, and performance in gender-specific roles, as I believe gender informs any navigational performance. Performance as movement implies the manner in which a process is carried out. Performativity suggests doing according to prescribed ritual; it can also mean "to give a rendition of." So performance as "a rendition" through movement seems appropriate because first, it adds the element of experience that a piece of visual or auditory nature at each viewing event; and second, because it changes from viewer to viewer, from time to time, because the narrative is constructed in an entirely different way each performance through the navigation. Lyotard focused upon the event and upon "performativity" as a working principle of knowledge—that a figure could claim its own descriptive space no more or no less "universal" than any other. "No single instance of narrative can exert a claim to dominate narratives standing beyond it."[11]

As far as gender in these online spaces, the move is away from the body of the enactor and much more towards identification and manipulation of the body of the digital characters or images onscreen. The body has been *the* important site for feminist analysis and performance study. By breaking away from the idea of natural sex, and male and female sexed bodies along with writers such as Judith Butler, we can think about gender as enacted, as multiple and fluid. The same distinctions could be extended to cyberspace—in cyberspace there is nothing that is not constructed and performed. The body is physically separate, and spatialized objects would not exist without navigation. As we move about a virtual space, our avatars or our perspectives become sites for performativity when we are using them in spatialized interactive texts.[12]

These possibilities help to shatter the subject position found in other forms of electronic storytelling, and indeed in other media forms. This challenge to the digital teller/told or storyteller/listener relationship offers a fissure at which new ways of identification in storytelling, especially for women and disadvantaged or disenfranchised groups, can develop. While virtual space may inscribe gender norms, performance through navigation may be the way to challenge or subvert these norms. Could it be that the performance of space will become the site for a feminist use of the Internet, computer culture, and specifically, of virtual space? Luce Irigaray notes that, "any theory of the subject has always been appropriated by the "masculine."[13] Yet perhaps exploring online worlds can center around receptivity rather than control of the experience and thus avoid such appropriation. For users, especially female users, the shattering or opening up of the position of receiver—of the subject position—offers a situation in which alternative ways of seeing, hearing, listening, and understanding can develop.

Example

Several projects have utilized online spaces for performances and are pertinent to the discussion of performance. Among other things, they rely on navigation to construct the story; therefore, a new story is found with each telling. For an example of a navigable narrative of this type, I'll use a piece of my own to show the ways in which unconventional ways of storytelling have emerged.

[the perpetual bed] is an online, virtual VRML world situated in the world of my grandmother's dreamstate in which users can interact with each other within a navigable, surrealistic narrative. This piece is about my 91-year-old grandmother's experiences when critically ill and hospitalized. She could barely feed herself from shaking so much (medication and lack of oxygen in the blood), but she could talk and drift in and out of sleep. She had terrible, fantastic, and funny dreams while ill, and the dreams acted out in the space of her room, a space which lost its taupe walls and hospital-huge doors to expand into a wake-dream world. In her less lucid moments, I could see Grandma staring off and silently wording things in this wake-dream state. These were interactions between the waking and dreaming world. Grandma mentioned that people kept coming up to her bed, many times, all kinds of people, and she'd give them chocolate chip cookies as they went on their way. Some of these people were dead; some were nurses or strangers. Sitting in the room with her, my skin tingled with the feeling of paths crossing, of energies exchanging, and I realized that even though there was a lot going on that I could not see, I could definitely feel it. But Grandma–she interacted. The idea behind performing the piece through movement instead of pre-scripted animation came to me as a result of my grandmother's interaction with her dream space. It seemed to me more than a nonlinear narrative–it was a spatialized narrative that took place around her bed during her illness.

The piece, a "virtual performance," is a hybrid between linear forms such as film and video, traditional oral storytelling, dance, installation, and animation. I call this type of story a "navigable narrative" because it takes the viewer literally into the story's space. This piece uses performativity as a general operating strategy–it's an activity that allows the operation of improvisatory experimentation based on the perceived needs and desires of a situation. I call it navigable because it also spatializes the smaller meta-narratives in the story, giving no one particular tract or story an inherent authority or truth. It is fluid and changes each time it is traveled. Through unhinging the static point of view common in two-dimensional spaces, the piece is a fluctuating series of pieces, objects, set in a changeable, scalable world. A hybrid between video, interactive art, installation, and animation, it relies on the movement of the user/viewer to encounter my grandmother's experiences with transparent yet tangible beings, memories, and places. Multiple people can also "inhabit" the space and leave their mark. Whether for multi-user or single-user, I am trying to create a new medium from the temporal and motion imaging elements of film and video, the accessibility of the internet, the user-centered narrative form from interactive art, elements of choreography, and user point of view. I wish to tell the story in an altogether different way using this technology—by allowing guests or performers to move through a story, to "happen" upon a scene and find their own meaning, and leave traces behind: a spatialized palimpsest. Some of the interaction takes place through a technology I have designed called Navigable Chat. Users can perceive each other through their textual presence, and the audience can perceive the different performers by their trails of text and their individual colors. My goal is to tell a story in a moving way—one that allows the users to move through a story, to "happen" upon a scene, and to find their own meaning in this ever-enacted place. Users can then leave their mark and become part of the story—leave hints, impressions, etc.—for the next viewer.

I want to stress that creating this kind of work is a process. All of the work I've discussed today has been a work in progress, both in terms of the "live" and exploratory nature of the work, and because there are no "right answers" about online narrative spaces. Progress by artists in the area of navigable narratives is slow because of the sheer amount of technical expertise and effort it takes to construct complex, spatialized narrative worlds. For [the perpetual bed], next steps will involve more direct interaction from image/characters and a physical interface, so users can manipulate real objects in order to garner different ways of understanding the link between cyberspace and the real world. Navigable narratives are one venue to reflect these shifting subjectivities and to destabilize historic use of navigation and spatial metaphors, in addition to reworking navigation and narrative as linear and bound to historic models. My goal as a storyteller and computer artist is to tell personal stories not generally represented by a technologically driven culture. I want to tell stories about ordinary people facing real struggles with things like illness, aging, dreams, and fading memory using the computer. I am trying to create a new media, whether multi-user or single-user, from the temporal and motion imaging elements of film and video, the accessibility of the internet, the user-centered narrative form from interactive art, and elements of choreography.

While Luce Irigaray notes that "any theory of the subject has always been appropriated by the "masculine,"[14] could it be that the complex subject/object relationship exemplified by the navigable narrative will become the site for a feminist use of the Internet, of narrative, of computer culture, and specifically, of virtual space? The junctions between surfaces, then, are fissures of possibility for exploring subjects and objects for women's narrative practices. As the writer J. K. Gibson-Graham notes, "the babble emanating from this discursive space is a political process without end, and without a (unified collective) subject."[15] My work, part of this babble, engages with the process and with the place of "the other" in cyberspace.

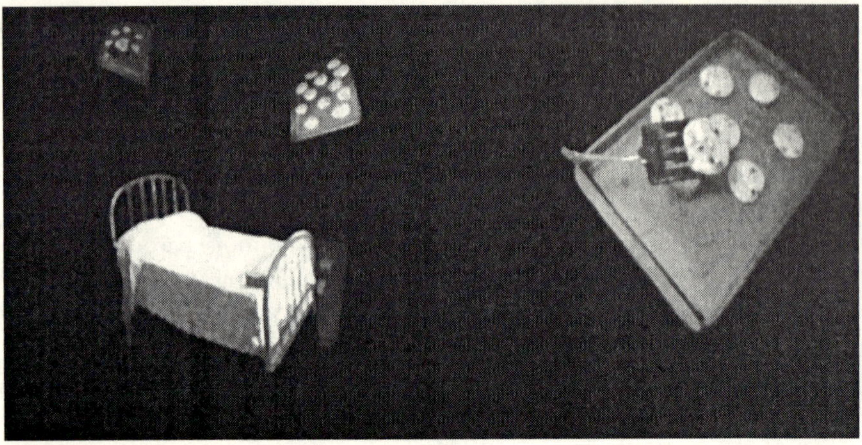

Endnotes

1. Cybernetics : the science of communication and control theory concerned especially with the comparative study of automatic control systems such as the nervous system, the brain, and mechanical-electrical communication systems both inside and outside the body.
2. Meese, p. 187, from the article "The Place of the Letter: An Epistolary Exchange," pp. 161-202, in Bammer, Gwin, Katz, and Meese, *Making Worlds: Gender, Metaphor, and Materiality*.
3. See Dibbel, Julian. "A Rape in Cyberspace," in *Internet Dreams*, ed. March Stefik. Cambridge: MIT, 1996, 293 - 315; Brail, S. (1996). The Price of Admission: Harassment and Free Speech in the Wild, Wild West. Cherney, L. & Weise, E.R *Wired Women:. Gender and Realities in Cyberspace*. Seattle: Seal Press, pp. 169 - 181; and Canon, M. (May 1995). Life in the big city. (Internet concerns). *MacUser*. 11:5, p. 17(1).
4. Linda McDowell, in her article," Spatializing Feminism: Geographic Perspectives" in *BodySpaces*, ed. Nancy Duncan, P. 28-44, concludes her discussion of feminist spatial practices by calling into question separatist movements and asking for the validation of multiple truths, not universalist tropes, as the closest constitution to truth we can have (42).
5. Grosz, p. 126, from *Space, Time, and Perversion.*
6. This is in reference to the argument that many concepts, at least in English speaking worlds, are associated with languages of geography and spatial metaphors. George Lakoff and Mark Johnson, *Metaphors We Live By*. Chicago: University of Chicago Press, 1980.
7. For a lengthy explanation see Pratt (1992).
8. Pratt, p. 13 in *Making Worlds: Gender, Metaphor, and Materiality*.
9. Novak, Marcos. "Liquid Architecture in Cyberspace." In *Cyberspace: First Steps*, ed. Michael Benedikt. Cambridge: MIT Press, 1991, p. 228.
10. Gender Trouble, p. 142.

11. Readings, Bill. *Introducing Lyotard: Art and Politics.* London: Routledge, 1991, p. 69.
12. Sue-Ellen Case notes that Eve Kosofsky Sedgwick would extend performativity to "coming out, for work around AIDS and for the self-labeled, transversely but urgently representational placarded body of demonstration."
13. Irigaray, *The speculum of the other woman*, p.133.
14. Ibid.
15. JK Gibson-Graham, p. 242.

Bibliography

Women and Geography Study Group of the Royal Geographical Society with the Institute of British Geographers. *Feminist Geographies: Explorations in diversity and difference.* Harlow: Addison Wesley Longman, 1997.

Bammer, Gwin, Katz, and Mees. "The Place of the Letter: An Epistolary Exchange." *Making Worlds: Gender, Metaphor, and Materiality*. Ed. Susan Hardy Aiken, Ann Brigham, Sallie A. Marston, and Penny Waterstone. Tucson: University of Arizona Press, 1998. 161-202.

Butler, Judith. *Bodies that Matter: On the Discursive Limits of "Sex."* London: Routledge, 1993.

Case, Sue-Ellen. Performing lesbian in the space of technology, part 1. *Theatre Journal,* March 1995 v47 n1 p1(18).

Grosz, Elisabeth. *Space, Time, and Perversion*. NY: Routledge, 1995.

Holtzman, Steven. *Digital Mosaics: the Aesthetics of Cyberspace.* NY: Simon & Schuster, 1997.

Irigaray, Luce. *The Speculum of the Other Woman*. Ithaca: Cornell University Press, 1985.

Gibson-Graham, JK. "Postmodern Feminist Social Research." *BodySpaces,* ed. Nancy Duncan. NY: Routledge, 1996. 234-244.

McDowell, Linda." Spatializing Feminism: Geographic Perspectives." *Body Spaces,* ed. Nancy Duncan. NY: Routledge, 1996. 28-44.

Lakoff, George and Mark Johnson. *Metaphors We Live By*. Chicago: University of Chicago Press, 1980.

Novak, Marcos. "Liquid Architecture in Cyberspace." *Cyberspace: First Steps,* ed. Michael Benedikt. Cambridge: MIT Press, 1994. 228-254.

Pratt, Geraldine. "Spatial Metaphors and Speaking Positions," *Environment and Planning D: Society and Space* 10 (3): 241-3.

Pratt, Geraldine. "Geographic Metaphors in Feminist Theory," *Making Worlds: Gender, Metaphor, and Materiality*. Ed. Susan Hardy Aiken, Ann Brigham, Sallie A. Marston, and Penny Waterstone. Tucson: University of Arizona Press, 1998. 13-30.

The Great Holy Woman Malka of Beltz: Women as Heroes and Storytellers in Hasidic Tales

Justin Jaron Lewis

Looking for Women's Torah

It's an honour to speak after Diane Wolkstein, and I'm glad that Diane mentioned the Ten Commandments in her talk. We're a few days from the Jewish holiday of Shavuot, which celebrates the giving of the Torah on Mount Sinai. According to the Bible, what God gave us on Mount Sinai was the Ten Commandments. But Jewish tradition understands that what was given on Mount Sinai was the whole Jewish tradition—especially the holy books, the sacred texts, beginning with the Bible and increasing from generation to generation. All these books are Torah, given on Mount Sinai, and the classic Jewish religious activity of "learning Torah," studying sacred texts, can be engaged in with any of them. Since the number of books does increase generation by generation, it is clear that the "giving of the Torah" means that the Torah is given to us to add to and to create, not as something static or unchanging.

But the question arises—it arose in past generations, and it is asked with increasing anger and pain in our time—whether this Torah is given to women, or only to men. The issue begins at Mount Sinai, with the Ten Commandments, which, as Diane pointed out, really do say "You shall not covet your neighbour's wife." They say nothing about "your neighbour's husband," because they are addressed to men, not to women. Also, the main human character in the story of Mount Sinai is a man, Moses, and the reputed author of the story is a man, Moses. So, the foundational story of Torah is presented by a male narrator about a male character for a male audience, and this continues to characterize Torah all through the generations. With few exceptions, Jewish sacred literature is written by men, about men and for men. Women's voices are hard to find; women characters, especially strong, independent characters, are few and far between.

So today there is a quest for women's Torah, Torah by and about women. I am part of this quest, along with many others, both through storytelling and through scholarship. In the course of this search, I have found that in Hasidic stories we have a genre of Torah, Jewish sacred text, which is relatively open to women's voices, as narrators, and to women as strong, central characters. I want to explore with you this phenomenon of women's Torah in the Hasidic tale, and some of its roots and limitations.

Background: Hasidic Judaism and Its Stories

Hasidic Judaism is a trend within traditional religious Judaism. Hasidic Jews are distinguished from other Jews today by their intense traditionalism. They are distinguished from other traditional Jews by their origin story and by their social organization. The Hasidic movement traces its origins to one man, the Baal Shem Tov, who lived in Ukraine and whose public career was in the 1740s and 1750s. There are various Hasidic groups, organized around spiritual leaders called Rebbes. The Rebbes are teachers, advisers, healers, and bestowers of blessings. All the Rebbes trace their spiritual lineage to the Baal Shem Tov.

The Baal Shem Tov was a storyteller, and stories were told about him, and this has continued with the Rebbes of following generations. Many of them have been storytellers, and stories are told about them—typically about their miracles, but also about their deeds of piety, their wisdom, and so on. Beginning with the Baal Shem Tov, and still today, the Hasidic movement gave storytelling higher status and greater prestige than it previously had in Judaism. Hasidic Jews consider storytelling by and about the Rebbes to be holy, a spiritual practice (Buxbaum discusses Hasidic sacred storytelling in detail). The boundaries of the kind of storytelling that is considered holy are not easy to define, but the core of the genre is clear: a story is certainly a holy Hasidic story if it is told by a Hasidic Jew in praise of a Hasidic Rebbe.

Fairly late in the history of the movement, books of Hasidic stories began to be published, most of them based on stories in oral circulation (Nigal summarizes the history of the genre and provides bibliographic information). Because of the holiness which Hasidic Jews attach to storytelling, these books of stories also have a certain recognized holiness; they are within the boundaries of sacred literature, Torah. In fact, because of the emphasis on texts and reading in traditional Judaism, when an oral Hasidic story is printed in a holy book its status as Torah is validated and given greater permanence since the book may be read for many generations to come. (I am simplifying a complex topic. Evaluations of storytelling, books of stories as a genre, and specific books, vary widely within Hasidic communities; the recognition of books of stories as holy contends with a disparaging view of them as merely "folksy" (Herskovic, June 7). For the purposes of this paper I have focused on the view that gives most honour to stories.)

Books of Hasidic tales are a crossroads genre. The period when most of these books appeared, between the 1860s and the First World War, was a time of increasing modernization and secularization for Jews in Eastern Europe, and the books respond to this context. Some were written by traditional Jews with the expressed intention of counteracting the charms of modern literature (as discussed by Robinson). Others, including the books that established the genre in the 1860s, were written by secularized Jews but addressed to a religious audience, essentially to take advantage of the gullibility of traditional readers eager for miracle stories (Joseph Dan explores this phenomenon). Such books by secular authors, based on the storytelling of religious people, were accepted by the religious audience and absorbed into the sacred literature. (Thus, they are among the sources credited by impeccably devout authors of recent books of Hasidic stories, such as Klapholz and Zevin.) During the same time period, oral Hasidic stories were being collected by secular folklorists and reworked by authors creating a secular, modern Yiddish literature. Their books were generally not accepted by the religious communities because they were clearly addressed to a more secular audience. In terms of what comes to be accepted as Torah in the traditional world, the core definition would be: a book of stories told by Hasidic Jews in praise of Hasidic Rebbes, addressed to a traditional religious audience. These books are the focus of my current research.

WOMEN HEROES: MALKA OF BELZ

In this genre of book, we find stories ascribed to women narrators, and we find stories whose main characters are holy women. These stories are treated by their authors as important and significant, although there are not many of them to be found. Let me illustrate with the example of Malka of Belz, the wife of Rebbe Sholom of Belz. I told some stories about her on the first night of this conference.

Malka died in 1852 (Klapholz 87). The first book containing stories about her was *Dover Shalom*, published in 1910. The book mainly consists of stories and information about Malka's husband, Rebbe Sholom. However, Malka is mentioned with the highest praise, and her husband's greatness is ascribed to her (Michelsohn 7).

The author of *Dover Shalom* is quite thorough in noting his sources for stories, written or oral. Several of the stories about Malka begin "I have heard" (Michelsohn 7, 20, 21, 30, 31, 142) and none of them is credited to a written source. When he mentions Malka for the first time, the author says, "the whole world knows of the greatness of her righteousness" (Michelsohn 7). So we learn two things: about sixty years after Malka's death, people were still telling stories about her; and, until then, no one had seen fit to write down these stories, unlike the many stories about her husband which the author cites from various written sources.

The next book to appear in the traditional community with stories about Malka came another sixty years later, in 1972. Again, Malka is presented with great respect. This book, *Admore Belz*, includes a number of stories about her that are not in *Dover Shalom*. So, people were continuing to tell stories about Malka 120 years after her death, but during whole generations no one in the traditional community had gathered the stories in writing. (Stories about Malka were written down for a non-traditional readership by Langer, 36-40.)

I am told by a Hasidic Jew that the followers of the Rebbes of the Belz dynasty, descended from Rebbe Sholom, are still telling stories about Malka (Herskovic, May 10). Perhaps in another sixty years there will be more stories about her in print.

Out of the 400 stories or teachings in *Dover Shalom*, about ten are mainly about Malka. This is a very small percentage, but it is a much higher proportion than what you would find about women heroes in most works of Jewish holy literature.

Roles of Women Heroes

What kind of roles do women play in these stories? Usually, the reason that a woman is the focus of a Hasidic story is her connection to a male hero, and her role is the classic one of the enabler: "Behind every good man there's a woman." This is the first story about Malka in *Dover Shalom*:

> I heard that every night she would wake [Rebbe Sholom] from his sleep, and say to him: 'Rise, Sholom, from your bed, to do the service of the Creator. Lift up your eyes and see that all the working men have already risen from their beds to do their work. You, also, rise to do your service, holy service.' (Michelsohn 7)

Malka's husband, Sholom, is doing the service of the Creator—meaning

Torah study and prayer. She is in the background, making sure he wakes up in good time to do it.

But there are also stories in which women like Malka act as healers or teachers in their own right, like the story I told earlier in the conference:

> Once a sick man came to Belz to see Rebbe Sholom, and Rebbe Sholom was napping. So Malka said to the sick man, "What do you need to see the Rebbe for?" and he said, "For a year now, my foot has been hurting, so badly I can hardly walk." Malka said, "For this you don't need to see the Rebbe. Go home to your town, and every day light a candle in the synagogue, to give some light for people who are praying and studying—and your foot will get well." The man went home and began lighting a candle in the synagogue every day—and his foot healed completely. When word got back to Rebbe Sholom, he said, "Malka, how did you come up with this cure? I've never heard of it." Malka said, "Sholom, Sholom. You call yourself a Rebbe—you don't even know the Bible. It's written in the Book of Psalms: 'Your word is a light for my feet.'" (Paraphrase of Michelsohn 22)

It is interesting to compare these two stories. In one, Malka wakes her husband from his sleep so he can do his holy work, while she stays in the background. But in the other story, when he is asleep, she can step into the foreground and be powerful in her own right, in a way that takes her husband by surprise.

(In response to a question: It is possible to see stories like this, with their humour and far-fetched miracles, as subversive examples of the carnavalesque, as in Bakhtin's thought. But this is not unique to stories about women, and the conference audience may be getting an exaggerated impression of this aspect of the stories, because of not sharing the firm belief of Hasidic Jews in the power of holy people to work all kinds of miracles. The question should be explored further, but relating to men's as well as to women's Hasidic stories.)

Women Storytellers

Books of Hasidic tales also include stories credited to women narrators. In *Dover Shalom* there are three such stories: one, a story told by Malka about her husband (Michelsohn 15); one, a story told by Malka's daughter Eydele about her father, which I will discuss later; and one told to the author by his own mother about her father's encounters with two great Rebbes

(Michelsohn 137f.) There are also quite a number of stories introduced by "I have heard" which may have been heard from women, by the author or by his informants. So, there is a small but significant presence of the voice of women as storytellers, which again is remarkable in the context of Jewish holy books. What is still missing in this sample, and in other books that I'm aware of, are stories told by women about women.

The Presence of Women's Stories

The limitations of the presence of women in this literature are clear, but I want to emphasize again that by comparison to Jewish sacred literature in general, there is a stronger presence of women heroes and women's voices in Hasidic stories than in nearly any other genre. (The major exception would be *tekhines*, Yiddish prayers written for and often by women; see Weissler's study.)

How do women's stories come to have a presence in books of Hasidic tales? In Hasidic communities, storytelling is something that women can do. The main reason why most Jewish sacred literature has scarcely any women's voices is that in virtually all Jewish communities, until the most recent times, women did not receive an education in the sacred texts. The typical genre of Jewish sacred texts is commentary on other sacred texts. Therefore, there was a vicious circle in place: in order to create sacred texts you have to be well versed in the sacred texts; women, because they were excluded from studying the texts, couldn't create them. But to tell a story of a holy person, you do not need to know the texts. The Hasidic movement, by recognizing the holiness of storytelling, made it possible for women to engage in a holy practice that could eventually become part of holy texts. The classic dichotomy between male text and female orality, very strong in Jewish tradition, began to break down.

The occurrence of strong women protagonists in the stories has at least something to do with the fact that there really were women leaders in the movement (Polen's "Miriam's Dance" is a recent discussion of some examples, with bibliographic information). Hasidic Judaism at its beginnings was a revolutionary movement. Its followers were excommunicated by the leading rabbis of their time, and the opposition against them was so widespread and bitter that eventually all non-Hasidic traditional Jews in Eastern Europe became known as "misnagdim," meaning "the opponents." Scholars disagree about what was so revolutionary about the movement, but it seems to have had something to do with a de-emphasis of Torah study in favour of ecstatic, holy-roller-style prayer, and a focus on the charismatic personalities of the Rebbes. The de-emphasis of Torah study and focus on personality were potentially favourable to women leaders in a culture where women were not deeply involved in study but could certainly have strong, devout personalities. And the general sense of being revolutionaries breaking new ground made it possible for people to take on unexpected roles. Hasidic Judaism has become much more established, restrained and conservative over the generations, but some of the revolutionary elan has remained with it and made it possible for recognized holy women to arise in nearly every generation.

It is also possible to explain this along more conservative lines. Nearly all the recognized holy women and women Rebbes had close family ties with male Rebbes, as daughters, or mothers, or wives. So, it is possible to see the recognition of holy women as a matter of the male Rebbe's charisma rubbing off on those close to him (Polen 2, citing Ada Rapaport-Albert). We see this in our own times in the political realm: women have risen to positions of high political leadership in some very traditional, patriarchal societies because of their close family connections with great men (or famous men, anyway). I wouldn't emphasize this too much, however, because the same thing can be said about Hasidic men: most recognized holy men and Rebbes are close relatives of other male Rebbes. There is an aristocracy of rabbinic and scholarly families in the Jewish world, and the position of Rebbe became hereditary in most Hasidic communities.

As for the presence of women's stories in holy books, which affirms their status as Torah in the traditional world-view, we have to take into account the impact of feminism in the surrounding culture. As I mentioned, books of Hasidic stories are a crossroads genre, coming into being where the traditional culture meets the modern world. Avraham Hayyim Simha Bunem Michelsohn, the author of *Dover Shalom* and several other books of Hasidic stories (some of them included in the anthology *Ohole Tsadikim*) gave a lot of attention to women. He included women in genealogical lists–in contrast with, for example, Biblical genealogies, which exclude women almost completely. He wrote about women in terms of great honour and consistently included strong women characters in his books. Writing in the teens of the twentieth century, he was surely influenced by the early stirrings of modern feminism in the surrounding culture. By 1972, Israel Klapholz, the author of *Admore Belz*, devoted a whole chapter to Malka–again, surely influenced by the impact of feminism in the general culture on himself and his intended audience.

The Absence of Women's Stories

What about the opposite question: why are there so few stories of women in these books?

As I mentioned earlier, the core definition of a holy Hasidic story is a story told by a Hasidic Jew in praise of a Hasidic Rebbe. Since almost all Hasidic Rebbes have been men, there is a vicious circle once again: there are far fewer stories about women Rebbes because there are far fewer women Rebbes to tell stories about. And the possibility of women Rebbes arising is limited by the lack of stories about women Rebbes who could serve as role models.

As for women as narrators, the social organization of Hasidic communities has to be taken into account. There is a very high degree of social segregation between the sexes. Women have much less contact with their Rebbe than men do; they may go to the Rebbe for individual advice but are rarely if ever gathered in his presence to learn, pray or eat together. Therefore women have less opportunity than men to witness deeds of the Rebbe which might potentially become stories. Also, male Hasidic Jews frequently, especially on the Sabbath, participate in male social gatherings in which storytelling plays an important part. These gatherings are not open to women and I do not think they have close equivalents among women. Further, because men and women rarely socialize, the opportunities for men to hear stories told by women are extremely rare—and men have been the authors and editors of all traditional books of Hasidic stories. Finally, there is the likelihood that male authors and editors would simply be less interested in stories by or about women than in male stories.

They may also have been fundamentally uncomfortable writing about women leaders. The one story we have about Malka's daughter Eydele illustrates the male narrator's ambivalence toward her:

> The well-known respected woman, Eydele of Brody, was a holy woman. She conducted herself as a Rebbe, and people brought her *kvitlekh* (petitions for blessings or healing). I heard that her father Rebbe Sholom said about her, "My daughter has everything but a Rebbe's hat." And I heard that there was a man in her town, Brody, who had been sick for years with an illness of the lungs, and the doctors had given up hope for him. And once the blood was flowing from his throat, and the doctors said that this blood was from the last remaining bit of his lungs, and that his moments were numbered. And his family ran with great tumult to Eydele and told her what was happening. And Eydele said, "Let me tell you a story."

> "The same kind of thing happened in the time of my father, Rebbe Sholom of blessed memory. And my holy father said: 'First of all, I don't believe the doctors when they say he has no lungs left. And second of all, suppose he has no lungs left? If God says we can live with lungs, God can say that he can live without a lung.' And that man was completely healed. And I hope with God's help that the same thing will happen now."
>
> And so it did; that man was healed completely, and he lived for many more years, telling this story. (Paraphrase of Michelsohn 15f.)

Eydele was an exceptional woman, taking on the role of Rebbe which was usually reserved for men. According to the story, her father says, "she has everything but a Rebbe's hat"—which was worn only by men. If she had that, she would be a man. The fact that she is not a man is a failing. Nevertheless, the story celebrates her as a recognized holy leader, and the author lets us know that he *heard* the story, that people were telling stories about her. But, this story about her entered printed form primarily because it includes a story about her father, Rebbe Sholom, the male hero who is the focus of the book.

Eydele conducted herself as a Rebbe—a teacher, healer, spiritual advisor. She must have been gifted in these areas, otherwise she would not have stayed a Rebbe for long; nobody would have continued to go to her. So, there must have been other stories about her. But as far as I know, none of them were included in this or any other book of Hasidic tales.

(Since I presented this paper, David Assaf of Tel Aviv University has referred me to a narrative about Eydele, not in a book of Hasidic tales but in a memoir [Sadan, 256-264], which emphasizes that her femaleness was seen as a flaw which prevented her from full self-realization as a Rebbe. Also, a recent Hasidic book, *Be-ohole Tsadikim*, Jerusalem 1993, does have some material on Eydele.)

The Future of Hasidic Women's Tales

What is the future of this genre of women's Torah? Let's imagine the ideal: a book of holy Hasidic stories about women, told by women, published by a woman author. Such a book does not yet exist, but I think there is room for optimism.

First of all, Hasidic women today certainly do tell stories. I subscribe to a Hasidic newspaper in Yiddish, *Der Yid*, which frequently runs long eulogies on honoured women in the community. Now and then, the eulogy mentions that the woman would tell stories, in a religious spirit, about her encounters with the Rebbe or about her own experiences.

Also, women are already editing collections of stories told by Hasidic Jews. A notable example is Yaffa Eliach's collection of stories she herself heard, including many stories told by women. Her book is not Torah from a traditional Hasidic point of view because it is written in English and because it is addressed to a general audience, not inward to the religious community. But it comes close.

Also, opportunities for Hasidic women to tell stories to each other are increasing. Into the twentieth century, there was little education for girls in Hasidic communities, but today there are large networks of girls' schools with women teachers, which must provide opportunities for storytelling. Among adult women, there are networks of women who support each other in doing acts of kindness: visiting the sick, providing clothes or food for the poor, and so on. This is a very important part of the social life of Hasidic women, and it is a context for storytelling. I just found out recently that there is a web site (shemayisrael.co.il/orgs/key, "Worldwide Chessed Project") with stories posted by women about deeds of kindness done by themselves and other women.

Finally, the ongoing influence of feminism cannot be discounted. Just as books earlier in this century included women's stories in response to feminist trends in the surrounding culture, so will holy books in the future, as women in all Jewish communities take a more and more public role in the life of the community.

What Counts as Women's Torah?

Still, there is not yet a real book of women's stories that would be recognized in the traditional Hasidic world as Torah, sacred text. I think that in time there will be. But in the meantime the rest of us, outside the closed world of the Hasidic communities, do not have to wait. Our definition of Torah can be broad enough to include what is already available in Hasidic women's storytelling, simply by shifting away from the traditional focus on the male Rebbe. We can recognize a newspaper article about an honoured woman who told stories of her life, or a web site about women's kindness to other women, as holy Torah, part of what was given to us on Mount Sinai. It is my hope that this recognition of the women's Torah, the holy stories of women, already available to us, will increase in the broader Jewish world, and perhaps in the broader non-Jewish world as well.

Works Cited and Suggested Reading

Assaf, David. Email to the author. June 6, 1999.

Bakhtin, Mikhail Mikhailovich. *The Bakhtin Reader: Selected Writings of Bakhtin, Medvedev, and Voloshinov.* Ed. Pam Morris. London: E. Arnold, 1994.

Buxbaum, Yitzhak. *Storytelling and Spirituality in Judaism.* Northvale, New Jersey: Jason Aronson, 1994.

Dan, Joseph. "A Bow to Frumkinian Hasidism." *Modern Judaism* 11 (1991): 175-193.

Der Yid (Brooklyn) [Yiddish newspaper].

Eliach, Yaffa. *Hasidic Tales of the Holocaust.* New York: Oxford University Press, 1982.

Herskovic, David. Emails to the author. May 10, 1999; June 7, 1999.

Klapholz, Israel. *Admore Belz* [Hebrew]. Bnei Brak, Israel: Peer Hasefer, 1972.

Langer, Jiri. *Nine Gates to the Chasidic Mysteries.* Trans. Stephen Jolly. Northvale, New Jersey: Jason Aronson, 1993 [translation of first Czech edition, 1937].

Michelsohn, Avraham Hayyim Simha Bunem. *Dover Shalom* [Hebrew]. Premyshl: Umkroit & Fraynd, 1910 (reprinted, Israel, n.d.).

Nigal, Gedalyah. *Ha-Siporet ha-hasidit, toldoteha venoseha* [Hebrew]. Jerusalem: Marcus, 1981.

Ohole Tsadikim [Hebrew]. Jerusalem: H. Vogshal, n.d.

Polen, Nehemia. "Miriam's Dance: Radical Egalitarianism in Hasidic Thought." *Modern Judaism* 12 (1992): 1-21.

Rabinowicz, Tzvi M. *The Encyclopedia of Hasidism.* Northvale, New Jersey: Jason Aronson, 1996.

Rapaport-Albert, Ada. "On Women in Hasidism: S.A. Horodecky and the Maid of Ludmir Tradition." *Jewish History: Essays in Honour of Chimen Abramsky.* Ed. Ada Rapaport-Albert and Steven J. Zipperstein. London, 1988. 495-525.

Robinson, Ira. "Hasidic Hagiography and Jewish Modernity." *Jewish History and Jewish Memory: Essays in Honor of Yosef Hayim Yerushalmi.*Ed. Elisheva Carlebach, John M. Efron, David N. Myers. Brandeis University Press, 1998. 405-412.

Sadan, Dov. Mi-mehoz ha-yaldut [Hebrew]. Tel Aviv: Am Oved, 1981.

Weissler, Chava. *Voices of the Matriarchs: Listening to the Prayers of Early Modern Jewish Women.* Boston: Beacon Press, 1998.

Zevin, Shlomo Josef. *Sipure Hasidim* [Hebrew]. Tel Aviv: Segulah, 1972.

Crafting Stories, Crafting Narrations of Being

Zabe MacEachren

To survive life as a graduate student living in a small bachelor apartment, without a TV, at the north end of the urban sprawl of Toronto, I have taken up walking to the weekly open mike storytelling event in the city core. I look for the greenest route marked on my map and four to five hours later find myself at my destination: A *Thousand and one Friday Nights of Storytelling*. I have a lot of time to think on these walks and sort out what I am doing. Why did I leave the northwoods that I love so much, to pursue doing what I joke is a PhD in "woodcraft lore." Why do I look forward to Friday nights so much, the main day in my week in which I turn off my computer and academic mind and venture off to fill myself up with stories instead? Why do I crave and value the time I spend walking along narrow remnants of forests which meander through a concrete jungle? When I reflect upon my interests and chosen paths I recognize my rambling to be a web which I have woven to catch stories by which to understand my pursuits. I would like to explain to you how I have woven this web of understanding.

To simplify a story often means to tell about a beginning, middle and end. In crafting we might call this triad gathering of raw materials, the preparing and transforming of the material, and then the bringing it all together in the completed craft and its use. Traditionally all of this knowledge was passed on orally. The concept of making something by looking at a blue print or reading directions only became a possibility for most people in the last century, when texts became more widely available to the general public. As technology continues to increase and remove our need to make things by hand, our crafting experience has declined accordingly and with it the oral traditions which preserved its knowledge base. Unfortunately written directions can not transfer the knowledge of a master carpenter's hands which can bend a piece of wood "just so" or "this much."

I understand this kind of knowledge because I have failed, or perhaps I should say learned, just how important "getting-the-feel-right" is. Despite my many "how to" craft books filled with directions and numerous diagrams, the "just so," bodily knowledge, was not conveyed to me through the texts alone. The intellect that can read directions is not the body that can understand what it takes to go with the grain, sense the fibers, extend your being into the wood's being in order to carve.

Crafting knowledge is embodied knowledge. As we make our busy minds soften so that we can attend to our senses and let our body engage in the work that needs to occur. Listening to stories is similar because it makes us familiar with traveling to places where the senses are attended first, the whole body confirmed and the intellectual facts no longer dictate. Oral narrations and storytelling invite us to open ourselves up so that we can sense the material we are working with as if we are it. Where does a crafter's body begin and end when s/he is bending a willow wand? Isn't knowing just when it is about to break an embodied understanding of sustainability? Can this understanding be truly expressed on a computer screen? As an environmental educator, I believe it is important to teach others to trust their inner senses, their embodied knowing, their ability to listen to the more-than-human world where their crafting material originates.

Telling a person to bend a branch until just before s/he "thinks" it will snap can't be recorded in a blue print, but the words "think" or "feel" may invite us to extend beyond our mental capacities and focus on our bodily awareness where our tactile sensitivity allows us to dissolve into a branch when we carve. Stories about animals, rocks, and plants that communicate with humans affirms our ability to communicate with the more-than-human and trains us to bring this awareness to the forefront of our understanding. A familiarity with stories is a familiarity with being sensitive to the unseen world where other phenomena must be respected. As hearing stories habituates us to listen to the voices of the natural world, crafting habituates us with holding and dancing with material of this world, allowing us to practice communicating in nonverbal motion. Clay, wood and skin begin to speak and share their magic. Such activities encourage an animistic perspective and invite the enchantment with the world to return to our lives. Using stories and narrations of women I will attempt to shape and flesh out the beginning, middle and ending of the crafting process and explain how crafting activities feast upon the sense of animism that storytelling encourages.

Before we can tell a story we need something to tell about. Characters and places are shaped as we learn to pay attention to their unique features and nuances. Likewise a craft cannot be completed until we have suitable material from which to shape and mold what it is that we intend to make.

Finding suitable material is like the quest or search involved in many stories where one must pay attention to the clues along the way in order to succeed in finding what one seeks. The oral traditions of many cultures have continued to pass on clues about gathering sustainably, and what appropriate passage and ceremonies should accompany the harvesting of certain plants or animals. Unfortunately, not all crafting texts mention this knowledge because usually they begin by first listing supplies, encouraging us to perceive everything as a commodity that can be purchased and sold.

Stories and narrations often encourage and preserve other perspectives and relationships with our materials. The writer Ngahuia Te Awekotuku explains the depth of this knowledge which is preserved and passed on by Maori women when she describes how flax is cut in the swamps near Maketu:

> Trimming cautiously, she ensures that the rito- the youngest, finest shoot that emerges coyly between two larger parent leaves–remains untouched and undamaged. The parent leaves are also respected, for they will keep the youngest warm, and ensure the life of the plant. Anyone who comes across the growing flax of a Maori weaver will immediately notice the quaint fanning of cut leaves, growing in a neatly chopped delta shape up from the earth...the roots themselves will be fed. Bundles, bound and rotting, are packed about the ground in browning, spindly piles. These are the offcuts–the threads and thinning extremities, the freckled unuseables, the blade spines and residue. Tied together, they are placed within the bosom of the plant–once again to ensure its life....A belief firmly held is that these beautiful fountaining leaves can only be picked when they are ready....Grasped resolutely with one hand, and turned against itself, the ready *kiekie* will snap off easily. Any resistance from the plant warns off the gatherer–she respects its growing, and seeks elsewhere, because *kiekie* that is unready can spoil, or split badly, and make one's work worthless. Taking from the plant as the plant offers itself makes the growth and ongoing lifecycles certain, and ensures further access to and use of these precious forest resources....For the future, despite the depletion and abuse of natural resources, we must find hope in the wisdom of the past. The past as it is preserved by the present–such as the work of the

> weaver of fibres, the woman who cultivates, gathers, recycles... the woman who knows and loves *Papatuanuku* and celebrates the bounty of the earth. This knowledge, if emulated and perpetuated, will serve as our strength and foundation for the times that lie ahead (140).

Unfortunately unless one has a grandparent who has passed on such knowledge, one must learn through trial and error: how much is too much to take? What offering, song or dance the little people like to receive who still live and bless a particular area where fine crafting material grow? As access to crafting material decreases, due to regulations and the loss of the principles of commonland ownership, we may feel inclined to wrestle back access of public resources just like old tricksters-mythological creatures. Florence Davidson, a cedar bark weaver from Masset, BC, remembers: "Take it while you got a chance; you don't get a chance like this again! This is what Raven taught the people in the beginning."

As a child I was once told a story about a group of children who played in a field full of flowers. One day they decided to pick some flowers and soon this activity became a contest for who could pick the most and the prettiest flowers. The contest continued for many days with no one noticing how quickly all the flowers were disappearing. That night one of the few remaining flowers in the field began to cry as it feared that the next day it too would be picked, but a voice from the night calmed the flower and said not to worry. The next day when the children raced to this remaining flower in the field and reached out to pick it they withdrew their hands in pain. Thorns now grew on the rose and pricked anyone who tried to pick it. I beaded a rose on my mukluks so that the moral of this story would walk with me into the forest. Whenever I see a rose it speaks to me of a conservation ethic about never harvesting for beauty's sake alone. Stories and oral traditions feed us a sense of respect and sustainability which are embedded in our body and surpass an understanding which is based upon numerical data alone. Listening to stories and crafting experiences condition us to keep the concerns of other creatures foremost in our minds so we can become environmentally aware through the wisdom they share.

When it comes to preparing and transforming material into a craft, the middle part of a story, I remember fondly the Anishinabe elders with whom I have had the opportunity to work and learn from. Their ability to weave stories and teachings throughout our making activities, instead of lecturing, has left strong impressions with me about how to teach. They submerge experience in stories. One elder I worked with taught me how to shape a birch bark basket full of a consciousness that the forest is alive and watching everything we do.

We had been sitting under a tree early in the morning at a camp I help direct for Native youth. The preceding day we had gathered birch bark from the trees after making the appropriate offering of tobacco and saying a prayer in an act of reciprocity for what we had taken. The staff had just informed me that they had suspected some campers had been up in the middle of the night eating the last of the cookies. I mentioned this to the elder in hopes that she would aid me in deciding what course of action to take on this matter. She simply began to tell me the following story:

> When I was young I asked my grandfather about stealing. He said that no one could ever take anything without someone knowing. I went off to think about this. I kept wondering who would know if I took something. Who would know? I went back to my grandfather later and asked him? Who would know if I took something? Who would know? He replied by saying "They'll know, they'll know." She said these final lines, patting the tree next to her.

Hearing this story left a great impression on me and a firm commitment to continue to tell stories. I couldn't help but wonder what it must have been like to grow up in a world where people encourage you to perceive the trees as if they were alive, conscious and always watching. Such animistic beliefs seemed familiar to me, but I suspect that I had abandoned them in my childhood about the time adults and teachers started telling me that "trees really don't talk." As an adult I now have to choose what types of stories to tell and share with others, influencing others' perceptions perhaps, as this elder's story had influenced me.

As I later sat under the same trees that she had patted, and completed making my birch bark basket, I recalled some of the things that other elders had said to me about crafting items: Never turn a branch upside down and stick it in the ground, that would be disrespectful to the tree; ensure that green wood cut for snowshoes stays covered in snow and is not burned by bringing it into a heated cabin. Remember that a drum is like a living person—an elder, never to be left unattended at a ceremony. I started to realize how these oral narrations about making things had all encouraged me to treat the material in a respectful manner, not to waste it, to treat it as if it was an extension of my own body—alive, living, sentient. Stories of making often warn us about difficulties that arise when we do not treat other phenomena with the respect they deserve.

Paula Underwood's sharing of the old Cherokee tale *Who Speaks for Wolf?* is an example of an old oral myth which encourages us to consider the more-than-human in our endeavors. She tells:

AND SO IT WAS
That the People devised among themselves
  a way of asking each other questions
    whenever a decision was to be made
      on a New Place or a New Way
We sought to perceive the flow of energy
  through each new possibility
    and how much was enough
    and how much was too much

UNTIL AT LAST
  Someone would rise
    and ask the old, old question
      to remind us of things
        we do not yet see clearly enough to remember
"TELL ME NOW MY BROTHERS
  TELL ME NOW MY SISTERS
    WHO SPEAKS FOR WOLF?"
(Punctuation Paula's, 38-39)

Stories and narrations can encourage us to extend rights to the material we use and they also encourage us to seek out the voices at the margins. When they were denied the right to publish, vote and express themselves orally, many women took their voices underground and stitched or wove them into crafts which conveyed who they were. Crafted items and crafting traditions often reflect the life or a voice which was far too often silenced and devalued.

Susan Glaspell's play, *Trifles*, recounts the conversation between two women who are able to uncover a murder motive after they first notice how the stitches in a quilt suddenly become erratic. The story is suitably called "Trifles" because that is what the county attorney, while also searching for the murder motive, thinks the topics of ladies' conversations revolve around. Like so many other stories, this story encourages us to pay attention to each single stitch, each daily task in order to eventually piece together the larger quilt or mosaic of our life experiences. Each stitch is like a little voice that is significant to the greater whole. We need to craft a culture that makes sure all voices are heard and that someone is always asking the question, "Who speaks for wolf?" Both storytelling and crafting experiences give us guidance in this area.

When we complete the made item, how do we embrace it in our lives? Will it be for display only, like a book forgotten and resting on a shelf? Will we somehow be able to clasp the items between our hands and continue to speak of it, know it, with our whole body? Will we see how it reflects who we are?

Sarah Hill's book, *Weaving New Worlds*, describes how the lives of Southeastern Cherokee women were built upon and interwoven with their ability to make baskets. As access to each preferred weaving plant was lost, a new material was found and the weaving technique and style adapted in order for the women to continue to make baskets and support their family. Hill not only collects narrations from women who weave baskets but also myths, which contain an understanding of how weaving came to the Cherokee people and the importance of this craft to their whole lives. She recounts:

> There they saw Selu standing in the middle of the room with a basket in front of her on the floor. Leaning over the basket, she rubbed her stomach-so-and the basket was half full of corn. Then she rubbed under her armpits-so-and and the basket was full to the top with beans....Mystery and magic permeate the myth. Selu's marvelous body brought food, actually was food, and from one container to another, from body to basket, the fertility of woman guaranteed a future...directly associated with Selu, with women performing their most fundamental tasks and assuming powerful responsibilities, was the basket that the first mother carried with her each day (Hill, 78-79).

As an outdoor educator I tell stories because they are like a huge knapsack I can take with me anywhere. I can pack it full of just about any place and any thing, yet it remains extremely light and easy to carry. To open up the pack I simply start telling stories and talking trees, magic pots, baskets woven by enchanted creatures start informing a room full of people. I can take people on walks in their imagination where they tune their bodies to understanding the ancient language of the trees and hear which ones whisper "I want to be a boat." Or they can snowshoe along beside me and let their whole body shiver with the anticipation of success when trying to kindle a fire with wet wood. Stories about crafting take us to where we can sense magic in the air and where our singing to a dark night sky may be heard and create dancing northern lights.

Crafting and storytelling are dependent upon learning with the whole being. They both encourage holistic brain activity in comparison to reading. When we read we scan from left to right, repeatedly triggering specific light receptors at the back of our eye to be react first. These specific receptors happen to be connected to the left hemisphere of our brain which prefers analytical and sequential understanding in comparison to right hemisphere understanding which is more synthesizing and speculative. So by reading we train ourselves to understand in an analytical manner.[1]

Although we can tell stories which emphasize and are derived from understanding the world in analytical ways only, (and this is what many feminist writers are often emphasizing) it is hard to condition ourselves to hear a story by only engaging one hemisphere of our brain. Crafting movements which engage our body all over, on a sensitive three dimensional plane, trigger and engage various aspects of our brain. Telling stories which encourage us to attend to all the manners of understanding which our brain is capable, supports the skills of crafts people. Telling a story may be the best way to teach someone a practical skill such as, how to work with the grain, how to center a pot, or how to stretch a hide.

I will end with one more crafting narration collected by Sarah Hill:

> A weaver's sister told this story: When they were very young, her sister (*e-do*) wanted to learn how to make baskets. It was their grandmother (*o-gili-si*) who told her what to do. To be a good weaver, the grandmother said, a woman must go outside early in the morning and find certain kinds of spiderwebs, those woven by spiders in the darkness before the dawn breaks, the webs that glisten with morning dew. When the woman finds the strong and shimmering webs, the grandmother continued, she must rub them on her hands. Then she would be able to make beautiful baskets. As the weaver's sister told the story thirty years later, she wondered if perhaps her grandmother's advice is what made her sister one of the best honeysuckle basketweavers among contemporary Cherokees (185).

I agree with this story that we all need to wash our hands with the sensitivity and the connectivity of a web that shimmers with new perspectives and resonates with the more-than-human world. Our grandmothers and mothers were wise to share all this wisdom with us not only in the tales they told, but also the quilts they stitched, the baskets they wove, and the lives they touched.

Note

1. For more information on this topic refer to: James Burke and Robert Ornstein. *The Axemaker's Gift*. New York: Tarcher/Putnam Book, 1997 (p.71).

References

Awekotuku, Ngahuia Te. "He Wahine, He Whenua, Maori Women and the Environment." *Reclaim the Earth*, Ed. Leonie Caldecott and Stephanie Leland. London: Women's Press, 1983. 136-140.

Glaspel, Susan. "Trifles." *Quilt Stories.* Ed. Macheski. Kentucky: University of Kentucky Press, 1994.

Hill, Sarah. *Weaving New Worlds.* North Carolina: University of North Carolina Press, 1997.

Steltzer, Ulli. *Indian Artists at Work.* Vancouver: Douglas & McIntyre Ltd, 1976. 35.

Underwood, Paula. *Who Speaks for Wolf.* California: A Tribe of Two Press, 1991.

The Native Voice: Preservation of a Culture

Petra Lina Orloff

Since Native America has only been recognized as historically viable through contact with Anglo-Europeans, contemporary historical representations of Native peoples are problematic. However, current Native authors are using literature as a means of reconstructing and reforming Native identity by combating Eurocentric viewpoints and historical representations. This type of self-representation undertaken by marginal groups is, according to several theorists, namely Molefi Kete Asante, indicative of postmodern history. Instead of proposing oneness, or a modern subject, oppressed peoples posit a dislocated subject which must inscribe itself into the dominant culture.

Molefi Kete Asante, in his book, *The Afrocentric Idea,* makes the point that "current literary theories—phenomenology, hermeneutics and structuralism, for example, cannot be applied, whole cloth, to African themes and subjects. Based as they are in Eurocentric philosophy, they fail to come to terms with fundamental cultural differences" (159). In the same way, incorporating Western Anglo theory into an exploration of Native life essentially revictimizes Native peoples and reduces their cultural standing to that of the traditional contact story, where again Native identity can only be represented as subject to white individuality.

Since the earliest colonization of North America, Anglo-Europeans have sought to erase and replace Native identity with non-Native representations. Linda Alcoff has stated that, "as philosophers and social theorists, we are authorized by virtue of our academic positions to develop theories that express and encompass the ideas, needs, and goals of others. However, we must begin to ask ourselves whether this is a legitimate authority" (7). Anglo-European scholars have presumed to reinscribe Native history into a linear form, which supposes that some events hold more significance than others, an assumption foreign to some Native concepts of time and history. In addition, Natives have been displaced from the sacred geography which constitutes Native historical sense and communities, further mystifying American Indian past. Anglo-Europeans have also attempted to represent Natives as "Europeans" by defining Natives in white terms: separating religion from daily life, terming Native artifacts "art," and most damaging, transforming Native stories, or histories, into "myths" and "legends." Even today, tribal membership is still based on blood quantum, which, as Vine Deloria has stated, prevents tribes from forming or reforming on sociological, religious, or cultural bases...Indian tribal membership today is a fiction created by the federal government, not a creation of the Indian people themselves" (56). Asante notes that such creations are not culturally reliable and that "the critic must ensure that his or her judgment, subjective as it must be, is grounded in the historical or cultural basis of the discourse" (178). Essentially, Native American identity, and therefore history, is still being controlled by Anglo-Europeans.

Furthermore, Native Americans are continuously defined in contrast to white culture. Clifford Geertz strictly warns against this: "If you want to understand what a science is you should look in the first instance not at what its apologists say about it; you should look at what the practitioners of it do" (5). In order to understand Native peoples and their history, we must first understand the importance of the oral tradition in Indian culture and how Natives use this tradition today. Considering Geertz's point, Anglo representations of Native cultures are essentially faulty. As William T. Hagan states in his essay "New Indian History," the film *Dances With Wolves*, which was written and directed by Anglo-Americans, prompted a resurgence of popular interest in the West and in Native America (29). Additionally, Susan Hazen Hammond's text, *Timelines of Native American History*, provides blurbs on Indian history only in reference to Anglo culture. Hammond also only notes that the success of athlete Jim Thorpe at the European constructed Olympic Games and the achievement of novelist John Joseph Mathews and his book, *Wah Kon Tah*, only after the fictional text became a Book-of-the-Month Club selection. Likewise, on the first page of Angie Debo's A *History of Indians of the United States*, she responds to the Western stereotype of Native America. These books illustrate that Native America and its representation are not characterized by a definitive historical moment, but rather consist of several moments which are noted in history only in reference to white authority. For instance, the Indian activist movement, which began in the 1960s, is not represented as a Native mobilization to reform and refine Indian identity. Instead, the movement is continually represented, even in Native authored texts, as a number of Indian led skirmishes which directly defy white authority. The movement, which inspired a generation of Native authors to take up their pens, is only remembered by the 1969 occupation of Alcatraz Island, the 1972 storming of the Bureau of Indian Affairs in Washington D.C., and the 1973 occupation of Wounded Knee. Similarly, contemporary Natives are represented in the same manner. Authors, such as Evan Connell, Ann McGovern, and Angie Debo, only permit Indians a speaking position when writing about white history. Whether it be discontent over issues of repatriation, land rights, or the recent popular media interest in the remains of Kennewick Man, Natives only gain a speaking position when at odds with white culture.

While the recent direction of ethnohistory, as explained in Donald Fixico's *Rethinking Native History*, has been to focus upon the various methods and theoretical trends in order to change the scholarly approach to representing Native America, the problem still lies in the fact that American Indians are inherently different from Anglo-Europeans in that their culture is oral, rather than written. Gayatri Spivak prefers that the intellectual "neither abnegate his or her discursive role nor presume an authenticity of the oppressed but still allow for the possibility that the oppressed will produce a 'countersentence' that can suggest a new historical narrative" (Alcoff 23). Yet, in presuming that new or old Anglo-European ways of representing will accurately depict Native identity and intrinsically, history, Anglo-Americans are still trying to form Indian identity, and failing to come to terms with the fundamental difference between the two cultures. Even David William Cohen's suggestion that historians "rework our logic of the production of historical knowledge" (110), does not alleviate the problems and complexities involved in representing an oral culture. As Linda Alcoff suggests, "the study of and the advocacy for the oppressed must come to be done principally by the oppressed themselves" (7). Hence, contemporary Native authors are acting as their own ethnographers and writing their own ethnohistories in order to assert the basic ideology of their culture. Here, Asante notes that rhetoric is grounded in the politics and culture of societies (166). By utilizing purely Native concepts, such as the oral tradition, to manipulate the English language, American Indian writers are finding a voice and successfully restoring a form of Native identity and spirituality in a non-Native world. Yet, written inscription still remains the antithesis of the Native way, and the attempt to document the oral form continues to be highly problematic. To borrow from Geertz, society's forms are culture's substance, and the need to communicate oral tradition into the current hegemonic structure is necessary for the authentic representation of Native peoples. American Indian authors such as Leslie Marmon Silko, Paula Gunn Allen,

Art

Greg Sarris, Sherman Alexie, N. Scott Momaday, and others, are developing new forms and frameworks of language in order to embody Native American tradition into the constraints of Anglo-European language, liberating English in order to suppress English representations.

According to Margery Fee, this outgrowth of language can be defined as *radical writing*, which is "writing that is struggling, of necessity, only partly successfully to rewrite the dominant ideology from within, to produce a different version of reality" (244). This version of reality is the Native experience.

White contact initially denied the voice of Indians, but Native literature being produced today is more alive and full with oral tradition than ever before. Take for instance, the anthology of contemporary native North American women writers, titled *Reinventing the Enemy's Language*. In the introduction, Joy Harjo and Emily Bird write that the enemy language is being used to tell truths, to sing, and to remember identity, all through literature. Both women make the point that the literature in the anthology places no mediation between art and the readers. Other than the language, there is no site of Western privilege to interfere with what the two editors consider telling and singing the collective voice of nations.

Paula Gunn Allen has done much work on the recovery of the feminine voice through Native authored literature. Allen defines the essential link between ritual, characterized by repetition in a text, and the oral tradition. She writes that the oral tradition of all tribal people is the literature of vision and its reality is social *(Sacred Hoop 22)*. Essentially, it communicates "an enduring sense of fluidity and malleability, the fragility and plasticity of the creative universe in which we live and dwell and have our being" *(Grandmothers 22)*. In the literary anthology *Song of the Turtle*, edited by Allen, she links questions of identity and boundaries of consciousness and race to all First Nations texts. For Allen, reidentifying the Indian is intrinsic to the oral tradition in which identity loss, identity development, and transformation in identity are major roles (*Turtle* 16).

The identifying relationship formed between audience and storyteller is perhaps best realized in Leslie Marmon Silko's *Storyteller*. In literary form, Silko weaves her family's history with photographs, which only heightens the personal character of the text, uniting storyteller and audience. Once immersed in the book, the reader forgets she is reading, Silko's voice is truly speaking to the audience and forming the story of her life. In the introduction to *Storyteller*, Silko remarks that as with any generation the oral tradition depends upon each person listening and remembering a portion and it is all of us remembering what we have heard together that create the whole story, the long story of the people (6-7).

According to Silko, the ancient stories are embedded in those stories being told now. She feels these stories have the power to bring people together even if they are preserved and passed down in the written form, like hers.

Much in the tradition of John G. Neihardt's *Black Elk Speaks*, Greg Sarris brings to life the stories and tradition of Mabel McKay, a Pomo basket weaver and medicine woman, in his oral history, *Weaving the Dream*. Here, Sarris preserves Mabel's words, her mythic vision, and her stories. In mixing first-person narrative and Mabel's own words, Sarris creates a story which not only details his and Mabel's personal histories, but reveals the history and tradition of a people as well. The same can be said of N. Scott Momaday's *The Man Made of Words*, a collection of essays, stories and passages which are inherently infused with the oral tradition. Sherman Alexie's poetry also incorporates storytelling. Each word Alexie writes is exact and essential; he chooses words and uses language as a storyteller would.

All of these authors, and many more, owe much to the devices of oral storytelling. Although the texts are written, the authors' voices are preserved so that the voices ring out in every word, and every nuance of the text, transforming these authors from mere writers into storytellers.

By preserving oral tradition by the form and theme which constitutes the standard partnership between storyteller and audience, and imposing essential Native identity by marking the distinct differences between the two audiences, these Native authors actually use the English language in order to write against the English language, which, in essence, decanters the non-Native reader and inducts him into the realm of the Other, which also constitutes a sense of the Native experience. Native rhetoric, unlike Western rhetoric, allows other cultures to exist. According to Asante, oppressed rhetoric cannot be imperialistic or oppressive.

Essentially, through their work, contemporary Native authors are seizing control of their own representations and dispelling stereotypes of Native motivations. Yet, even as Native authors use written English, they are still defining themselves against a European construction. Paradoxically, Natives can only form their own identity through the primary mode of communication within the current hegemonic structure, challenging the universality of Eurocentric concepts, but still mystifying Native American identity.

Work Cited

Alcoff, Linda. "The Problem of Speaking for Others." *Cultural Critique*. 4 (1991): 5-32.

Allen, Paula Gunn. *Grandmother of the Light*. Boston: Beacon Press, 1991.

________________. *The Sacred Hoop: Recovering the Feminine in American Indian Traditions*. Boston: Beacon Press, 1992.

________________. ed. *Song of the Turtle*. New York: Ballantine Books, 1996.

Asante, Molefi Kete. *The Afrocentric* Idea. Philadelphia: Temple University Press, 1987.

Ashcroft Bill, Gareth Griffiths and Helen Tiffin, eds. *The Post-colonial Studies Reader*. London: Routledge, 1997.

Debo, Angie. A *History of the Indians of the United States*. London: University of Oklahoma Press, 1970.

Deloria, Vine Jr. *God is Red*. Golden, Colorado: Fulcrum, 1994. Fee, Margery. "Who Can Write as Other?" In Ashcroft 242-248.

Fixico, Donald J., ed. *Rethinking American Indian History*. Albuquerque: University of New MexicoPress, 1997.

Harjo, Joy and Gloria Bird, eds. *Reinventing the Enemy's Language*. New York: Norton, 1997.

Momaday, N. Scott. *The Man Made of Words*. New York: St. Martin's Griffin, 1997.

Sarris, Greg. *Mabel McKay: Weaving the Dream*. Berkeley: University of California Press, 1994.

Spivak, Gayatri Chakravorty. "Can the Subaltern Speak?" In Ashcroft 24-28.

"Mami Wata and Mari Jo"

Mumbi Jonson

If you're not afraid to lookI'll invite you to my underwater nook where time stands still and years pass in seconds come on, Mami Wata beckons I first met her when the moon was roundI'd no idea what I'd found Are you ready?....Are you listening?Turn the rock the rock spins This is how my story begins...

On a typical day at home after schoolI came home and found my brother breaking all the rulesI told him to stop but he would notI told him to stop but he would notHe pushed him backUntil he upset Mother's antique porcelaine rackJust as the priceless porcelaine smashed to the floorMother came in through the door"She did it, Mom!" said my brother to my Mother I wanted to reply, "Momma He is lying"zzzoom- she sent me to my roomI was so angry my ears were steamingI hit my pillo_w before the tears started streamingMy brother had blamed <u>me</u> for the very last timeI packed my things and left without a dimeDusk was dusking and I just went to the seaI'm still not sure what possessed meThe wind was singing through my hair and earsSuch sweet music I felt no fear

My little dog Pagi had run awayI wondered why he didn't stay?And there I wasby the edge at nightPeaceful and warm in the absence of lightA cloud rolled away and Grandma moon came outThe lake had a voice like a long silent shoutThe waves rippled gently

perfect rhythm with the wind. Daunting and beautiful I wanted to swim

Come, look a little closerWhat do you see?Come sit nearbyand stare at meCome face the moonand face the sea and soon the face you'll seeis me....

I stared at the moon and the sea and the skyI stared at them for fourteen sighsI saw my reflection on the seaI felt like the sea was speaking to meThe water parted and bobbing on the glowing wavesshe spoke to me in silent tongues

.... Come face the moonand face the sea and soon the face you'll seeis me.... "I am Mami Wata."

Perched on rippling wavesby the glow of Grandma MoonI knew my time was coming soon

Entranced by her motionNo words were spokenI plunged straight into nature's rhythmand rhyme

Past seaweed and dolphins and schools of fistPast canvas, rock sculptures and someone's wish

Mami Wata, Goddess tureTeach me to swim just like you.Her movements graceful and gestures strongHer hair so rich and black and longI copied her bob and followed her twirls and off we swamin a Sirenian Swirl

Mami Wata said "Pretty Jo, you're a natural you knowyou must be hungrylets go..."

We travelled over hill and dale If only tales could tell a tale

We swam through French water in the Bassin BleuJean-Louis, Mami Wata's coming back for youWe supped on seaweed and spinach and grapes For desert we picked crystal rock candy carved into shapesWe swam with penguins in the arctic sea Playing Qallupilluit Qallupilluit you can't catch me....you can't catch me...In the Isle of Spice It's really un-im-agi-nably nice

We helped Aglo and Petal swim to the raft

Those town people are so selfish and daft

In Sirenia, schools of fish only study fun and everyone talks to every other one

But. At the intersection of Bread Street and RockMami Wata came to a sudden stopI bobbed in a closeA sign was posted on the doorI squinted my eye's to find out more....

Frisk to frolic and frolic to friskEnter - at your own RISKWELCOME TO THE MERMAID TAVERN

Mami Wata looked at me longAre we going in? I knew I had to be strong.Inside we saw a strange looking crowd. It was smoky and foggy and deafening loud

Old men and young were boasting and brash Laughing and drinking and clanging their glass Mami Wata reached out and touched my arm

Down here at the Mermaid TavernOn each high tide, fools gather

and smile on the outsideBrashful braggingRidiculous jestersTelling things they've never seenTelling things they've never doneClinking glasses toCelebrate lies Down at
the Mermaid Tavern
Why did she bring me here?This is not fun? Mami Wata lets go

While swimming away from this
cavernous Tavern You'll never guess who we meet... But my very own brother Bragging about his latest feat I stared in shock and tried to call outMy voice would not whisperMy voice would not shoutand
all of a sudden I felt a confusion
Suddenly, Mami Wata whisked us away Helpless, in her wakeWe swam fast and dartedWe swam and swam
so long I started...
On the borderof the other worldI heard sounds and splashing I swirled and bobbed and pushed to the topI was tired and weak but I couldn't stop
That voice? My brother? "come on Mari Jo It's not time to go
Grab the branch
I am sorry I am"
I swirled and bobbed and pushed to the topI felt so weak,
but I couldn't stop Mami?
Pretty Jo, I'd love you to stayBut you need to decide
where you want to play In Sirenia we
swim and bob
and swirl and sup Eat crystal rock
candy
and have tea and trumpe.....
And I heard waves thrashing and arms flailing andAngry
shouting, crying and wheezing, "Come on Mari Jo It's not time to go
Grab the branchI am sorry I am"
Should I ? Could I try once more?I swirled and bobbed and pushed
to the top
As suddenly as he disappeared my dog Pagi bit me on the earPulled from the water in that beautiful seaGrandma Moon smiled at me
When I met my brother this time
I was no longer a young girl of nine
My hair was long and clothes too small We both had grown very tallSo, when the moon is full and round I remember what I found A strange thing happened when I got homeNear my mirror, I found a combWater dripped off as I picked it upIt spoke to me...silentlyA soft wind blew past my ear

and on my cheek I felt one tear
Farewell my sister Pretty Jowhen is dusking and your spirit is lowCome join Mami Wata in the SeaWe'll swim and bob and swirl and supUntil it's time to go back up.

Step on a tin the tin bends, this is how my story ends.

Cultural Representation and Oral Literature: Mami Wata and Mari Jo

Mumbi Johnson

"Myth Helps you put your mind in touch with this experience of being alive."

Joseph Campbell

Because that moment was so racially infused (my revulsion at what my school friend wanted: very blue eyes in a very black skin; the harm she was doing to my concept of the beautiful) the struggle was for writing that was indisputably Black. I don't yet know what that is...

Toni Morrison

Especially important in the coming Millennium and beyond are the stories our female children will recall when they look back on their childhood. Consider the stories of Cinderella, Rapunzel, Snow-white and a whole host of romantic happily ever after stories. Are these the only stories our children will remember? Furthermore, will Western classics infect the minds of our African children? The word infect may seem strong, but is entirely appropriate. Children's literature based on romantic European Monarchial power structures infects the minds of all children because they diminish and ignore the strong leadership of women in earth-based culturally-rich African perspectives. The attempt to exclude the African female makes it essential to publish Afrocentric and female-centric texts for children. The idea is simple. When our children recall stories from when they were growing up, they should be able to recall positive memories and representations of themselves in their childhood stories.

Children's literature mirrors adult literature because they both reflect current norms and mores in society. In universities, in the workplace, and in politics there is often a cursory or imposed recognition and inclusion of the marginalized other. The development of a female-centric African cannon for children is an effective response to the exclusion of women of African descent in children's literature in our changing world.

This story for children of all ages contains sibling rivalry and escape, time-space mysteries, unconscious problem solving and rebirth, and moral insights. Cumulatively, these ideas illustrate how African mythology can provide an educational and entertaining text from which children can form a healthy respect for African spirituality and, at the same time, identity with and enjoy the positive representation of the mythological African female.

I am offering the story of Mami Wata and Mari Jo (the story you have just read) as such a story, one that can initiate North American children into female-centred African narratives. The audi version, complete with sound effects, can, in ten minutes, take listeners on a journey with language and rhythm which initiates fantastic visual images unique to each listener. Mami Wata engages the imagination.

A Story of Sibling Rivalry and Escape

Mari Jo is wrongly blamed for her brother's mischief and runs away to the one place she finds solace, the sea. While there, Mari Jo meets a Yoruba mermaid and travels to another world. In this story poem, Mari Jo is an authoritative, female, first person protagonist who tells her own story which is implicitly immersed in the world of a Yoruba water spirit, Mami Wata.

This story is multi-layered and meaningful to listeners of different ages and insights. Adults may revel in the symbolism of Mami Wata, while children may enjoy the escape via the creative use of language and rhythm or the thought that you could escape from your brother. Older listeners who study African religion, mythology and poetry will find their own meanings, meanwhile the child listener will also find significance in the story. A young girl may identify with Mari Jo, her relationship with her brother and the desire to escape. A younger child may enjoy the sheer fun one experiences as the language and rhythm of the story mimic their lives' or the water's rhythm, the fun of "eating seaweed and spinach and grapes" and picking "crystal rock candy/carved into shapes." Children may not know what frisk actually means, but may enjoy saying the words, "Frisk to frolic and frolic to frisk/enter at your own risk."

Time Space Mystery

A time space gap occurs when Mari Jo resurfaces older than the nine year old girl who entered the water...

> When I met my brother this time
> I was no longer a young girl of nine
> My hair was long and clothes too small
> We both had grown very tall

When Mari Jo re-enters her original world, her hair and her body have grown. Notice though, that Mari Jo and her brother are taller. The moment when Mari Jo is struggling to the surface we assume she fell in the water, nearly drowned and was saved by her brother, the same person who made her mad enough to run away. How could it be possible that Mari Jo was missing long enough for her body to have matured into that of a young woman? Is it possible that you could just turn your head and several years pass by? How was she able to re-surface if she was missing for that long? The power of mother nature, Mami Wata, Grandma Moon and potentially Pretty Jo/Mari Jo all come into question.

Unconscious Problem Solving and Rebirth

The problem solving and ultimately the decision made by Mari Jo are an interesting aspect of the text. The locus of decisions appears vague at first. Key windows of movement in the text are: when Mari Jo makes her entrance into the water; her exit from the underwater world; and her entrance back to the land. Who makes the decision to act? Did Mari Jo decide to jump in the water or was she entranced by Mami Wata? Was it a kind of suicide jump or was she seduced by Mami Wata? "...entranced by her motion, no words were spoken, I plunged straight into nature's rhythm and rhythm and rhyme." Perhaps Mari Jo simply followed with blind faith the same way a child assumes an adult will lead them to safety.

As Mari Jo resurfaces she is forced to reflect on her physical and intellectual limbo three times. Mari Jo is first led into the underwater world by Mami Wata where she is "Helpless in her wake." After they leave the Mermaid Tavern, Mari Jo is suddenly startled by the speed of their movement because they seem to move very far, very fast. Mari Jo is startled, when she finds herself on the border, between two worlds, virtually in limbo. At one point she hears her brother's voice. Once again, the sound seems new to her, as if she was hearing her brother's voice for the first time. The next time, Mari Jo calls out "Mami," again a vagueness of recognition. At this point, Mami Wata tells Mari Jo that she has to decide.... "Pretty Jo, I'd love you to stay/But you need to decide where you want to play..." The third time, Mari Jo hears herself thrashing and flailing and realizes that she should grab the branch her brother is extending into the water. She gradually gains consciousness and comes to understand that she is the one struggling in the water. Mari Jo's delivery onto the land may be compared to the trauma of birth. Mari Jo is renewed and reborn as Mami Wata allows for her delivery back to the people of the land.

Mami Wata trusts Mari Jo to decide. Mari Jo is probably aware subconsciously that she must decide to go back to her family on land. Perhaps she just trusted her gut and also understood that eating rock candy cannot last forever. Mami Wata facilitates the maturation which leads Mari Jo to comprehend her moral insights.

Moral Insight

Mari Jo's moral insights are triggered by noise. In the tavern scene, noise pollutes the serenity and utopian bliss of Sirenia. Sounds of laughter and men drinking and clinking their glasses, the toasting and boasting, telling of stories and lies fill Mari Jo's head like a migraine headache. The Mermaid Tavern is a stressful place to be, but Mami Wata shows Mari Jo the flip side of this underwater paradise on purpose, for to understand peace, one must experience fear and anxiety.

Loud noise is also present when Mari Jo is struggling at the surface, "at the border of the other world/I heard sounds and splashing....heard waves thrashing and arms flailing and/Angry shouting, crying, and wheezing." Only after the third attempt does Mari Jo have a clear idea it is her own self who is making the noise of struggle.

The realization that her brother may be one of the men imprisoned in moral death row at the Mermaid Tavern remains an unconscious fear which resolves itself only when she grabs the branch and hears her brother apologize. The noise and the struggle end when she is standing on land. Mami Wata has placed Mari Jo/Pretty Jo back on the earth, where she reconciles with her brother and returns home.

Serenity and Stress

Journey stories take the child on a journey which start and finish in the same place, but the child taking the journey is markedly changed on her return. The journey enriches the child and teaches her to see and appreciate she already had but was not able to see or appreciate.

Mari Jo, a young African girl, is no different than Alice, or Tom, or Dorothy, but the context and intent of her journey story, in which she travels from point "a" to point "b" is very different. She left home without a dime and came back with a rich perspective on life. The journey is not an adventure to find a lost treasure and become wealthy; instead, the journey brings about an understanding of wealth as family and culture. Mari Jo is enriched by her new ability to celebrate her female African self as a valid part of her family, community and world. Mari Jo must make a leap of faith. The argument, the anger which made her leave her house, and the unexpected adventure are all parts of the risk-taking that is life. The greater the risk we take, the greater the reward. She accepts the invitation of risk, experiences the journey and returns enriched.

Her journey with Mami Wata represents the finest aspects of nature's power. Grandma moon watches over Mami Wata and Mari Jo as they travel and learn about the complexity and the beauty of the natural world. Mari Jo's journey awakens her social perspective. She comes to understand the fact that one can be happy in water or on land, but each person, male or female must and can decide "where they want to play..." Mari Jo/Pretty Jo appreciates herself, and herself in the world.

In the end, Mari Jo is changed, she discovers that she can find solace in the sea and also on land. The mythology of Mami Wata and Mari Jo shows Mari Jo/Pretty Jo the strength and the modesty of African culture, spirituality, and the human connection with the land. The journey with Mami Wata has allowed Mari Jo to experience frisk, frolic, rock candy, the Mermaid Tavern and the cumulative knowledge of all that fosters her contentment.

In her bedroom, which I imagine to be just as she left it as a nine year old girl, she looks at her new self in the mirror. Her hair comb transports her back to her time with Mami Wata, and she is quietly sad and glad, "...and on my cheek, I felt one tear." Mami Wata, consistently with her dual nature, both says goodbye to Mari Jo and offers her a silent promise, the possibility of return...

Farewell my sister Pretty JoWhen dawn is dusking and your spirit is low.Come join Mami Wata in the SeaWe'll swim and bob and swirl and supUntil it's time to go back up.

Step on a tin the tin bends, this is how my story ends.

Telling Moves, Transmitting Embodied Stories[1]

Tomie Hahn

When the Japanese government banned women from the stage in 1629, women's performance became marginalized from a very visible and economically lucrative position to a private, hidden domain. This did not stop women from performing, however. This paper examines how women have, and continue to teach women embodied cultural expression through storytelling in nihon buyo (a Japanese performing tradition dominated by women).

To convey the story in this tradition a vocalist narrates the plot and provides the voices of the individual characters. In turn, performers express the narrative with their bodies. Often one storyteller/dancer shifts smoothly yet convincingly between a wide variety of characters to unfold the story.

This paper proposes that the trained storytelling ability to "shift" between characters metaphorically mirrors a social coordination of self present and respected in daily life in Japan. Social anthropologists have noted that "self" in Japan is relational, and that the conceptual flexibility of self permits individuals to interact in a wide variety of social levels.

I have observed that performance training, as a means of transmitting embodied cultural knowledge, simultaneously transmits gender ideologies—concepts of a shifting, or flexible sense of self within the aesthetic structures of this storytelling genre. Performers pass down the tradition through oral, aural, kinesthetic, and tactile modes of transmission. Through the process of sharing movement expression, bonds between teacher and student are reinforced. Further, as this dance is transplanted and taught in the United States, a second level of identity shifting is layered onto the performance.

I will perform a brief dance which illustrates the metaphoric shifting present in *nihon buyo*. I believe involvement in these performances offers women an embodied understanding of multiple identities as well as flexible notions of self within a society which has historically restricted their expression.

Note:

1. Unfortunately, only Ms. Hahn's proposal was available for publication.

LIVES OF THE STORYTELLERS

DAN YASHINSKY

"Listen your way in/with your mouth."
Paul Celan

What do I do now?!? I'm hosting an open session at the Toronto Festival of Storytelling, and a little boy just took the talking stick, perched on the stool, and proceeded to tell, in a shrill, unstoppable voice, an absolutely appalling story:

Once there was a little boy
and he was running away
and he came to a big dark forest
and there was a big hole in the forest
and then he fell in and he couldn't get out
And then his Mommy was looking for him
but she couldn't find him
But then she did and she looked in the hole
and the little boy looked up at her and said:
"GET ME OUT YOU FUCKING BITCH!"

Now we are sitting shell shocked, stunned by the little boy's last few words. He, in the aftermath, is swinging his legs back and forth on the stool, knocking my talking stick against his shoes, oblivious of the havoc he's just wrought.

People are starting to look at me, waiting for some hostly word or gesture that will repair the damage. Trouble is, I am just as speechless and horrified as my audience. The boy's blast of harsh language has thrown me for a loop. I feel as helpless as the mother in his story, too late noticing her son's absence, too late to the rescue. And I notice the young storyteller's mommy isn't looking so very pleased herself just at the moment. This is awful. The silence is excruciating. What does a host do in case of emergency?

It had been such a pleasant gathering so far. There are people here from every part of Canada, storytelling pilgrims who have made it to our quiet library room on this February afternoon. When I opened with my usual emcee shtick—"Who's come to the Festival from somewhere far away?"—I was amazed by the answers. They have been a terrific crowd, lively, articulate, full of stories, and they are good listeners: patient and generous even for the boring storytellers—and this, being an open session, has had its share of those. And now this.

What do I tell my dazed tribe?

My Romanian grandmother, of blessed memory, used to say: "When in doubt, fake it. Go through the motions. Act like you know what you're doing and wisdom—sometimes—will follow." It seemed to work for you, Grandma. You outwitted death many times, pretended to be people you were not, hunted and gathered supplies for yourself and your daughter in a bombed-out Bucharest. You never lost your courtly, gracious, and famous hospitable ways no matter how many wolves or Nazis howled at your door—and, as my mother has told me, you were rewarded by being liberated by an officer of the Red Army who happened to be a Jew. Benign survivor, refujew par excellence, my granny trés civilisée et bien rusée, I will take your advice. Something has to be done. I recall now that you also used to tell me that the recipe for the sweetest Romanian Egg Cake began, "steal two eggs." Very well, Granny, I will try to steal whatever wisdom I can find to make things sweet again.

Fake it.

The motions.

I get up and walk over to the boy. I take back the talking stick. Invite the customary applause. Desultory; it quickly dies away. I escort the boy over to his mother. Moments later, she slips from the room, an unreadable expression on her face, kid in tow.

But the rest of us are still here, wondering what hit us. And I am still standing holding my hosting prop, this long piece of wood with strange faces carved on it—my "talking stick." It's fake, of course. I borrowed the idea from oral cultures around the world—that part is real enough. The old tradition was that the storyteller would hold a ceremonial stick as he/she spoke the words the tribe had gathered to hear. This one I acquired at a Latin American craft store for twenty bucks. I asked the clerk if the designs meant anything, but he said, no, it was just a fancy post for tethering goats in the highlands of Peru. Now I am clutching it in the suburbs of Toronto, wondering what tethers storytellers to their listeners, hosts to their communities, little boys to their hero-swallowing stories.

The stick stands for protection, I suppose—a kind of guarantee that the host will keep life at a certain distance while the stories are being told. My Romanian grandmother used to begin her fairy tales by saying, "Once something happened. If it hadn't happened, how I could tell you about it?" Which makes, I see now, its own Romanian egg-stealing sense. Stories mark the happened somethings that make up whatever is most memorable and valuable about our lives. A woman gives birth, and it is the most astounding story in the world. But we do not expect her to tell it while she is still in heavy labour. The story is for afterward, when she draws a frame of memory and language around the miraculous event. The little boy's ending seemed to break that frame, his words sounding too real, that blast of rage and terror coming too ??shary and spontaneous—a cri de coeur from the heart of a five-year-old's worst nightmare. That is why the reverie of our listening has been so badly shattered. We do not feel embarrassed. We feel betrayed.

It would have been easier to deal with if the kid had been trying to discomfit us. Hell, I am generally pretty good with rude kids. I'm an American-born, civic-minded—my Canadian wife would add, with vigilante tendencies, but then her background is United Empire Loyalist—individual. I like to see a certain order observed in public life. I do not hesitate to point out in a raised voice the mistakes I see other drivers make on city streets. I break up school yard fights. I go up to groups of loud, rough-talking teens and request of them, in my polite, bespectacled, 40-something way, to please amend their vocabulary and volume. For reasons I—and probably they—do not fully understand, it works every time. But this is different. My little boy hadn't been trying to offend, just trying to tell his story. But the story had too much panic in it. He fell in the same hole as his hero, and now the rest of us are gathered at the edge, speechless.

The roof of the sanctuary's just blown away, and it is up to the host to protect his group, and I'm the host, and now what do I do? I need the counsel of my elders and betters. I need a tradition!

Motions, gestures, a fake talking stick, my threadbare, catch-as-catch-can understanding of how storytelling used to work in societies that truly valued it. And my desire to hear a story, a good story, a fresh story. A story, as Scheherazade's little sister Dunyazad used to say, "to make the hours of night pass pleasantly." See, I'm new at the business, barely versed in the customs and thoughtways that once governed my long-lost art. Or not so much lost as abandoned, dropped down its own mysterious cold dark hole in history, practically unfindable in the age in which I live in.

Storytelling? Isn't it something from long, long ago?

Or is it? I mean, here we are, a ragtag and unlikely band of partisans fighting their resistance struggle in a Toronto library on a dusk-lit afternoon at the far end of the twentieth century. We're here to remember not only stories, but storytelling itself, to welcome the storyteller home again, back to the hearth, the council-fire, surely a noble and romantic enterprise, no? It's just that half the time it feels ridiculous, like we've all wandered in from the set of a remake of Fahrenheit 451, or like I've time-travelled up from the ancient past or down from some possible but not probable future, a self-proclaimed bard who memorizes wonder tales and voice-casts them directly by word-of-mouth into the narrative-starved ears of his data-blasted, microsoftened, amnesiac fellow-nomads on the wanderground of modernity.

Or something like that.

It's all just a half-baked—though whole-hearted—improvisation, this attempt to build a new habitat for my long-exiled but not-quite-forgotten storytellers, griots, grannies, bards, and elders. Should I be hopeful or utterly hopeless? Yesterday the grade five students I visited told me 95% of them watch TV before school and from home-time to bed-time. Hearth? Ain't no such thing anymore, just the blue-flickering likenesses of TV draining the reality out of our watching—erstwhile "living"—rooms, silencing the talk and muffling the spirits of the nation.

Maybe I learned the romance and necessity of remembrance from you, my Romanian grandmother of blessed but elusive—you died when I was six, and most of what I remember was told to me afterwards—memory. In your family just about everyone and everything disappeared, thanks to fascists and fate, down the coldest, darkest, most lost hole humanity ever fell into. Stories are all you brought over with you from Europe—and a couple of intricately woven Romanian rugs. I grew up feeling like I'd been delegated by a host of vanished and war-scattered ancestors to stay tuned to the wavelength of word-of-mouth stories. If I lost the signal in the static, entire histories would stay unfound, unremembered, untold. You made sure that I listened my way in with my mouth and memory, that I felt responsible for keeping alive the stories of the gone ones. Even if the story was only one word long: "The property depot, or 'Canada,' was the last sector immediately behind our sick bay, in between crematoria 3 and 4, from which it was separated only by a non-electrified fence"—this from Wieslaw Kielar in *Anus Mundi—Five Years in Auschwitz*. This was apparently the best place to work in the concentration camp because you could organize extra clothing and food. It was only a temporary sanctuary, of course; the work details would be periodically murdered, along with everybody else. How odd to be thinking of their "Canada" this afternoon, as I host my storytellers in my own Canada, so many years later. It was their name for a place of shelter, a dream of peace and blue lakes and beneficent forests and prosperous towns, a word that echoes up from Auschwitz to remind me that I must not stop listening, even if the stories are almost impossible to tell or hear.

Down the hole, and nobody left to come looking for them.

Except for us, I suppose, here in our nice library with the late February light fading outside, and the echoes of the child's terrifying story only now quieting. I mean, nobody's left the room yet, everybody's still hoping the stories can continue, that the shelter can be rebuilt, the sanctuary re-sanctified. Suddenly, I'm pleased that no one has left.

This isn't, after all, the first time an open storytelling session ran into trouble. I'm thinking of you, Harry Bailly, keeper of the Tabard Inn on the high road to Canterbury. According to Chaucer, you were the greatest storytelling host who ever lived in either fiction or real life. You were generous, bluff, irresistible, as you cajoled, persuaded, bribed, teased, and generally compelled your fellows pilgrims to tell each other "tales of best sentence and moost solaas"—of wisdom and solace. But then it was the Pardoner's turn. He was drunk and obnoxious, and he began by boasting to you all about how he makes his living conning stupid peasants with nonsense about his phony holy relics. "I preche nothyng but for coveitise"—I preach only for covetousness, was his foul and cynical confession. Then he told his story, all about the three drunken, boastful youths who scoff at the power of death, only to bring fatal calamity upon themselves through their greed, sacrilege, and violence. And at the end of the story, this beer-fuelled con artist got caught up in his customary commercial spiel. Carried away by his narrative momentum, the Pardoner started in on you, Harry, of all people, as if you were not a discerning and hospitable story-loving host, but just another 'lewed' ignorant paysano ready for the gulling: "Come forth, sire Hoost, and offre first anon/And thow shall kisse the relikes everychone,/Ye, for a grote! Unbokele anon thy purs!"

Wrong move. Beloved Innkeeper, your righteous indignation echoes for six centuries into my own recollection this February afternoon. "Nay, nay," you quod, "thanne have I Cristes curs! ... Thou woldest make me kisse thyn olde breech [undies]/And swere it were relyk of a seint, /Though it were with thy fundament [shit] depeint!" And after your rage at this fool who treated his listeners like customers and his art like an ad for indulgences, you told him, quite literally, to get stuffed: "I wolde I hadde thy coillons [balls] in myn hand /In stide of relikes or seintuaries/Lat kutte hem of, I wol thee help hem carie; /They shul be shryned in an hogges toord!" Yes, enshrined in a hog's turd. So much for storytellers who betray the trust of their listeners.

You had a drunken Pardoner; I just have a five-year-old who got lost in his own scary story. And, as I recall, with the Knight's courtly mediation, you kissed and made up with the vile creep who so rudely broke the ancient decorum of storytelling. I should be able to make room for my little boy's story, however harsh and untoward his way of telling it. And even the Pardoner's transgression was nothing compared to what they dealt with in Boccaccio's *Decameron*. The ten storytellers in that book told their stories while the Black Death raged outside their villa. Pampinea, you were the host who made your fellow-survivors tell stories. The plague had devastated your city of Florence, broken every bond of civil order, left most of your families dead or dying; yet you insisted that the company tell each other stories, not about death, but about amore, trickery, horny priests, crafty lovers, desire in every colour and fullest consequence. You kept listening to their stories with chaos just beyond the gates. The stories were the seeds you could carry, if you lived, into whatever future you were able to dream for yourself.

Pampinea of the Black Death, Harry Bailly of the Tabard Inn, my own Romanian grandmother, who kept the stories of her missing tribe and, now dead, needs someone to keep her story—you are my illustrious ancestors. If I have a tradition as a storytelling host, you are my elders. I'm not as alone as I thought when I took the stick back from the little boy. In fact, I think I know what needs to happen next. I can see my audience is waiting for a word from their sponsor, and, now that I know what the host must say in a situation like this, I can take a breath. No rush now. I want to say it right. The late afternoon light at the window; the festival crowd audible in the rooms around us; the shockwaves slowly settling from our minor calamity. There's time for a last conversation with the greatest listener of all, before I talk to the audience.

Let me remember the story properly.

Once something happened. If it hadn't, how could I be remembering it now, when I most need a host's best sentence and moost solaas? A sailor was shipwrecked on an island. A princess found him and brought him to the king and queen. They offered him their hospitality, but strangely enough, he didn't tell them his true name; just made up a yarn about a storm, a distant war, a bewitched island, a god-cursed effort to reach his home. Only when Demodokos the bard began to sing did the stranger drop his mask. The bard sang of a warrior-king named Odysseus, and the guest wept secretly behind his cloak. Only you, Alkinoos, great and kingly host, noticed those secret tears. After the banquet, there was track and field, then circle-dancing, then back for more barbeque; and now the bard took requests, and the stranger asked for another tale about that selfsame hero: "Sing only this for me, sing me this well,/and I shall say at once before the world/the grace of heaven has given us a song."

He, even knowing how hungry freelance storytellers can get, sent a plate of choice meat to sweeten his request. The bard tuned his lyre and began to sing; and this time the castashore could no longer hide his tears. Finally, Alkinoos, you demanded to know the truth: "You must not be secretive any longer! Come, in fairness, tell me the name you bore in that far country..." And to complete your hospitality, you promised your guest safe passage home on one of your magic ships, vessels that moved as swiftly as their navigators' dreams.

He began by praising you, great king, and the way you celebrated the storyteller's art:

> Alkinoos, King and admiration of men,
> how beautiful this is, to hear a minstrel
> gifted as yours; a god he might be, singing!
> There is no boon in life more sweet, I say,
> than when a summer joy holds all the realm,
> and banqueters sit listening to a harper
> in a great hall, by rows of tables heaped
> with bread and roast meat, while a steward goes
> to dip up wine and brim your cups again.
> Here is the flower of life, it seems to me!

A fine praise-song, wrought by Homer and translated by Robert Fitzgerald; and having paid this eloquent due to the art that has released his tears and is about to release his name and story, the stranger said, 'I am Laertes' son, Odysseus.'

Halfway through his epic tale—for Odysseus went on to tell his adventures—he stopped, afraid his audience might be getting bored. But you, most noble of listeners, reassured the storyteller with words that still reassure me, your distant cousin, nearly three thousand years later:

> Here's a long night—an endless night—before us,
> and no time yet for sleep, not in this hall.
> Recall the past deeds and the strange adventures,
> I could stay up until the sacred Dawn
> as long as you might wish to tell your story.

And when the story had come to an end, you gave the wanderer a dream-guided ship to carry him home: "Clear sailing shall you have now, homeward now, however painful all the past."

Ancient and honourable host, your humble twentieth-century descendant is awe-struck by your epic hospitality. You gave both the story and the storyteller a safe harbour. You promised to listen "until the sacred Dawn," until the whole story could be told, for only so could the teller bring his whole life to the telling, his troubled history and his dreams of home. In your noble sanctuary, story and life became both frame and force-field for each other. From the shore of his own story, Odysseus could finally sail dream-swift and with your blessing home to Ithaca.

So the story shelters life, and the telling of the story is indeed the flower of life, the moment when we know what brought us here, and when we dare to imagine the home we seek. And you hosts, the ones who keep listening, Alkinoos on your magic island, Harry with your pilgrims, Pampinea with your plague-survivors, and Grandmother with your most Romanian cake of memories stolen from oblivion—all of you, dear ones, give me the courage to bring the little boy's story home, to hear and accept its violent and undeniable truth.

With the blessings I imagine I've inherited from you all, I hold my store-bought goat tether, my host's antenna for all the broken and hard-to-tell stories in the world, and say to my tribe what I think a storytelling host must say: "We've just heard the essence of all fairy tales: I'm lost! Find me! It is the oldest story ever told, and our young friend gave it to us straight from the source. I thank him for telling it. Now who has the next story?"

References

Celan, Paul. *Poems of Paul Celan*. Trans. Michael Hamburger. Persea Books, 1988.
Homer. *The Odyssey*. Trans. Robert Fitzgerald. Anchor Books, 1963.

Violence and Remembering: The Culture of Multiplicity

Emma Zevik

I begin this essay with a story I wrote in 1988. Before I do, a brief introduction: I am the oldest daughter in a family of seven. My parents were high school sweet-hearts. My father, youngest in a poor Portuguese family living on the wrong side of the tracks, and my mother, who was Irish and French, the favorite daughter of the local judge, grew up in a small town outside of Boston. Although I am divorced now, I was married for ten years to an Egyptian man from Cairo. So you see, I am a child of a mixed marriage, from before the "M-word"—multicultural—was fashionable. And I followed that experience into a mixed marriage, in which I thrived as did my former husband. I wish to speak to you today from personal experience as well as from a more traditional academic posture.

Elegy No. 8

Uncle Armindo always receives the same gifts on Christmas Eve. A plaid flannel shirt, a case of Black Label, and a carton of Winstons. Every Sunday we visit Vovo, who stuffs us full of linguica and rice, rabbit, calamari, sweetbread, watermelon and garden-fresh tomatoes. Uncle Armindo sits and leans heavily on the kitchen table tap, tap, tapping his foot in time to the old radio. I am the one to sit and talk with him. He quizzes me on my music scales. His big beer belly shakes like a tub of orange jello when he laughs and wheezes. He scares the others. But I am the one to sit and visit with him. It is my duty. This pays my passage into the family. I earn my keep as a member of the clan taking care of Uncle Armindo during Sunday afternoon family visits. He was the talented one whose life was cut short by his father's early death. Quit high school and violin lessons too, so he could help his mother, his two sisters, his baby brother. The big war came. Off he went. Came back not the same, never the same. No one ever told us what really happened. We just could tell when Uncle Armindo was remembering the war talking to himself, shouting a little, pacing back and forth.

Aunt Mary has been shut away for years, taken out on Thanksgiving and Easter where she sits plopped in a chair all day. Humming this, humming that. Faded paisley dress draped over her, white buttons down the front, white hankie in the pocket, white hair soft smooth shiny. Her eyes blue, deep Irish blue. Nylons bunching up round her ankles like the camel with the wrinkly knees in my storybook. We all speak loudly to her: "Happy Easter, Aunt Mary!"

They were all afraid of you, Uncle Armindo. I was their buffer, camouflaged as a little girl in pink. We talked about your music. You gave me my first violin. With that gift came the legacy. You had 15 years in the loony bin from the war. Never played the violin again. With me they wipe, wipe, wipe away all they couldn't face about you and your life. Twenty years later, off I go to play little Carnegie Hall. But it was you they came to see, to hear, to applaud. I sit today listening to your record, your violin singing Clair de Lune—a pale green melancholy. And I see you clearly standing on that stage next to me. Even though you never played for me, my life was marked to become what you might have been.

"Happy Thanksgiving, Aunt Mary!" No one ever tells us stories about your early Irish days. We don't even bother to make any up. Slowly, over years, you and your stories have been forgotten, never told, erased from the family. There are no pictures of you even. I am your namesake and your shadow. You are my vision and the warning. Aunt Mary—you are what I am to become if I don't behave, keep the secrets. No one ever visits you, the place is just a mile down the street. No one even knows you're there.

I am the metronome, a maypole never winding down, measuring out the back and forth tick-tock tick-tock, caught in-between the beats of all the clan conductors, perched on the edges of two sad iniquities.

This story is a remembering. It hints at a reality of trauma and fright, threats and violence. Yet, there is an air of innocence and childlike wonder which seems unreal, even surreal, as it is juxtaposed with an aura of destruction surrounding the child telling the story-memory.

Trained as a composer, I have experienced multiple shifts in my own creativity, both process and products, as I moved away from working with sounds and towards working with poetry, visual art and movement. Now, as a researcher in the fields of ethnomusicology and cultural studies, I am intrigued with exploring a topic I call "The Community of Self." Somewhat like an archeologist, let me sift through the art and artifacts of my own music, drawings and poetry, looking for clues in my life's journey. The sketchbooks and notebooks along the way serve as signposts in a world fraught with violence and despair as well as academic achievement and artistic accomplishment.

In 1985, I completed an introductory study of Arab music in Egypt—my first field experience. Ten years later, I found myself embarking on new fieldwork in Western China. I lived there from 1995 to 1997 and, as Visiting Professor at Sichuan Conservatory of Music, I taught in the composition and musicology departments. My ethnomusicological research there took me to the northern Sichuan mountains, where I collect the mountain songs of the virtually unknown Qiang people.

I slip easily in and around, across and beyond borders—geographical, cultural, linguistic, musical—I have long called myself a "border-crosser." It is as easy and natural for me in my professional work as it was for me to wander back and forth across the train tracks in my hometown between my Portugese Vovo, Uncle Armindo and the dozens of newly arrived relatives, and the Irish-French, well-off family on my mother's side. I believe this early life experience provided both a world view and navigational skills that serve me in my chosen fields. Clearly, my abilities to hold and to exist within juxtapositions—of class, of ethnicity and heritage, of language—are my most valuable tools for my life's work.

At the same time, and seemingly unrelated to my work and life accomplishment, I, like others described in the Virginia Foundation for the Humanities (VFH) 1996 Call for Papers, "carry in my body and my memory overwhelming experiences of violation and trauma. Like entire populations moving across borders in the wake of war and famine, I am a bereaved citizen of a world born of extremity and wounding; the displacement has its basis not in natural disasters and environmental crisis, but in human brutality and violence. This is a crucial body of knowledge. Those who know violence most fully are those of us who have experienced violence and reside in the world as survivors, for whom the meaning of violent experience is more embodied than intellectual, more felt than told" (2).

Co-Existence vs. Assimilation. Multiplicity vs. Integration. Independence vs. Interdependence.

Societies around the world today face difficult and painful issues, articulated with this terminology, as they seek solutions in the process of developing or rebuilding their communities. This is also the terminology used in psychological discourse in working with people who have Dissociative Identity Disorder. DID (formerly known as Multiple Personality Disorder - MPD) is a diagnosis for individuals experiencing extreme and prolonged traumas, many originating in childhood. DID is characterized by "the presence of two or more distinct identities or personality states (each with its own relatively enduring pattern of perceiving, relating to, and thinking about the environment and self)," according to the Diagnostic and Statistical Manual of Mental Disorders or DSM/IV published by the American Psychiatric Association.

I suggest a different perspective: it is my contention that MPD is not a *disorder*, but a *response*—creative, imaginative and extremely practical—to intolerable trauma. As such, the individual, with accompanying response, can be viewed as possessing important skills and abilities, rather than (as in a society such as North America where a high premium is placed on a ruggedly individualist Self) as someone who is disordered, disabled and dysfunctional. And since the diagnosed person is actually a collection of several inside-people, it is an easy step to view this person-containing-many-others as a *person-society*. Perhaps, then, there are other ways to understand developing person-societies as well as other developing cultures across the globe, *world-societies*.

Might the struggles of multicultural world-communities find some commonality with the experiences of people who are multiple? What can be learned by exploring multiplicity from other perspectives? How might a multiple's experiences be constructed or valued or "diagnosed" in non-Western cultures? Though the cultural contexts may be divergent at first glance, there may be some underlying similarities.

Consider this. As a former multiple or person-society, I offer first-hand testimony and understanding of the struggles to accommodate Self as well as Other(s), all existing within one physical body. This is similar in many ways to cultures where there is a dominant group with many (multiple) entirely separate ethnic groups within the same physical geographical boundary (body). As a singularity, I now see that the integration process does not end with integration. Indeed, integration brings with it entirely new and different sets of difficulties and issues, so much so that I do not believe that integration is (or must be) the one and only goal of healing in these societies—whether the disrupted development has occurred in a person-society or a world-society.

Indeed, imagine the possibilities in terms of exchange. I wonder what new learning might come about if the research practitioners who study world-societies were to be brought together with those healing practitioners who work with person-societies. What might be gained if multiples could have some interchange with anthropologists, ethnomusicologists and others, whose work has been focused on world-societies, fragmented or otherwise? How might the skills and experiences of counseling professionals, who work with person-societies in the clinical arenas, inform the work of these cultural researchers? And what perspectives might disrupted world-societies absorb directly or indirectly from person-societies?

Just as particular family systems shape and silence accounts of violence, so do entire societies. As a former multiple, I still struggle to reconstruct the human connections that were ruptured and severed and replaced by violence (VFH, CFP). Now, as a singularity, I am living and learning to navigate in the collective society that is China, which in many ways is much healthier that my life-long struggle to live in the United States as a multiplicity.

The perspective of multiples, as survivors of violent family systems, is unique. The authors of the VFH CFP suggest that "Survivors know critical dimensions and effects of violence which elude formal studies. Precisely because survivor understandings of violence are different from those of non-survivors, they must be included and examined." From my own experience, since my healing took place entirely within artistic circles, I have absolutely no experience with treatments involving hypnotherapy, drugs and medication, hospitalization. My process in working through traumatic experience has been entirely through the creative arts—music, art, poetry. In one sense, then, my journey is a testimonial to the power of the arts in healing.

Understandings of violence and memory are complex; yet the complexities are quite different for survivors and nonsurvivors. Again, I quote: "Violence and its memory can be approached in many ways. The experience of violence, and its memory and (re)telling, takes us immediately to the crossroads of the body, emotion and culture that is at its core. Everyday we are confronted with testimonies of violence—of war and genocide, rape and torture. But of those of us who know violence first-hand experience the ways in which violence moves through and consumes social systems. We survivors know it in the body. Just as the actual experience of violence is beyond words, so too is its telling" (VFH CFP). In this essay, I take no part in the theoretical debate surrounding on memory and remembering, although my treatment of the subject has, inevitably, been influenced by it.

The story of Uncle Armindo with which I opened this essay recollects the traumas and violence he experienced and the effect war had on him and his family. The story attempts this remembering from the viewpoint of the little girl and presents her understanding of his early life. "We just could tell when Uncle Armindo was remembering—and forgetting—the war, pacing back and forth, shouting a little." In fact, there are layers of remembering here. Indeed, the narrator is herself a witness to Armindo's remembering and in the poem she is remembering *his* remembering as well as re-constructing her own memories of childhood. Just as importantly, in telling this story, she is remembering the silencing at the same time—the silencing of Armindo's traumas as well as her own.

How might my experiences (as the poet), the shifting back and forth within my internal community as well as the integrations, inform other such developing communities in the world? What might I, as well as other multiples, learn from these kindred-soul societies that can ease my own struggles in the path of continued good health? For example, imagine the depth of my new learning as I experience living and teaching, as an integrated singularity, in a collective society such as China, and how does this compare to my struggles growing up, as a multiple, in the individualist culture of America?

"Though we are often silent or silenced, survivors often try to tell what we know—to bear witness. Working through violence and its effects is a fragmentary process at best, full of contradictions. The epistemology of violence cannot be separated from the interpretation of its memory—nor should it be. Our personal, sometimes impassioned accounts are generally not considered precisely scholarship, however, which tends to begin its work from less intimate perspectives" (VFH 1996). Silence often operates as a survival strategy; however, silencing is a powerful tool of control.

In Elegy No. 8, the voice of the little girl describes the mechanism of the family system and its techniques for silencing. Beginning with Uncle Armindo, the narrator explains: *No one ever told us what really happened.* Although it is never articulated in words, she knows exactly what the rules are and consequences of breaking the silence: *if I don't behave, keep the secrets.* Even Armindo's music is silent, save for an old scratchy recording. At least Armindo has his soldier effort to carry some degree of respect for him. For Aunt Mary, the silencing extends beyond words—there are no photos of her in family albums and no stories about her. One would imagine that such a figure would have been, at a minimum, the object of children's ridicule and imaginative taunting. In this family, the silencing of Aunt Mary is all-encompassing.

There is a common link between survivors, and a distinction between them and non-survivors, according to the Call's authors: "As survivors, we ourselves often find it difficult or inappropriate to speak of what we know of violence and its effects, in words sufficiently detached and academic to be considered scholarly. Non-survivors usually find survivors' knowledge and language either too aversive and intimate or too detached or surreal to be considered real *knowledge*, however much it may be *experience*" (VFH CFP). The emotional intensity of the events and haphazard circumstances of ongoing survival characterize our intepretation and re-telling of our stories. And often, when the telling is beyond belief- when listeners cry, "That's not true!"—survivors fall back into silence.

In the story, I tell some facts about my life. I describe my grandmother's house and meals. I continue with some facts about my uncle's life and his music. This recollecting, autobiographical in essence, describes—beyond the facts—how these family visits *felt* . This memory is not a single, unique event, but rather, it is the sum of many occasions. The memory of visiting Uncle Armindo is the memory of many recurring events, woven together into one impression, thereby indelibly etched into my memory, like the tick-tock of the metronome.

Personal testimony *is* evidence. Bringing the personal into scholarship is more than mere autobiography. That is why, "We need a wider scholarship, an opening and expanding of research study, to the true nature of the experience. The search must be more than just listening. This involves questions of what and how survivors know, how others hear survivors as well as how cultural explanations configure violence and shape its telling" (VFH CFP). It seems remarkable in my own case that what I shared with my uncle was a communication beyond words, experienced in the mutual exchange of simple music. This is listening on a different level, beyond words and beyond the body, and "it is this expanded context which survivors seek to report. Locked in the body and away from words, it is precisely this kind of discourse that needs to inform the academy. Perhaps, if we survivors are involved in this kind of scholarly inquiry, then we can more fully develop the connections between body and conflict, suffering and social order" (VFH CFP). The results should prove to be useful to both survivors and non-survivors alike.

Intriguing questions. And I offer few definitive answers. Indeed, it seems no coincidence that my own professional and academic endeavors have found me in the fields of folklore, cultural studies and ethnomusicology—I am a border-crosser instinctively and, though not by my own choice at first, I've been conducting fieldwork almost since birth, as I moved through a rebuilding of the community of Others contained within my multiple Self.

Notes

1. This paper was first presented in an early version in Finland at the Crosswords in Cultural Studies International Conference, 1996.
2. In this essay, I combine direct quotes and free paraphrases from a 1996 Call For Proposals issued from the VFH Center for the Humanaities. Violence Studies and Survival Studies as fields of study can now be found in several academic programs, notably but certainly not limited to Carnegie Mellon University; Emory University; University of California, Davis; University of Colorado; University of Minnesota; University of New Hampshire; University of Western Ontario, Fanshawe College.

Storytelling Within Texts

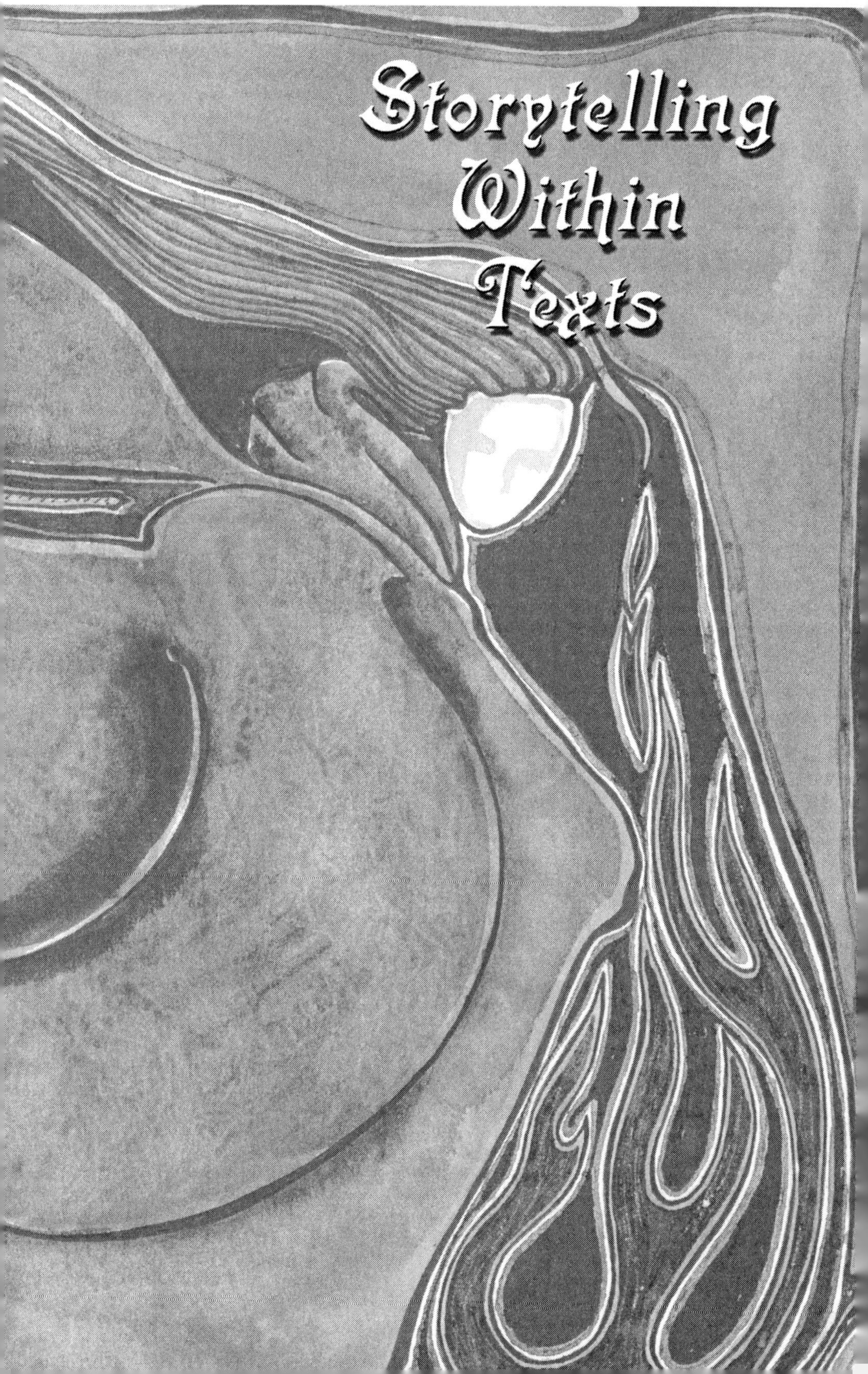

An "Acadia Within:" Carnivalizing the Epic Impulse in Antonine Maillet's *Pélagie*

Cheryl Cowdy Crawford

"Only along the shores of the mournful and misty Atlantic
Linger a few Acadian peasants, whose fathers from exile
Wandered back to their native land to die in its bosom."
Longfellow, *Evangeline*, 126.

Pélagie, "widow of the Great Disruption," (36) has spent several years leading a group of dispersed Acadians back to their former home in an oxcart when she pauses to celebrate the marriage of her daughter. Jean-Baptiste Allain, a religious member of the cart's community, advises the new groom to expect love, honor and obedience from his wife, since he is "the chief who in the Garden of Eden received the baton of authority over the whole family" (169). The comment causes Pélagie to "cock an eyebrow," since it has been her leadership that has been responsible for the carts' progress and survival (169). Smiling knowingly to herself, she contemplates the ways in which the culture and society of the Acadians have been changed by the "Great Disruption," the name used to refer to the uprooting and deportation of approximately ten thousand Acadians in 1755 by the British government:

> Her daughter Madeleine hadn't known the old ways before the Great Disruption. Most family chiefs had perished in the catastrophe, carrying their batons of authority received in the Garden of Eden with them to the depths of the woods or seas. As a result, the women had to face the enemy and adversity alone and wield the scepter of the head of the family. As

> posthumous child of her father and ancestors, Madeleine knew only this regime. Pélagie could count on her to continue the line (169).

For Pélagie, the Great Disruption was an event, much like the Fall in Milton's *Paradise Lost*, that profoundly changed the social order of a society.[1] As Michèle Lacombe has remarked, in Antonine Maillet's epic tale, "the myth of the fortunate fall acquires new meaning and poetic resonance in her iconoclastic treatment of 'le grand dérangement'" (52). With the patriarchs scattered across the continent and the sea, or killed during the Disruption, women such as Pélagie had to appropriate the patriarchal "batons of authority" and act as the heads of their families. In contrast to Longfellow's epic poem about the Acadian dispersion, *Evangeline*, it is the mothers in Maillet, more than the fathers, who have "from exile/Wandered back to their native land." Although some, like Pélagie, may "die in its bosom," they have their daughters to "continue the line," to create a new tradition of female authority. This necessity of appropriating a traditionally patriarchal "baton of authority" also means that Antonine Maillet's epic novel *Pélagie* will be very different from the conventional epic tradition to which writers such as Milton belong.

As a genre that is, according to *The Penguin Dictionary of Literary Terms and Literary Theory*, "a polygonal, 'heroic' story incorporating myth, legend, folk tale and history," (284) the epic is particularly well suited to the history of the dispersal and return of the Acadians. It is also an effective genre for representing the myths, legends and folklore so rich in the Acadian oral tradition of storytelling. Moreover, epic conventions add a heroic dimension to the story of Pélagie and the group of Acadians she leads back to the "Promised Land." However, as a woman writer who belongs to a linguistic and cultural group that has been marginalized within the dominant English-speaking Canadian culture, Maillet's relationship to the epic tradition is somewhat ambivalent. At times, the epic structure of the story seems in conflict with the carnivalizing tendencies of the novel, a conflict that is represented in *Pélagie* by the competition between the two primary storytellers of the cart—the centenarian Bélonie, and the fool, Pierre-à-Pitre.

Descriptions of the two storytellers provide the reader with a key to understanding the novel's relationship to the tension between its serious epic impulses and the carnivalizing spirit of the novel:

> For here is the lasting difference between the two greatest Acadian storytellers of the journey home: Whereas for almost a hundred years Bélonie faithfully passed down to his line a repertory of tales and legends from the time of the Great Rains, Pierre-à-Pitre, the people's fool, went spilling into this reper-

> tory such versions, variations, improvisations, and elucubrations of his own fabrication that it isn't easy today to know what's authentically old (68).

Bélonie and Pierre-à-Pitre represent two often-opposing ways of telling a story, and each spins a tale for a very different purpose. For Bélonie, storytelling is a serious trade. He rarely speaks (except for an occasional "Hee!"), preferring to save himself for his stories. As the narrators explain, he "never wasted saliva on foregone obstinacies" (5). When he tells a story, the "old chin-wagger" enters into a trance-like state, demanding his audience's absolute attention (48). It is his responsibility to keep safe the legends, stories and histories of the Acadian people—a very grave responsibility given the effects of the dispersion. As we are told in the Prologue, "without these storytellers and root-delvers of Bélonies, sons of Bélonies, and the sons of sons of Bélonies, History would have rolled over and died at the end of every century" (3). Not only the history, but the very survival and future of the community depends on the seriousness of Bélonie's vocation, and it is for this reason that I have chosen him as a representative of the serious epic impulse.

In contrast, Pierre-à-Pitre descends from a tradition of Rabelaisian fools. For Mikhail Bakhtin, fools are "the constant, accredited representatives of the carnival spirit in everyday life out of carnival season" (*Rabelais* 8). Like his antecedents, Pierre enjoys turning the traditional stories of Bélonie and Acadia upside-down. He is quintessentially irreverent; a "taletelling-chinwagging-legpulling-trickplaying genius" (69). A genius because he represents the power of a folk humor that not only denies the authority of official culture, but "revives and renews it at the same time."[2] Frequently, Pierre's storytelling is inspired wholly by pleasure: "Pierre-á-Pitre's stories were pure invention, everyone knew that and only listened for entertainment. But Bélonie's tales were something else" (217).

It is important to note that although Bélonie and Pierre represent opposite storytelling tendencies, neither is strictly confined to his type. Bélonie's story of the White Whale, for example, is infused with folk humor and profanation. He even changes the ending after the carts end up in prison and the Acadians consume a strange elixir, created by Célina the medicine woman, that is meant to incite the jailers to free them. The new ending to Bélonie's story is full of bodily images of the whale that are, like Bakhtin's grotesque body, concerned with the "material bodily principle"; hence, they have "a cosmic and at the same time an all-people's character" (*Rabelais* 18-19). Likewise, Pierre-à-Pitre's stories occasionally gain some authority as those "which the hearth could no more do without than soup on the table" (136). As Bakhtin points out, this "double aspect" is essential to the carnivalesque: "But at the early stage of preclass and prepolitical social order it seems that the serious and the comic aspects of the world and of the deity were equally sacred, equally 'official'" (*Rabelais* 6). In the carts of the dispersed Acadians, Antonine Maillet creates in microcosm such a "preclass and prepolitical social order," for the Great Disruption has turned the class and political hierarchies of the community upside-down. This enables her to write an epic novel that embraces the double aspect of Bakhtinian carnival.

Maillet strategically uses the conventions of the "high" epic genre to confer authority on her heroes, her narrators and their collective stories. In order to create a work that will aid the process of maintaining Acadian culture (a project that continues today),[3] Maillet undertakes to write an epic in the tradition of such past writers of the genre as Homer or Virgil, each of whom helped form a national epic past and tradition for their own cultures. On the other hand, *Pélagie* also follows the tradition of Pierre-à-Pitre; it is a carnivalization and a novelization of the epic impulse that parodies the official culture of the epic canon with its often masculinist and "Anglocentric" conventions.

Bélonie and the Epic Impulse

"He, Bélonie, would never improvise like that, to the whim of the wind and the sway of the oxen. He held his tales from his father who had got them from his. You didn't go passing themaround like chewing tobacco" (94). As a storyteller, old Bélonie treats his materials as sacred. He only deals "in the authentically true," even if that truth is as fantastic as hearing the bells of Grand-Pré church "ringing on the high seas in the middle of a hurricane" (136). Although the stories he tells the carts are hardly of the "high" epic type, he functions as the oral chronicler of the carts, turning events of their journey into legendary episodic tales. He gives them names such as "the combat of the carts," "the Baltimore Striptease," or "the Charleston Whiskey Carnival." This role makes him a suitable representative for the novel's more serious epic impulse.

Bakhtin's influential essay, "Epic and Novel" is useful for theorizing the tension between epic and novelistic impulses. For him, the epic is a genre whose development is complete (3). Three "constitutive features" characterize it. First, its subject matter is "a national epic past" or "the national heroic past," a world that Bakhtin describes as one "of 'beginnings' and 'peak times' in the national history, a world of fathers and of founders of families, a world of 'firsts' and 'bests'" (13). Second, the epic is grounded in "national tradition" as opposed to "personal experience," the latter being more characteristic of the novel (13). Lastly, Bakhtin suggests that there is "an absolute epic distance" that "separates the epic world from contemporary reality, that is, from the time in which the singer (the author and his audience) lives" (13). The key feature of these conventions is that they are "valorized" categories; epics are not simply about the past or tradition, but an idealized, valorized heroic past and tradition. And, as Bakhtin explains,

> This idealization of the past in high genres has something of an official air. All external expressions of the dominant force and truth (the expression of everything conclusive)were formulated in the valorized-hierarchical category of the past, in a distanced and distant image (everything from gesture and clothing to literary style, for all are symbols of authority) (20).

For Bakhtin then, this valorization of a national past and a national tradition is intimately connected to the "authority" that high genres such as the epic are granted by official culture.

Other theorists of the epic help to round out Bakhtin's formulations. In "Criteria for the Epic: Borders, Diversity and Expansion," Van Kelly both agrees and disagrees with Bakhtin. Unlike Bakhtin, Kelly does not view the epic as a completed genre, but as one that is capable of a "diverse unfolding of...potential"(1). Kelly seems to agree with Bakhtin's suggestion that the epic has been changed by its contact with other genres. However, while Bakhtin speaks of the "novelization" of the epic, Kelly reminds us that the epic has also "gradually redefined its borders with other genres and discourses–the lyric, tragedy, medieval *geste*, saga, the novel, memoirs, chronicle, and historical document" (1). He suggests that it is characteristic for both past and contemporary epics to combine mnemonic with regenerative traits (4). He defines "mnemonic traits" as "segments of the genre's prior evolutionary history," while "regenerative traits" are "characteristics taken from non-epic sources" that work in combination with the former to "furnish mixes that progressively redefine epic" (4). Kelly's most interesting suggestion in terms of *Pélagie* is to make a connection between a historically progressive expansion of epic topics and the importance of such works to the societies that produce them. As he explains, "expansion in the scope of its topics, and the increasing repertory of works recognized formally or instinctively over time as belonging to the genre, have tended to transform the epic into an estheticized historical and cultural memory" (16). In many ways, Maillet's *Pélagie* could be described as just such "an estheticized historical and cultural memory," for the motivation driving her epic impulse is to cure our nation's historical and cultural amnesia of the story of Acadian survival.

Both Kelly's and Bakhtin's observations on the nature and characteristics of the epic genre help readers of *Pélagie* to appreciate the advantages to

Maillet of working within the tradition. By utilizing both mnemonic and regenerative traits, Maillet's epic novel helps to create a cultural epic past and tradition for a people whose way of life was forever changed by the Great Disruption.[4] Some of the "mnemonic traits" Maillet uses include epic conventions, such as lists, and epic similes. She also includes many of the themes common to the epic, such as war and the conflict between love and duty.

Maillet uses conventions that are recognizably epic to create an authoritative space for her novel within the "high" generic canon. Previous criticism on *Pélagie* has noted the novel's many allusions to biblical, mythical and epic materials.[5] Michèle Lacombe identifies many instances when Maillet uses conventions such as epic lists and similes, and includes traditional epic themes such as war in her narrative.[6] At the most obvious level, the narrative is structured, in the tradition of *The Odyssey*, as a return home, including the many trials and tribulations that Pélagie and her fellow members of the cart must overcome. The first chapter begins *in medias res*, with a conversation between Bélonie and Pélagie on the subject of Bélonie's "Wagon of Death," a phantom cart that introduces a supernatural element into the story.[7] This conversation is immediately followed by Pélagie's shouts of "Hue!" and "Dia!" as the oxen get the cart "moving again" (6). Aside from the odd scattered reference, this beginning "in the midst of things" does not tell the story of the Great Disruption, nor does it narrate the experiences of the Acadians during their exile in Georgia. It is a deliberate use of a mnemonic trait of the epic that alerts the reader she will not be reading an ordinary story; this is an epic novel whose heroic protagonists are the stuff of legend.

As Karolyn Waterson points out, however, Pélagie and the other characters in the novel are not ordinary epic heroes: "Maillet's folk heroine leads a collectivity which is neither traditionally heroic nor anti-heroic, but otherwise heroic" (56). They are, however, valorized characters in the Bakhtinian sense. For their descendants, the collective narrators of *Pélagie*, they are legendary. For example, Broussard-called-Beausoleil, captain of the *Grand'Goule* and lover of Pélagie, is described at the end of the novel in language that is highly heroic, conveying the reverence of later generations for this legendary character:

> And he set to sea again, the captain did, with his giant and his fool in his fourmaster without flag or home port, absurd, intrepid, heroic, swooping like an albatross over the scud of waves, flying toward impossible horizons, toward lost kingdoms, entering upright into the legends of his land (246).

Beausoleil is no ordinary man; his feats of heroism, such as his rescue of the carts from the Salem swamp, confer legendary status on him as a "Robin

Hood of the Seas," (70) and future generations do not doubt his ability to perform the impossible. He is a quintessential epic hero. As Bakhtin says, "There is not the slightest gap between his authentic essence and its external manifestation" (34).

Pélagie, however, is a slightly more human epic heroine. As Marjorie Fitzpatrick suggests, her "triumph depends on her moral force rather than physical strength" (143). Yet even Pélagie's physical description conveys her humanity: although Acadia's storytellers give her the "Golden tresses and fairy fingers" (80) of folklore, she is also "a woman with laughter in her eyes besides" (81). Like any good character in a novel, the genre whose heroes Bakhtin refers to as those "of a life process" in contrast to the epic heroes "of tradition," ("Epic and Novel" 36), Pélagie has moments when she doubts her own ability to lead her people back to Acadie. She also experiences a conflict between love and duty when her passion for Beausoleil causes her to wonder, "Hadn't she earned a single day of life, of life for herself, this Pélagie, after a whole existence given over to saving others?" (121) This theme is common to many epics, as in *The Aeneid*, when Aeneas neglects his duty during his tryst with Queen Dido. It also occurs in *The Odyssey*, when Circe distracts Odysseus from his return home. Unlike these masculine heroes, however, Pélagie does not choose a love interest that threatens the success of her journey. Although Beausoleil often attempts to convince Pélagie to join him on the *Grand'Goule*, he understands her drive to bring her group of Acadians back to their former home, an objective he shares:

> . . . What a woman, this Pélagie! Capable single-handed of bringing her people home. And of bringing them back against the current. For the current ran south in those days, and Beausoleil had seen half his people slip into it and let themselves be carried along to the Antilles or Louisiana. But now who had crossed his path but this stiff-necked, proud-browed woman who dared stand up to her people... (77).

It is, in fact, Pélagie's strength and tenacity Beausoleil admires most, and the journeys of the Cart and of *The Grand'Goule* become parallel.

Marjorie Fitzpatrick sees Pélagie as "mother of a whole race" (148), a traditional role, actually, for heroines of epic literature, such as Virgil's Lavinia, Spenser's Britomart or Milton's Eve. The difference, however, is that Pélagie recognizes that "If Acadie hadn't perished body and soul in the Great Disruption, it was thanks to women" (112). Unlike their literary ancestors, Acadian heroines are not metonymically reduced to their wombs, and Pélagie can count on her daughter Madeleine to continue her tradition of female authority and leadership. The above comment also implies that Pélagie differs from previous women of classical epics like Dido, Circe, or the women of Troy who set fire to Aeneas' ships. While these women commonly frustrate the hero's attempts to return home or found a new city, Pélagie's leadership and strength is responsible for bringing the Acadians home. In this way, Maillet's epic contests Longfellow's immortalization of the Acadian fathers who "only" wander back from exile. It also contests the assumptions underlying Bakhtin's assertion that the epic past is about "a world of fathers."

When Pélagie finally arrives in Acadia, she realizes that her epic journey has succeeded in bringing about the impossible: it has transformed the splinters of many families into a people:

> . . . Her people. For the first time Pélagie realized it. Now that the family who had left Georgia by cart had reached Acadie, they had become a people. In ten years she had made a clean sweep of the land of exile, bringing back whole tribes of her countrymen and women to their own lands by the back door (243).

Similarly, by turning the many narratives of return into an epic story, Antonine Maillet contributes to the regeneration of a culture whose survival has been threatened by the dispersion of its people. As Pierre Anselme Chiasson observes, Acadian literature since the deportation has served as the primary means of holding Acadians together as a people:

> Paris is the metropolis of French literature; Montréal, of Québec literature. Acadian literature has no metropolis. Its centre is the admirable, stubborn will of Acadians themselves. Geographic Acadia is lost, but the world of literature now offers a spiritual Acadia to replace it.

This compensatory "Acadia Within" that is offered by literature helps us to appreciate the profound importance for Maillet of conferring the authority of the epic genre and its conventions on the story of Pélagie.

Pierre-à-Pitre and the Carnivalesque

> It must be said that Pierre-à-Pitre Gautreau, known as the Fool, had fewer scruples than Bélonie when it came to the storyteller's trance; let's say he was more accommodating to his public. He could spin you a tale as well by day as by night, at twilight or dawn, standing, fasting, eating, walking, jumping, farting... (94).

Although every character in *Pélagie* displays the humour that is such a part of the Acadian cultural identity, it is the fool, Pierre-à-Pitre, who represents it most. Bakhtin says, "It is precisely laughter that destroys the epic, and in general destroys any hierarchical (distancing and valorized) distance" ("Epic and Novel" 23). He traces the source of this laughter and the development of the novel to the Socratic dialogues, positing Socrates as the first "bewildered fool" to appear in Western literature (24). In *Rabelais and His World*, Bakhtin suggests that "A special carnivalesque, marketplace style of expression" emerged during the Middle Ages and the Renaissance that was also to have a profound effect on the development of the novel (10). This "carnivalesque" style of expression is based on a folk humour that displays a "peculiar logic of the 'inside out,'" (11) a logic that certainly appeals to Pierre-à-Pitre, and, at times, to the collective narrators of *Pélagie*.

For Bakhtin, "parodic stylizations of canonized genres and styles occupy an essential place in the novel" ("Epic and Novel" 6). The result, he argues, is that,

> They become more free and flexible, their language renews itself by incorporating extraliterary heteroglossia,[8] and the "novelistic" layers of literary language, they become dialogized, permeated with laughter, irony, humour, elements of self-parody and finally—this is the most important thing—the novel inserts into these other genres an indeterminacy, a certain semantic open-endedness, a living contact with unfinished, still-evolving contemporary reality (the open ended present). ("Epic and Novel" 7)

If we agree with Bakhtin's characterization of the novel as "a genre of becoming" (22), then we can see how the conventions of this genre also lend themselves well to Maillet's purposes. Unlike the stories of classical epics like *The Aeneid*, the return to Acadia and its spiritual "refounding" are not "complete" in the sense that Bakhtin uses the word. Although the novel is set in a valorized past, it is not the "absolute past" of the epic world, but one that continues to influence future generations of Acadians. As the direct descendants of the carts, Maillet's narrators have a more direct relationship to the represented world of *Pélagie*. By "novelizing" her epic story, Maillet is able to utilize the conventions of laughter, folk humour, and parody in a manner that is consistent with the Acadian oral tradition. At the same time, as Lacombe suggests, "The oral tradition becomes part of the canon questioned by subsequent generations of chronicler storytellers, and joins the classical texts (all epics traditionally situated at the margins of the oral and the written) parodied by the author through her primary narrator" ("Narrative" 44). Most importantly, Maillet's epic-historical narrative maintains "a living contact with unfinished, still-evolving contemporary reality" essential to a "still-evolving" culture.

As previous critics have noted, Maillet wrote her doctoral dissertation on Rabelais,[9] and her work has certainly been influenced by his carnivalesque qualities. In her essay, "Narrative, Carnival, Parody: Intertextuality in Antonine Maillet's *Pélagie-la-Charrette*," Lacombe argues that *Pélagie's* complex narrative structure, with its multiplication of narrators and "combination of framing and Chinese box effects" (45), assists the reader's entry into "the narrator's "carnivalesque world" (47). As descendants of the carts, moreover, the narrators also ensure that the story of the return remains in contact with contemporary reality.[10]

According to Bakhtin, certain forms of folk humour and "genres of medieval and Renaissance familiar speech" are associated with the culture of the marketplace (*Rabelais* 15), and it is in marketplaces that many of Maillet's most carnivalesque episodes occur. Perhaps the most memorable is the "Baltimore Striptease" that Pierre-à-Pitre contrives in order to keep the carts in town as Pélagie awaits a rendezvous with Beausoleil and his ship, The *Grand'Goule*. Pierre convinces the women of Baltimore that he knows how to turn hemp into silk, initiating a frenzied, Rabelaisian striptease that is also a parody of the epic list:

> All the women in Baltimore market tore off their collars, their bonnets, their aprons, their skirts, their petticoats, their bodices, their sabots, their laced boots, their garters, and besieged the upturned barrel. It was the first and only grand public striptease to be recorded in the annals of the town of Baltimore. Shoes, hats, and *déshabillés* flew in the air revealing underthings never before revealed even to husbands in the intimacy of alcoves. The Fool cast the spell, and the Marys of Maryland let themselves be bewitched. They tore the hair and skirts from one another, shouting and yelling and trampling their old clothes underfoot as if they never again intended to wear homespun or cotton. They had just discovered the court of miracles where a wizard could change pumpkins into golden coaches and Cinderellas into princesses (128).

With the striptease, Pierre-à-Pitre recreates the culture of medieval and Renaissance carnival that celebrated, according to Bakhtin, "temporary liberation from the prevailing truth and from established order" and "marked the suspension of all hierarchical rank, privileges, norms, and prohibitions" (*Rabelais* 10). In the Baltimore Striptease, hierarchies are turned so upside-down that even the governor's wife is not immune to Pierre's bewitching magic.

The Charleston Whiskey Carnival, a carnivalesque parody of the Boston Tea Party, is another episode that the narrators compare to "a kind of Mardi Gras or April Fool's Day" (140) and characterize as "a veritable carnival of the sea, which emptied casks and starred the heavens with fireworks" (142). In the text, such "revelry" is actually a strategy of survival for the resourceful Acadians:

> Everyone knows that Acadie was never equal to defending herself in equal combat since she was never on an equal footing with anyone. She managed just the same, like Pierre-à-Pitre, by brushing up on the gift of the gab and by learning that the way out of an impasse is sometimes by way of a cul-de-sac (140).

This episode illustrates the strong, almost urgent connection between survival and language for the Acadians. When the English navy captures Beausoleil during the American Revolution, it is his "amplifying, doubling, tripling, ruminating" ability as a storyteller that saves him and his ship. For the Acadians then, it is their "gift of the gab," their dexterity as storytellers and root-delvers, in addition to their inimitable ability to carnivalize and turn established orders inside out, that ensures their cultural survival.

This connection between story and cultural survival is most powerfully conveyed by Agnes Dugas Landry's stories of the Virginia Acadians and of the massacre at Cap-de-Sable, two episodes that are rarely included in historical accounts of the Great Disruption. As Agnes tells the carts, families who had been exiled to Virginia suffered a further disruption when they were taken to London, where they were imprisoned then exchanged for English prisoners and sent back to France. The Cap-de-Sable Acadians suffered horrendously during the Disruption when a Major Prebble ordered his troops to set fire to houses, slaughter animals and deport the wives and children of fishermen who were out to sea at the time. It is believed many of the men "went mad" when they returned, or perished in attempts to get to the schooners in their boats. As the primary narrator explains, these families, unlike many descendants of the carts, could never hope to reassemble their families:

> They would wait for years, those survivors of Cap-de-Sable, a whole lifetime; but according to my cousin Louis-à-Bélonie, they could wait an eternity and it still wouldn't be long enough. And when I asked what he meant...
>
> "It wouldn't be long enough to reassemble the families," he explained, "or to make them forget. I've heard say that the massacre at Cap-de-Sable was the last shameful act the En-

> glish could swallow, because six generations of storytellers and root-delvers vowed to pass on the true story from forbear to father to offspring, which means that Major Prebble's descendants will have to stay clear of Cap-de-Sable for a long time to come" (108).

As this episode demonstrates, the oral tradition of storytelling is a powerful means of countering a dominant culture's versions of History, another of the high genres, like the epic, whose valorization of the "national past" is granted authority by official culture. It also demonstrates how the narrative structure of *Pélagie* contributes to Maillet's "novelization" of the epic. While this is a large topic that exceeds the bounds of this essay, it is important to note that Maillet's narrators,[11] with their multiple voices and contributions to the Acadian historical and literary canon, contribute to the dialogization of the story and the epic genre. For Bakhtin, this is one of "the salient features of [the] novelization of other genres" ("Epic and Novel" 6), a process that renews and transforms the epic's relationship to contemporary reality.

"Acadia Within"

Ironically, it is when the cart reaches its geographical destination that Acadia becomes a "Paradise Within," just as the Garden of Eden does for Milton's Adam and Eve at the end of *Paradise Lost*. Standing at the edge of the decimated and deserted town of Grand-Pré twenty-five years after the Great Disruption, Pélagie exclaims, "I'm carrying my Grand-Pré with me in my apron" (242). Pélagie's apron pocket thus becomes a repository of the Acadian culture, history and language. As she explains,

> they've taken our Grand-Pré from us, with its apple trees in flower and its fresh cod and its wild strawberries. They've taken our lands and our boats. And once againwe must wrap our Acadie in homespun cloth and bury it deep in our chests and move it on a bit more to the north... (242).

Pélagie knows that it is the power of language and story that will ensure the survival of an "Acadia within." Into her pocket she stuffs "a stock of words, ancient words sprung naked from her grandsires' gullets, words she wouldn't leave as a heritage for foreign throats." She also includes "all those legends and tales, marvelous, terrifying or prankish, that her line had been passing on since the beginning of time." Most importantly, she puts in history, personified as female: "the history of her people, begun two centuries before, then whirled around by the four winds and left for dead in the gutter... till one day a passerby picks her up and brings her back to life and leads her, by force, back to her own country" (242). History becomes synonymous with the title character of Antonine Maillet's cultural and feminist revision of the epic. Tenacious by force of necessity, both have an amazing ability to survive, even if they constantly swim against the current like the salmon "remembering their spawning grounds" (77). Although the Acadians will never again be a nation like the Trojans who were led by Aeneas to found the site of Rome, the tenacity of their culture and traditions will ensure their survival as a people.

Notes

1. There are many allusions to Milton's epic, *Paradise Lost*, that invite comparisons to that text. For example, Acadia is frequently referred to as "the paradise lost" (8), or as "a lost paradise" that has been "buried in the depths of her [Pélagie's] entrails and loins half her life long" (121). The Bourgeois' chest also evolves into an epic simile, functioning as a symbol in later times for their heirs as "that treasure that was beginning to look more and more like a paradise lost" (161), signifying the Acadians' continuing quest to maintain their culture after the loss of a geographical Acadia.
2. As Bakhtin explains, "All the symbols of the carnival idiom are filled with this pathos of change and renewal, with the sense of the gay relativity of prevailing truths and authorities. We find here a characteristic logic, the peculiar logic of the "inside out" (*à l'envers*), of the 'turnabout,' of a continual shifting from top to bottom, from front to rear, of numerous parodies and travesties, humiliations, profanations, comic crownings and uncrownings" (11).
3. As the entry on Maillet in the Gale Infobase explains, the repercussions of the Great Disruption are still felt by contemporary Acadians: "Acadia today exists mostly as a subculture in parts of Nova Scotia and New Brunswick and is comprised of descendents of Acadians who either avoided La Dispersion or returned afterward. Today the colony is not recognized as a viable, cohesive political force; nor can its identity be defined in terms of territory or community. Acadians, however, have retained a shasred [sic] heritage, passed on largely through storytellers, and a language derived from seventeenth- and eighteenth-century French that is different in many ways from both the French spoken in Quebec and that spoken in modern France."
4. I hesitate to use Bakhtin's terms "national past" and "national tradition," since the events of 1755 effectively foreclosed the possibility of a future Acadian nation. According to Pierre Anselme Chiasson, "the nationalist debate dominated Acadian thought and writing" between 1881 and 1966. However, he credits Maillet with being one of the first within the literary world to turn away from it, presumably because nationalistic novels of the past "concentrated on the deportation, making it live again." In *Pélagie*, Maillet is far more concerned with focusing on the return and survival than on identification with the trauma of the deportation. For this reason, I would characterize her project as cultural rather than national.

5. See, for example, the essays of Lacombe, Waterson, Socken, Herz and Fitzpatrick listed in my Works Cited.
6. For example, in "Woman and Nation," Lacombe suggests that the catalogue of clothing removed during the Baltimore striptease episode and the genealogical lists of the Epilogue recall the convention of lists common to the epic (155, 157). She also points out that Pélagie's cart and handkerchief function as extended epic similes (158). The American Revolution and the Battle between the Acadians and Bostonians in Chapter Thirteen enable Maillet to include the war theme in her epic. Lacombe also suggests that this theme is covered by the "friendly internal battles of will between the men and women of the carts for their eventual place in the legendary history of the people," citing the "war of the pinchers" in Chapter Four as an example (157-8).
7. As Marjorie A. Fitzpatrick points out, Bélof Death symnie's Wagon obolically parallels Pélagie's Cart of Life: "As Pélagie is to her Cart of Life (alive, active, generative of hope), so the Cart of Death is to Bélonie (resigned, passive, prepared to be trundled to his death)" (144). For Karolyn Waterson, the cart also recalls medieval mythology. As she says, "Pélagie's cart is to her what Durendal and Veillantif were to Roland" (45). Michèle Lacombe compares the oxcart to "the classical war-chariot" of Homeric epics ("Woman and Nation" 158).
8. Heteroglossia: "A term coined by Mikhail Bakhtin (1895-1975) – the Russian is *raznorecie* – to describe the variety and diversity of languages used in epic and in the novel (*qq.v.*). He distinguished between the language used to represent the attitudes and opinions of the author and that used by individual characters in fiction and epic" (Cuddon 409).
9. Lacombe, Herz and Waterson all point this out, with Lacombe going so far as to suggest that Maillet substitutes "Rabelais for Longfellow in her quest for origins" (50). This idea is supported in the text, when the narrator suggests that "Beausoleil-Broussard, like Bélonie, sprang from a people of storytellers and chroniclers who had produced Gargantua and his noble son Pantagruel" (140).
10. As Lacombe notes, "The fact that Bélonie I descends from a Parisian immigrant named Antoine Maillet, really the author's ancestor, like the dedication of the novel to the memory of Virginie Cormier, the name of Maillet's' mother but also of the character who becomes the cart of life's mascot, underscores the interpenetration of real and imaginary" (47).
11. The narrators include the cart's storytellers, as well as their descendants, most notably Pélagie-the-Grouch and as well aLouis-à-Bélonie, s a primary voice identified with the "I" of the text, who seems to be a fictionalized version of the author. For a comprehensive study of *Pélagie's* narrative structure, see Michèle Lacombe, "Narrative, Carnival, and Parody: Intertextuality in Antonine Maillet's *Pélagie-la-Charrette*."

Works Cited

Bakhtin, M.M. *Rabelais And His World.* Trans. Helene Iswolsky. Bloomington: Indiana UP, 1984.

Bakhtin, M.M. "Epic and Novel: Towards a Methodology for the Study of the Novel." *The Dialogic Imagination: Four Essays by M. M. Bakhtin.* Ed. Michael Holquist. Trans. Caryl Emerson and Michael Holquist. Austin: U of Texas P., 1981. 3-40.

Chiasson, Pierre Anselme. "Acadia, Contemporary." *The Canadian Encyclopedia Plus.* CD-Rom. Copyright © 1995 by McClelland & Stewart Inc.

Cuddon, J. A. *The Penguin Dictionary of Literary Terms and Literary Theory.* Third Edition. London: Penguin Books Ltd., 1992.

Fitzpatrick, Marjorie A. "Antonine Maillet and the Epic Heroine." *Traditionalism, Nationalism, and Feminism: Women Writers of Quebec.* Ed. Paula Gilbert Lewis. Westport, Connecticut: Greenwood Press, 1985. 141-155.

Gale Research and Gale Canada. "Antonine Maillet." Canadian Periodical Index – Full text. Thomson Canada Limited, 1998.

Herz, Micheline. "A Québécois and an Acadian Novel Compared: The Use of Myth in Jovette Marchessault's *Comme une enfant de la terre* and Antonine Maillet's *Pélagie-la-Charrette.*" *Traditionalism, Nationalism, and Feminism: Women Writers of Quebec.* Ed. Paula Gilbert Lewis. Westport, Connecticut: Greenwood Press, 1985. 173-183.

Kelly, Van. "Introduction: Criteria for the Epic: Borders, Diversity, and Expansion." *Epic and Epoch: Essays on the Interpretation and History of a Genre.* Eds. Steven M. Oberhelman, Van Kelly, and Richard J. Golsan. Lubbock: Texas Tech UP, 1994. 1-21.

Lacombe, Michèle. "Narrative, Carnival, and Parody: Intertextuality in Antonine Maillet's *Pélagie-la-Charrette.*" *Canadian Literature* 116 (Spring 1988): 43-56.

Lacombe, Michèle., "Woman and Nation: Epic Motifs in Margaret Laurence's *The Diviners* and Antonine Maillet's *Pélagie-la-Charrette.*" *Multiple Voices: Recent Canadian Fiction.* Ed. Jeanne Delbaere. Australia: Dangaroo Press, 1990. 146-160.

Longfellow, Henry Wadsworth. *Evangeline: A Tale of Acadie.* Introduction by Dr. C Bruce Fergusson. Halifax: Nimbus Publishing, 1991.

Maillet, Antonine. *Pélagie.* Trans. Philip Stratford. Toronto: Stoddart Publishing Co. Ltd., 1994.

Socken, Paul G. "The Bible and Myth in Antonine Maillet's *Pélagie-la-Charrette.*" Eds. Jorn Carlsen and Bengt Streijffert. *Essays in Canadian Literature.* Lund: Nordic Assn. For Can. Studies, 1989. 103-115.

Waterston, Karolyn. "The Mythical Dimension of *Pélagie-la-Charrette. Francophone Literatures of the New World.* Ed. James P. Gilroy. Denver: U of Denver Dept. of Langs. And Lits., 1982. 43-69.

Julia Hart's Telling Stories of the Nation

Pilar Cuder-Dominguez

In June of 1823, Kingston's newspaper, the *Upper Canada Herald*, published a "Proposal for Publishing by Subscription," a novel that the editor advertised as being a purely Canadian product. According to Hugh Christopher Thomson:

> No country presents more interesting subjects for the pen of a novelist, than Canada. The romantic scenery, the history, and feudal character of the early colonists, their peculiar institutions and customs, the state of society, the habits and manners of the religious orders, the noblesse and the peasantry, derived from their ancestral connexion with France, and their own colonial circumstances, and modified by the introduction of British laws, example and intercourse, in consequence of the cession of the province to Great Britain, afford ample and appropriate materials for a novel.

Interestingly enough, the items Thomson lists here are, to say the least, very disparate. What to us may seem odd, was nevertheless perfectly understandable for an early-19th century intellectual, since variety, understood as a wealth in the number and quality of its components, was one of the most sought-for qualities in literature, and especially in novels. The fact remains, nevertheless, that the only feature the items in Thomson's list have in common is their assumed "Canadianness." Thus, a Canadian identity seems to be necessarily multifaceted, a composite of sometimes conflicting fragments: romantic scenery versus colonial circumstances, religious orders versus British laws, etc.

The young woman who would come down in history as the first Canadian-born author and the first to try her hand at making sense of this mosaic in a national novel, was herself the product of such a complex and rich background. Julia Catherine Beckwith was born in New Brunswick in 1796, of both French and English descent: her father a Beckwith, her mother a Lebrun. In 1820, she moved to Kingston, where she opened a school for young ladies and married an Englishman, George Henry Hart. Her *St. Ursula's Convent, or the Nun of Canada* (1824) was followed one year later by her second novel, *Tonnewonte, or the Adopted Son of America*. It is believed Julia Hart might have started a third novel, but if she did, it was never published.

Despite its author's efforts, *St. Ursula's Convent* merited at the time only indifferent reviews, and has to date received very little attention. Contemporary criticism has followed the lead of those early reviewers, and pointed out that the novel deserves to be remembered solely on the grounds of its chronology. T. D. MacLulich, for instance, must grudgingly accept that *St. Ursula's Convent* predates the publication of Richardson's *Wacousta*, but it helps that "Hart's story... is more important for its chronological priority than for its intrinsic merits" (16). Another case in point is John Moss's *A Reader's Guide to the Canadian Novel*, which summarily comments: "According to the author's preface, Hart was seventeen when she wrote it. After a careful reading, there is no reason to doubt the sincerity of her claim" (123).

What critics find fault with is, most of all, the implausibility of the plot, which, in accordance with the conventions of the romance, has many twists and turns, and unfolds in episodes rather than with a realistic, cause-effect linearity. The main storyline follows the life of Adelaide de St. Louis, a French-Canadian of good birth, from her uneventful childhood in the Quebec countryside to the discovery of her real identity—she is Lady Louisa Dudley, daughter to an English aristocrat—and her marriage in Britain. Along the way, however, she will form many acquaintances, whose life stories she will also get to share in some extent. Nearly all of those acquaintances are linked to her two companions at St. Ursula's Convent in Quebec City, where she is educated: her tutor, Mother St. Catherine, and her classmate Charlotte Turner. Through them, one of French stock, the other of English stock, and both with friends and relatives on the other side of the Atlantic, the scope of the narrative will be enhanced until it comes to enclose an amazing number of parallel stories.

It is precisely this multiplicity of stories, and their many loose ends that lead back to Europe, which critics seem to find decidedly wrong, since it suggests that the novel is correspondingly less Canadian. "Canadianness" in that sense is understood above all in terms of location, as having an exclusively New-World setting. If more are included, then the Canadian location becomes a mere exotic backdrop to more important endeavors. Carole Gerson argues to this effect:

> The breathless pace of Hart's narrative allows little opportunity to develop character or setting. Her many characters, all from upper-class French or British families, spend a limited if complicated time in Canada straightening out their true identities and finally retire to the luxury of Old World estates. Quebec provides a tinge of indigenous romance with its contented *habitants* and a conniving Jesuit. For Hart as for most subsequent Canadian writers, the novel was a European literary artifact. The way to write a Canadian novel was to find or invent Canadian equivalents for European romantic conventions—in Hart's case Quebec's Catholicism could furnish a convent and a treacherous priest—or to import European characters or situations and simply impose them on the Canadian landscape (22-3).

Nevertheless, I would like to contend here that bringing together so many disparate elements, settings, and characters shows that Hart does not conceive of a stable, unitary identity, and especially not one that can be pinpointed to a certain location. On the contrary, the author's deployment of these items highlights their close interrelatedness at all levels, as I will explain.

As regards characterization, Julia Hart thematizes the plight of three different generations. First, there is an older generation of French people who came to the New World to improve their prospects, like Mother St. Catherine's own parents. Their emigration meant a first rupture in the family, since a branch stayed behind. A second, parental generation, that of Mother St. Catherine herself, has suffered the effects of the Seven Years' War: they have either lost a partner, a child, or close relative, or else they have lost touch with the members of the family on the European continent. Finally, the third generation, represented by Adelaide de St. Louis, will be the one to repair the ruptures in the familial and national fabric by renewing contact among its scattered members and restoring social harmony.

Traditionally, marriage has been the symbol of the harmonious union of diverse natures, an image particularly apt for the Canadian case, so the author closes her narrative with a succession of carefully balanced marriages. These unions bind together the three families involved: the French de Montreuils to which Mother St. Catherine belongs by marriage, the English Turners to whom Charlotte belongs, and Adelaide's French-Canadian de St. Louis. Moreover, Hart has taken pains to ensure that five out of these six marriages are cross-cultural, in that one of the partners is English and the other is French or French-Canadian, either by birth or by education. As

Murphy has pointed out, the union of French and English in marriage is the "perfectly Canadian story" (8). This suggests that the offspring of these marriages will embody the best of both cultures and nations, and thus bridge the latent discord between them that resulted from the war.

The second aspect where the interrelatedness that is Hart's purpose truly shows is in the many settings chosen for the novel. Though the action starts in rural Quebec, it then moves to the streets of Quebec City, and then proceeds to Britain and to France. However, each of these locations is more an imaginary space than a tangible perception. No realistic depiction is even attempted, for it is manifestly not necessary: each place matters only for what it represents to the characters (and, by extension, to the community of readers, with whom they share a cultural space). Thus, the countryside of Quebec is seen as an Arcadian landscape, inhabited by contented farmers: "The weather was delightful, and the country people busily employed in collecting the fruit autumn liberally bestowed; and by their whistling and singing, appeared as happy as peace and plenty could make them" (61). Quebec City stands for education and religion, and the convent, the cathedral, and the college are the only places ever mentioned. When the action happens in England, it is in London's gardens and parties, or else in the drawing-rooms of its high society. Finally, only the manors and castles of the French aristocracy are taken into account when the setting is that country. This idealization is not only due to the author's inexperience or her ignorance of those places, but also to her choice of characters, the land-owning aristocracy of both countries, which restricts her to a handful of appropriate locations.

The novel focalizes much more the traveling from one setting to another than the settings themselves. Although some critics have no patience with Hart's descriptions of long sea voyages and with her tales of storms and shipwreck—and notwithstanding the fact that this is also a device to produce suspense,—its main effect is to highlight the distances between the characters and the stories, consequently reinforcing the notions of togetherness and separateness. Traveling serves to separate families, by emigration, war or shipwreck, while in other cases it brings long-lost relatives back to each other's arms. The links that bind the characters crisscross an ocean that they must necessarily traverse, in one or the other direction, in order to fulfil their destinies and set things right. Ultimately, no story can be completed, no family reunited, without a transatlantic voyage.

Finally, the narrative itself devolves around the notion of interrelatedness I suggested above. Although Julia Hart uses a third-person omniscient narrator throughout for her main storyline, that of Adelaide de St. Louis, the other stories are told by their protagonists, in the first person. Thus, for instance,

Mother St. Catherine tells Adelaide and Charlotte the story of how she lost all her family and decided to become a nun. Later on, her supposedly lost husband tells to an audience how he was captured and put to work as a slave in a mine. Even later, the woman who nursed Adelaide's nurse reveals Adelaide's true identity, by explaining how she swapped babies in their cradles. And so on.

However, all of these first-person accounts are only provisionally complete. Mother St. Catherine has not really lost her family, and the narrative will in time restore her husband and children. Her husband, in telling his misfortunes, is unaware that among his audience are those that will give him news of his family, and thus complete his tale. The revelation of the nurse needs to be checked by talking with the nurse of the other child on the other side of the Atlantic.

In so doing, the novel focalizes the weaving and unweaving of these tales, the very process of constructing a web of events and connections, just as it focalizes the story-teller, who in telling the story constructs a self for others to identify, recognize, and even embrace as the father long-gone, or the mother only just now discovered. Typically, the scenario for these narratives involves an audience that is sympathetic to the teller and that is willing to help him/her fill in the gaps of the broken puzzle that is identity.

I argued above that *St. Ursula's Convent* was received as a "national" novel, but Hart's vision of the nation was unpalatable to some and not Canadian enough to many. It remains so. One cannot avoid noticing, for instance, the erasure of the First Nations in this supposedly "all-Canadian" tale. This is because Hart's positions can be best understood as "imperial nationalism" (Monkman 80). Her notion of a national community is molded on the relationships established inside the western family, and perhaps even her own family. Her model is that of an extended family, whose members may be often different but always equal—since, after all, they share a common European heritage—, and who make sense only in their togetherness. Hart thus delineates a pan-European kind of differential identity for her young nation, insofar as she believes Canada is the meeting point (and indeed the product) of all the best Europe has to offer. Nevertheless, rather than a stable identity she endows it with an intensely relational pattern. Take away one piece, and the puzzle just does not make sense. For Julia Hart, Canada occupies a space on both sides of the Atlantic.

Works Cited

Blodgett, E. D., and A. G. Purdy, eds. *Prefaces and Literary Manifestoes.* Edmonton: University of Alberta Research Institute for Comparative Literature, 1990.

Gerson, Carole. *A Purer Taste: The Writing and Reading of Fiction in English in 19th Century Canada.* Toronto: U of Toronto P, 1989.

Hart, Julia Catherine Beckwith. *St. Ursula's Convent, or, The Nun of Canada.* 1824. Ed. Douglas G. Lochhead. Ottawa: Carleton UP, 1991.

MacLulich, T. D. *Between Europe and America: The Canadian Tradition in Fiction.* Toronto: ECW, 1988.

Monkman, Leslie. "Prefaces, Politics, and Julia Catherine Hart." Blodgett and Purdy. 72-81.

Moss, John. *A Reader's Guide to the Canadian Novel.* Toronto: McClelland and Stewart, 1981.

Murphy, Carl. "The Marriage Metaphor in Nineteenth-Century English Canadian Fiction." *Studies in Canadian Literature* 13.1 (1988): 1-19.

The Recuperation of Aboriginality Through Storytelling in *My Place*: Discourse and Contexts

Kofi Campbell

The Australian novel *My Place* is a collective story-telling occasion brought about through unusual circumstances. The author and protagonist, Sally Morgan, was born and raised in Australia. She lives with her mother Gladys and her grandmother Daisy, or Nan as they call her. Her life is fairly normal for the first fifteen years until, towards the end of her third year of high-school, she makes an astonishing discovery. She tells us:

> I arrived home early one day to find Nan sitting at the kitchen table, crying. I froze in the doorway, I'd never seen her cry before.
> "Nan, what's wrong?"
> "Nothin'!"
> "Then what are you crying for?"
> She lifted up her arm and thumped her clenched fist hard on the kitchen table. "You bloody kids don't want me, you want a bloody white grandmother, I'm black. Do you hear, black, black, black!" With that, Nan pushed back her chair and hurried to her room.
> For the first time in my fifteen years, I was conscious of Nan's colouring. She was right, she wasn't white. Well, I thought logically, if she wasn't white, then neither were we. What did that make us, what did that make me? I'd never thought of myself as being black before (97).

Confused, Sally asks her sister later that night if she knew that Nan was black. Incredulous, her sister replies:

> "You know what we are, don't you?"
> "No, what?"
> "Boongs, we're Boongs!"
> It took a few minutes before I could summon up the courage to say "What's a Boong?"
> "A Boong. You know, Aboriginal. God, of all things, we're Aboriginal!"
> "Oh." I suddenly understood (98).

Sally did not know she was aboriginal because all of her life her mother and grandmother had told them that they were in fact Indian. Aware of the hard life facing any aboriginal, they had decided to spare the kids from that life by keeping the fact of their aboriginality hidden from them. As Sally grows older, however, she becomes increasingly dissatisfied with this state of affairs. She wants to discover her roots, and she begins a personal quest to unearth the story of her family. Her search is not an easy one. She finds that those who know the most about the history of the family, namely her mother and Nan, both refuse to speak about that past. It is only with a great deal of effort and perseverance that she finally persuades first her mother, and then her grandmother, to teach her that history. And, because Australian aboriginal society is mostly an oral one, that history takes the form, not of a set of written documents, but of stories told by the two older women. Therefore, it is through acts of storytelling, both her own and those of her mother and grandmother, that Sally Morgan begins to construct her aboriginality. That construction, as represented in this novel, takes the forms of both an autobiography and a family history. It is a distinctly female history. With one exception, the stories are all told by women.

The one exception is the story told by Nan's brother, Arthur. His is the first story of the family's history that we are given; he is the first to speak to Sally about the old days. Arthur's dialogue with Sally is important in giving us a view of the complex place that stories and storytelling have within aboriginal culture. In the first place, such stories have a physical element which is alien to the Western conception of abstract and distanced narratives. When Arthur is finished telling his story he says to Sally, "Anyway, I told you my story now. You'll look after it, won't you?" (164). His story is a tangible thing to him, something which requires respect and care. It is not merely something which describes his life; in a very real way it *is* his life. At the end of his narrative he makes this connection quite explicit: "I'm at the end of my life," he says contentedly. "I want to get my land fixed up so my children can get it and I want my story finished" (210). His story can only end when his life does, because they are one and the same. Arthur also leads us into another important consideration in the discussion of this novel. He says, "And I got Daisy's grand-daughter writin' my story" (210). As I have said, Australian aboriginal culture is primarily an oral one; yet what we have before us in *My Place* is a novel, a written text, a decidedly non-oral document.

In discussing Morgan's construction of aboriginality and history, then, we must consider carefully the notion of genre. The major genre within which this text can be placed is that of the autobiography, a genre which does not exist as such in aboriginal culture. Aboriginal narratives are either "true," or "of the dreaming."?[1] They are either "real" stories or stories passed on from the spirit world. Why, then, does Sally Morgan use what is essentially a European discourse to accomplish a purely aboriginal project? Here we must follow Stephen Muecke's advice and consider the contexts within which this text was produced.

In order to disseminate her text to a larger audience, indeed to be published in the first place, Morgan is to a certain degree forced to use European discourses. She cannot, for example, use the usual method by which aboriginals record long messages in Australia today, the tape-recorder, as it is too impractical. Likewise she cannot tell her story in the form of a Dreaming Song, because this would make it inaccessible to a wider audience. She is, in fact, forced to use English, the language of the powerful printing press administrators, and one of their modes of writing, the autobiographical/historical novel. She must, in other words, accommodate herself to the white Australian power-bloc and its hegemony. Muecke in fact argues that Morgan's text is possible *only* with the permission of this power-bloc.

The first aboriginal to publish a novel was Mudrooroo, in 1965. Before this point aboriginals had been denied a part in any significant (from the European point of view)literary activity, and from public life in general. However, changes in the world, decolonization, and pressures from outside sources changed that. The power-bloc was forced to allow a voice to aboriginals or risk facing the censure of the world. Once such changes were forced upon it, the power-bloc had to make other concessions as well. Aboriginals had to be not only allowed, but indeed encouraged to publish, as it is "in the interests of the power-bloc to minimize the perception of social difference and to emphasize consensus because the reduction of contestation secures [its] own position" (Fiske 22). By allowing aboriginals to publish, the hegemony reduces friction and allows for another visual representation of its legal, if not actual, equality. Muecke's argument is for the most part correct, if somewhat conservative. His schematic gives no place to the notion of aboriginal agency, to the role that aboriginals themselves have played in opening the possibilities for self-expression and self-fashioning. He is, though, accurate in describing the influence of the power-bloc on Sally Morgan's text.

In order for her stories to be heard and published, Morgan must use those genres which will make money for the publisher; she is subjected to the surrounding economic discourse, as well as to a market that is hungry for just this type of autobiography, which is assumed to contain "a truer truth [about aboriginality] than documentary or... academic texts" (Attwood 302). Thus, even the possibility of a construction of aboriginality by aboriginals is made possible only by "adjacent discursive formations; a market enthusiastic about autobiography, the development of courses in 'post-colonial literature,' multiculturalism, a bicentennial year, and so on" (Muecke 137). Morgan, however, takes full advantage of these discursive formations and genres, subverting their traditional usages and aboriginalizing them.

Traditional autobiographies, for example, are narrated by the author. In traditional aboriginal culture, though, the concept of the author is absent. Authorship is deferred, and the producers of a text think of themselves as the guardians of a text given to them by some source exterior to themselves; hence Arthur's request that Sally "look after" his story. Under this system, no-one may speak a text, or story, belonging to another person without that person's consent, and in some cases without the right to speak that text, whether granted through age, ceremony, or some other means. This idea is evidenced quite clearly in *My Place*.

In her quest for the past, Sally runs into an insurmountable obstacle, namely her grandmother Nan's refusal to speak. Sally finally asks Nan's brother Arthur for Nan's story, but he refuses to speak it. He tells Sally to keep asking Nan and she, frustrated, asks "But Arthur, what if she won't tell us?" Arthur remains resolute: "Then I can't, either. There's some things Daisy's got to tell herself, or not at all. I can't say no more" (156).

The idea that a story can only rightly be spoken by the person who owns it is also evidenced in the over-all frame and structure of the book itself. Although Sally is the author of this book and the teller of her own story, pieces of the family history are told by Arthur, Gladys and Nan. Although this is an autobiographical text, Sally does not tell those stories; she does not own them. Even though Arthur has given her permission to do so, she refuses to tell his story choosing instead to transcribe it from her tape-recorder directly onto the page, more or less exactly as he told it. She does the same when first Gladys, and then finally Nan, tell their stories. Arthur, Gladys and Nan tell their own stories, stories of which Sally is only the guardian. In this way Sally turns the text into a collective story-telling occasion, and the stories follow one upon the other. It is interesting to note that, although Sally's narrative encloses the other stories, it is in no way privileged over them. They are all part of a continuous his (her) story.

Interesting as well in this story-telling novel is Nan's continued reluctance to speak. Muecke posits somewhat convincingly that her refusal to speak is also a refusal of genre, the genre of "the confessional (a non-aboriginal genre) and the power relation which it implies....A possible Aboriginal discursive strategy... would take the form of non-disclosure in the face of the demand to speak" (128). This does ring true in the case of Nan. Being the oldest surviving female member of the family she has perhaps the greatest cause to remember and fear the missionaries and their power relations with the aboriginals. Beyond this, though, Nan obviously fears the repercussions for Sally if her grand-daughter should stir up too much trouble by revealing the extremely dark underside of the missionary days. Speaking of the silence surrounding many of her generation she chides Sally, "Course they wont talk, Sally. They frightened. You don't know what it was like. You're too young... you dunno what you're doin' writin' this book. Bad things might happen to you. If I tell you some things, next thing you'll be telling everyone" (313).

Daisy displays what might be called a discourse of silence, for there are very specific rules which govern her silence. There are things which must be told to explain that silence, things which can never be told, and situations under which the silence may partially be broken. The discourse of silence does not only limit what Daisy can say but also what she can know. Her silence does not consist simply of not speaking certain things, but also of not hearing, or listening to, certain things. It is only after a long time that Sally learns to respect Nan's silence, realizing that some stories cannot be told, and that her right to autobiography and history do not supersede her grandmother's right to silence. Daisy's silence is not in fact simply a refusal of genre, but an awareness of the power and potential consequences of storytelling. "I know you," she says to Sally, "next thing you'll be telling everyone" (313). She is rightly concerned not only with the construction of aboriginality, but with its portrayal and reception.

The construction of aboriginality in contemporary Australia is a site of great contestation. The production and widespread distribution of texts by aboriginals is an emergent and indispensable means through which these authors can, for the first time, promote their own conceptions of aboriginality. The voices of these lost, dispossessed others have recently begun to make themselves heard, and to make the world see them through their own eyes, rather than through the gaze of white Australian discourses. These constructions of aboriginality are therefore fraught with political implications, as Nan realizes. Any such construction that is mass-marketed to a large non-aboriginal audience must acknowledge that it is creating an idea of aboriginality that will, in all likelihood, help to create much of White Australia's, and the world's, understanding of aboriginals. Eric Michaels acknowledges this fact when he says that "Many more people will read these texts than will ever encounter an Aborigine or an ethnography. The image of the Aboriginality constructed by them will have considerable popular force" (Attwood 302). Nan worries about precisely this. What effect will her story have? How will the world view the history of the aboriginals in light of her secret, which we finally piece together at the end of the novel? What will it say about aboriginals in general when people learn that her father is also the father of her child? Will this knowledge evoke sympathy and understanding, or contempt and reprisals from a society which would prefer to have its secrets remain buried in the past?

As such, the construction of aboriginality becomes very political, for now questions must be asked concerning the nature of the aboriginality to be constructed: whose construction will be privileged? what effect it will have on the position of aboriginals within Australia, and how such a construction can be made in the first place? *My Place* offers one possible answer to this last question, in that Sally Morgan constructs her sense of aboriginality through storytelling. And Nan was right about the potential power and influence of that storytelling. Since being published in 1987, *My Place* has sold an incredible number of copies and been translated into seven languages. As such, it is a novel which has had much to say to the world about aboriginality, and which has therefore influenced a large number of people's conception of aboriginals in Australia. For this reason the discourses and contexts behind its construction through storytelling demand more detailed analysis.

Stephen Muecke argues that aboriginality is constructed in discourse, and that "it has never been the same thing from one tribal group to another, from ancient times to the present" (19). As I said earlier Muecke tends towards conservatism at times, but his discussion of the discourses which govern both white and black Australian ways of looking at the world are both helpful and enlightening. Discourse theory, which drives Muecke's analysis, tends to dismiss the notion that language exists independently of ideology, and that it is an instrument which humans use to express ideas and to order the world around us. Rather, it sees language as a signifying system into which we are born, and which carries certain pre-conceived notions into which we are, therefore, also born. We have, furthermore, no say in the formation of the language into which we are born; we do not shape it, it shapes us. These ideas concerning discourse and language can be readily demonstrated through an examination both of this novel and of contemporary Australian linguistic tendencies.

Muecke notes that the language into which a white Australian child is born constructs that child so that it tends to speak *about* rather than *with* aboriginals. He says that:

> the third person plural here is both objective (accusative) and beneficiary: you do things *to* them and *for* them...you hardly ever report them as saying *I* or *you*. That is, you don't report yourself as being in a position in which you are addressed by an Aborigine....Aboriginals don't call out "Hey you!" (this would be insolent); nor do they state their intentions in terms of *I* or *we*. The Aboriginal *we* is a positive political threat. Already, even in a pronoun system, your language has positioned a people (23).

Thus, language begins to construct a certain way of thinking about aboriginals before a child is even aware that s/he is being so shaped. Language, of course, was and is an important element in colonialist strategy, and if a child could be taught to use the colonial language then s/he could be taught to see the world through the ideologies of that language. Thus, s/he learns to see him- or herself as the colonizer views him. The original white Australian settlers realized this, as Arthur demonstrates in his story. He tells us that once he was shipped off to be educated, "I wasn't allowed to talk blackfella after that. If I did, Dudley beat me. I like my language, but I got a good hiding if I spoke it. I had to talk English" (176). Of course most people probably did not realize the reason they were forced to speak English. It is a function of language, in fact, that it tends to hide the ideologies behind it through a process of naturalization. These ways of talking about aboriginals have been present for a very long time, and as such tend to be blindly accepted; it is simply the way things are, and there is rarely cause to question a language if one conceives it as natural and is brought up in its traditions.

Discourse theory, however, realizes that language is a perpetuator and disseminator of ideology. The various ideological and state apparatuses at work in a given society produce various discourses which are then articulated in language. As such, in discussing Morgan's construction of aboriginality through storytelling we must examine the discourses which create a language system such as the one just discussed. Muecke posits that white Australians tend to regard aboriginals through the lens of three traditional discourses, namely the Anthropological, the Romantic, and the Racist. As *My Place* and the stories within it demonstrate, though, these discourses are not found only within the white, hegemonic culture. Morgan's project is to chronicle the construction, or more accurately the re-construction, of aboriginality, and specifically *her* aboriginality. She does succeed in doing so, more or less to her own satisfaction. It is a testament to the power of the three traditional discourses of Aboriginality outlined above, however, that they can be seen to inform the thought processes not only of whites, but of an aboriginal woman engaging in a purely aboriginal act of reconstruction and remembrance. The three discourses permeate the stories we are told.

The first of these discourses, the Anthropological, refers to "a set of discursive practices that depend on relationships of dominance...ethnology is situated within the particular relation that the Western ratio establishes with all other cultures; and from that starting-point it avoids the representations that men in any civilization may give of themselves" (Muecke 25). This approach traditionally neglects or dismisses dialogue with the other who is the subject of investigation. It asks the question "who are they?" and then proceeds to answer it from its own, and only its own, point of view. The aboriginal viewpoint is usually ignored, or acknowledged only after the white discourse has made it fit for consumption by submerging it in its own language. The Anthropological discourse, by virtue of its ostensible seeking after authoritative and objective knowledge, has shaped a great deal of white Australia's attitude towards aboriginals.

Morgan also relies on the Anthropological discourse in this novel, and in her search for aboriginality. As is the case with many of the discursive formations she bows to, however, she also tends to subvert it. The discourse is evident as she goes about reconstructing her past. She begins to examine aboriginals, the way they live, speak and interact; she assumes, in other words, not only that aboriginality is something that can be known, but something that can be known by someone who has had no previous experience of it. Here she is much like the missionaries and anthropologists who invaded the aboriginals. Morgan also bows to all three discourses by focusing on difference. All three discourses are predicated and "articulated on perceptions of difference. Each of these discourses starts with one point of difference between 'us' and 'them'" (Muecke 27).

Having allowed the Anthropological discourse to inform her vision thus far, however, Morgan proceeds to resolutely ignore one of its traditional tenets. She speaks to the people she is trying to know. She learns aboriginality from aboriginals, rather than imposing her own view of what aboriginality should be. She listens to the aboriginals and hears their stories, she submits herself to their questions in return and thereby engages in a two-way communication, which allows her and those to whom she speaks to move closer to a common understanding. Furthermore, she does not encode their responses into what Muecke calls "the Standard English of the academic paper" (26). Rather, she allows the aboriginals with whom she speaks to tell their own stories in their own way. She does of course transcribe their narratives into a genre which is traditionally European Australian, but as I have discussed she does this in such a way as to subvert and aboriginalize that genre.

If the Anthropological discourse proclaims its ability to *know* the aboriginal, the Romantic and the Racist do not, nor do they care to. Both are based on a displacement from any desire to know. The Romantic discourse tends away from the search for knowledge towards a mythologizing of the other. Often, this discourse looks to a utopian past in order to mystify, and lend an air of nostalgia to the present. This discourse essentializes on the basis of genetics, and so aboriginals are perceived as doing things as a result of primitive drives which they are unable to control. This type of essentialism, by locating problems at the genetic level, intimates that socio-economic solutions to the hardships of native life need not be sought. Rather, aboriginals cannot hold jobs, and have problems with alcohol, drugs and family because that is the way they are, and no amount of analysis will change that. Therefore, why bother to analyze?

Morgan, again, is guilty of succumbing to and perpetuating this discourse, while at the same time subverting it. She does not locate the problems of aboriginals at a genetic level. On the contrary, the stories told in *My Place* underscore and emphasize explicitly the social, political and economic forces that determine and affect aboriginality. This said, it should also be noted that Morgan, and these stories, do not hesitate to essentialize and mythologize in other ways. She tends to perpetuate the civil/savage binary with her notions that aboriginals are somehow closer to the land than whites, in a way that extends beyond the historical and physical closeness that their history and lifestyle dictates. Aboriginals have a *natural* affinity to the land; this sentiment is echoed throughout the novel. As well, Morgan's conception of aboriginality is centred on the ideas of kinship, religion and spirituality, Romantic conceptions that do indeed tend to mystify aboriginals.

This mystical spirituality is demonstrated clearly at the end of this novel. The night before Nan dies, Sally's sister Jill hears a bird call which no one else hears. It is the call of a spiritual bird which aboriginals can hear, and no one else. It takes Sally a while, but she eventually does hear it. The novel ends with these words: "I heard the bird call, I heard the bird call. Around and around. "Oh, Nan," I cried with sudden certainty, "I heard it too. In my heart, I heard it" (349). Her ability to hear the call represents the aboriginal blood coursing through her veins, marking her indubitably as a member of the mystical brother- and sister-hood of aboriginality. The fact that the mystical force has now touched her means that she is truly aboriginal. This mysticism is portrayed in these stories as a necessary and defining characteristic of aboriginality.

If, however, it seems that such a process of mythologizing narrows conceptions of aboriginality through a process of essentializing rather than seeking after multiple, perhaps infinite determinations, I would argue that that is not the case. Sally Morgan, having grown up thinking she was white, then Indian, and now seeking after aboriginality, is very aware of the quicksand spaces of identity construction. She already lives within a frame of multiple determinations. I would argue that she stresses these particular aspects of those determinations because they are the ones she needs to address at this particular time, and not because she believes that they are the sum total, or the final determination, of aboriginality.

The displacement from a real desire to know is also characteristic of the Racist discourse. This discourse, rather than mythologizing, works through "a series of metaphoric displacements, [and] functions to designate a people as something other than an ideal... adult, white perfection" (Muecke 31). Needless to say, the Racist discourse also tends to essentialize, to put it mildly. This discourse is also present in the text, but in a slightly different way from the others. Neither Sally Morgan nor the aboriginals that she meets succumb to it directly. Where it is evidenced is in the language used in the stories themselves, and we must examine that language in light of Muecke's assertion that white Australian language serves to position aboriginals in certain ways. Note the following exchange between Sally and some of the aboriginals at Corunna, where her mother and grandmother grew up:

> "Oh yes," the other smiled, "your mob's from Corunna..."
> "You lookin' for your mob, now?" asked another kindly.
> "Yes," I replied. "My Grandmother was taken from here many years ago."
> "That's right," he agreed, "hundred of kids gone from here. Most never come back. We think maybe some of them don't want to come home. Some of those light ones, they don't want to own us dark ones"...."Light-coloured ones wanderin' around, not knowin' they black underneath" (219).

Note firstly the use of the word "mob." It conjures up images not of a people, but precisely of a mob, a vague quantity not really worthy of further definition. As well, they do not travel, but "wander," which has a quality of unthinking aimlessness to it. Finally, throughout the book the aboriginals speak of "owning" each other. The word obviously has a different meaning when used by an aboriginal than by a European, but what is important is that such a word, obviously used by the original settlers in reference to the aboriginals who worked for them, has moved into the everyday language of the aboriginals themselves. The words themselves, though, obviously have different connotations to the aboriginals. The word "mob" refers more to solidarity and communal associations. "Wandering" refers to the loss of traditional belief systems and lands, and spiritual loss. "Owning" is synonymous with "responsible for," or "looking out for," with the full kinship connotations that those phrases conjure.

The problems arise when a white Australian hears an aboriginal using these words. As Muecke has noted, white Australian discourse already positions aboriginals a certain way through its racist language, and that racist strain can only be intensified when a white Australian hears aboriginals continually referring to themselves, for example, as a "mob." The question this problem begs is "how do you toilet-train your language to dodge the arbitrary interpretations, fueled by racism, which white Australians may put upon it?" Sally Morgan's unspoken answer to this question is, "you don't." This text is in many ways about reclaiming language and discourse, and Morgan's ultimate message may be that white Australians will have to face up to their brutal history and see it from an aboriginal point-of-view, rather than only their own. She has no intention of accommodating European discourses any more than she absolutely has to. She is writing a history of aboriginals for aboriginals as well as for white Australia. As Nan says finally, "could be it's time to tell. Time to tell what it's been like in this country" (341). Gladys echoes this sentiment: "If I stay silent...it's like saying everything's all right. People should know what it's been like for someone like me" (234).

What we are presented with in *My Place*, then, is a representation and reconstruction of aboriginality through storytelling. Certainly Sally Morgan is to be commended for what she has done. Not only has she broken ground for other female aboriginal writers, she has given us a glimpse into the brutal, oppressive and hidden history of aboriginals in general. She has demonstrated that an aboriginal heritage is nothing to be ashamed of; in fact, she actively seeks it out. She has helped to raise the social consciousness of the world by displaying the raw abuses that were the past and that still inform the present of aboriginals in Australia. And she offers hope by showing how those who have suffered supremely can be proud of what they have survived and made of themselves, not necessarily in the white man's world, but in the world of the aboriginal and of aboriginality.

On the other hand, Sally Morgan's construction of aboriginality still bears traces of the old, oppressive discourses. She still succumbs to the easy answers of aboriginal essentialism at times, still mythologizes the aboriginals and thereby helps to continue their identification as mystical other. She still considers aboriginality to be something that can be known and fixed. Karen Jennings in fact argues that Morgan reduces "the complexity and heterogeneity of [aboriginality] to a single, homogenous (and repetitive) function" (10). This, I think, is somewhat unfair. The valorization of multiple, infinite determinations is a postmodernist/postcolonial consideration. But both postmodernism and postcolonialism are largely academic institutions. Who exactly is Jennings, or myself, or indeed anyone, to direct their agendas at Sally Morgan, whose life is in a volatile, searching, shifting and shaping relation to that genealogical/political/poetic complexity that we call being aboriginal in Australia?

Morgan's construction, then, is problematic, especially to scholars of the Western academies. Thus the question "is her construction of aboriginality a good one or a bad one?" is, I think, largely irrelevant. What is truly important is first, that such at least partly good representations by aboriginals exist, and second, that we examine the discursive contexts surrounding the production of such a text, as I have tried to do. This latter is important because such an examination moves away from the binary conception of good or bad representations which, after all, usually only involves a shift from one form of essentialism to another. What is important is not so much that people understand what aboriginality is, since no one can truly do so, but rather that spaces are opened within which aboriginality can express itself in its infinite variety.

Sally Morgan is an aboriginal woman writing the history, indeed the stories, of three female generations of her family, a black act of remembering and remembrance. By recognizing the need to accept certain discursive formations, and the equally pressing need to subvert them and bend them to her purposes, she continues the process of opening radical spaces from within which aboriginality can resist the institutional closures of white Australian discourses. She is an aboriginal speaking on her own terms. As Arthur says, it's time for the blackfella to enter history: "I want my story finished. I want everyone to read it. Arthur Corunna's story! You see, its important, because then maybe they'll understand how hard it's been for the blackfella to live the way he wants. I'm part of history, that's how I look on it. Some people read history, don't they?" (210).

Indeed they do: and thanks to Sally Morgan, they read her story too.

Works Cited

Attwood, Bain. "Portrait of an Aboriginal as an Artist: Sally Morgan and the construction of Aboriginality" *Australian Historical Studies* 25.99 (1992): 302.

Friske, John. *Power Plays, Power Works.* London: Verso, 1993.

Jennings, Karen. *Sites of Difference: cinematic representations of Aboriginality and gender.* Australia: Australian Film Institute, 1993.

Morgan, Sally. *My Place.* Australia: Fremantle Arts Centre Press, 1987.

Muecke, Stephen. *Textual Spaces: Aboriginality and Cultural Studies.* Australia: New South Wales University Press Ltd., 1992.

Margery Kempe and the Medieval Author as Reader

Laurelle LeVert

Since the discovery of the *Book of Margery Kempe* in 1934, scholarly attempts have been made to fit her into a sequence of holy women, saints or mystics. Her very life is a reformation through emulation of the affective ideal—courting shame, humiliation and pain for the love of Christ. Kempe's suffering, however, is a suffering re-produced according to her own mental criteria. She is a woman steeped in the tradition and texts of affective piety, and thus her experience is valuable primarily as a personal, religious experience which is defined by affective devotion to the humanity and suffering of Jesus Christ in fourteenth and fifteenth century England. Kempe's personal "rhetoric" of affective response is the primary method she uses to tell her "story," using both the privileged word, and affective experience. Kempe is a "reader" in that she internalizes a vast corpus of devotional, meditative, and didactic literature of her age, and in turn lives a life which demonstrates those teachings. She sees and portrays herself as a messenger and model (the role of an author) in a very public way, and she is consistently aware of her contemporary audience—those around her who witness her experiences and react to them. This witness is an important part of her experience as well, since she herself often displays an authorial "awareness" of the effect she is having on her own viewing audience and, by extension, her reading audience.

Kempe's visions of the Passion exemplify the experiential faith which is demonstrated in Passion narratives and meditations which flourished from the thirteenth to the fifteenth centuries; they call upon a reading and listening audience to imagine themselves as spectators at the drama of salvation, and to invent or "fictionalize" scenes which are intimate and personal. Kempe's written text was compiled with the intent of instructing and affecting an "audience" through the experience of her life. She re-writes her sources and her scriptural knowledge as her own experience. She claims to have read (that is, she had read to her) many devotional works including Richard Rolle's *Incendium Amoris*; Hilton's "Boke," probably the *Scale of Perfection*; the *Stimulus Amoris* (attributed to Bonaventure); some of St. Bridget's *Book of Revelations*; and work by Marie of Oignies. She had ample material upon which to construct a devotional life, and many exempla to follow. She is an "oral" reader, and yet Jesus tells her to "write" her experiences down for others to access, privileging the permanence of the written word over the ephemeral nature of human experience.

But Kempe's public is uncertain about the validity of her experience, an uncertainty which is paralleled by her own need for continual reassurance of the authenticity and orthodoxy of her visions. At times she claims to be, or behaves as though she were, uncomfortable with the "trewth" of her visions, and so she looks to the sources of her scriptural and devotional knowledge for confirmation —her scribes, preachers, and confessors. It is of course impossible to know whether this is a rhetorical ploy on Kempe's part, or the "trewth" as she believes it. Her grace-imbued nature competes with her human quest for tangible authority represented by books, books which represent for her the mediated, divine Word in its most concrete form. It is this knowledge that she desperately craves, imparted not divinely but humanly:

> "Alas, Lord, as many clerkys as [th]u hast in is world, [th]at [th]u ne woldyst sendyn me on of hem [th]at myth fulfillyn my sowle with [th]e word & wyth redyng of Holy Scriptur, for alle [th]e clerkys [th]at prechyn may not fulfillyn, for me thynkyth [th]at my sowle is euyr a-lych hungry."[1]

She internalizes scriptural and devotional sources and re-writes them as her own. Margery Kempe's experiences were first published by Wynkyn de Worde in 1521, in a small pamphlet called *A shorte treatyse of contemplacyon*.[2] The variety of texts being published with the advent of printing included many devotional and didactic tracts, and so Margery's first literary appearance into the public realm was not as a unique nor an inspirational model. In its first published format, Margery's life appears as that of a devout English woman, and indeed in its very manner of transmission, her story (in its limited form) appears as a practical handbook for personal devotion. Scholars were surprised when the actual text discovered in 1934 proved not to be the work of a devout anchoress or mystic, but of a woman very grounded in the social and economic milieu of late fourteenth and early fifteenth century England, who had been married, given birth to fourteen children, run a variety of businesses, and traveled widely.

The physicality of Christ's suffering and its imitation are central to medieval affective piety, and to Kempe's own experience of it. Her experience represents an extensive array of forms of *imitatio Christi*; however, she "imaginatively" allows her *imitatio Christi* to evolve into much more physical manifestations.[3] In addition to seeing images or reminders of Christ in everyday life, she also somehow projects the person of Jesus onto her very self, and some elements in the *Book* are strangely reminiscent of Jesus' own life, ministry and death—her quest for public humiliation, her Job-like patience in the face of slander, and her use of parables, for instance.

More than twenty years after her visions began, she claimed she was instructed by Jesus to write down her "felyngys & reuelacyons & [th]e forme of her leuyng [th]at hys goodnesse myth be knowyn to alle [th]e world" (3-4). This activity took more than four years, and the difficulty she encountered was great. The initial text (Book 1) was dictated to one scribe, and then transcribed and expanded (Book 2) by another, after passing briefly through the hands of a third. How much, if any, revision occurred in the transcription process is unknown; all we know, and that only from the text itself, is that Kempe told her story in the form of "very trewth schewyd in experiens," and in the order that she remembers it occurring to her (124). For Kempe, "trewth" is often manifested and demonstrated in "experiens," but this is a tenuous and sometimes unstable association. It is not my purpose here to delve into the hermeneutic difficulties involved in attempting to differentiate or explicate the roles of Kempe's scribes in the final version.[4] The issue of scribal interference and influence is perhaps too complex ever to solve unless more evidence comes to light; several scholars have suggested stages of influence, but in reality such hypotheses serve only to complicate the already-complex text at hand. I will thus take Margery Kempe's *Book* at face value, and treat her story as it is written on the page. To doubt her written version of "trewth" is fruitless. Kempe's scribe explains that:

> "Thys boke is not wretyn in ordyr, euery thyng aftyr o[th]er as it wer don, but lych as [th]e mater cam to [th]e creatur in mend whan it schuld be wretyn, for it was so long er it was wretyn [th]at sche had for-getyn [th]e tyme & [th]e ordyr whan thyngys befellyn. And [th]erfor sche dede no [th]ing wryten but [th]at sche knew rygth wel for very trewth."[5]

Kempe tells the events of her life as they occur to her when she dictates them, not necessarily as they were lived; in addition, she picks and chooses among her memories and recollections for the most effective, and affective, models and exempla which will be of service to her audience. Her experiences themselves thus manifest a tension between the historical "trewth" of her life and the "fiction" of her interpretation of it; her own sense of reality often merges the two. In the sifting process of her recollecting the events of her life, she shapes her past, and thus her story, to create the meaning it holds for her now, not then. For Kempe the storyteller, historical truth is elusive and relative, and determined by her purpose at the time of writing the *Book*, which is a collection of experiences, musings, and reflections which have been modified, interpreted, edited or expanded to give us what Kempe, in her later years, thought of the life she had lived—the truths and fictions which make up a life.

Kempe reconciles notions of truth and fiction in several ways, the most prevalent being her ability to visualize scenes from Jesus' life and Passion, participate mentally in these scenes, and "fictionalize" them for maximum affective and didactic benefit. Her experience of the Passion is always very dependent on her imaginative involvement, but also on her own ability to re-write the event in order to place herself anachronistically within its context. Thus her very act of recalling the events becomes in her mind part of Jesus' divine plan for her.

But unfortunately, not everyone who witnessed or read her story agreed that her connection with the divine was legitimate. Kempe's notorious, seemingly shameless exhibitions of piety (a very important part of her storytelling) have served to ostracize her from much serious critical consideration, both modern and medieval. She has been labeled at once unconventional, hypocritical, possessed, eccentric, manipulative, a histrionic individual and a holy fool. The authenticity and sincerity of her grief and tears, even what are called her "boistows sobbynges" have been questioned, and much has been made of her decidedly intimate and "homely" relationship with Jesus, but these are all elements of her story. Kempe has the ability to outrage medieval and modern audiences alike; the role she sets up for herself is a combination of Old Testament judge, prophet and seer, and benevolent holy woman whose words of comfort touch many. She is anxious that her story be seen as an example of pious living and affective devotion for others, and claims that Christ said to her: " [th]ei [th]at worshep [th]e [th]ei worshep me" (23); and " [th]u art myn & I am thyn, & so xalt [th]u be wyth-owtyn ende" (182).

She willingly weeps for others' sins and prays for mankind continually, chastises bishops, castigates priests, defeats charges of Lollardy and is granted many special privileges in the male hierarchy of the Catholic Church; but she is never really accepted, especially in her home country of England, primarily, it seems, because her personality gets in the way. There is often an inability on the part of her audience to separate the message from the messenger, and in her efforts to teach by example, Kempe alienates people from her message. She is examined several times for heresy, most notably by the Archbishop of York (123), but also at Canterbury. Kempe claims to find personal joy in public censure, and reassures everyone that her didactic role in displaying the virtues of patience and charity under such conditions are in fact a blessing, not a curse.

Anachronistic and homely domestic constructions are an integral part of Kempe's devotion, and Jesus plays the part of personal savior and protective husband. Indeed, Jesus at times even plays a subservient role in Kempe's world; their relationship is very nuanced, and the balance of power constantly shifts. She claims that her own affection for Jesus' humanity pervades her every moment, such that, for instance, when she saw a woman in Rome carrying a baby, she imagined it to be the Christ-child, and describes how she would: "cryin, roryn, & wepyn as [th]ei sche had seyn Crist in hys childhode" (86). Her experiential re-enactments of all aspects of Jesus' life are triggered by the most homely and domestic scenes, and so she cannot escape the affective connection she has to Jesus' human manifestation because she is constantly surrounded by reminders of it.

For Kempe, even adult males (especially the attractive ones) seem to pose a perception-problem for her. When she sees:

> ... a semly man, sche had gret peyn to lokyn on hym les [th]an sche myth a seyn hym [th]at was bo[th]e God & man. & [th]erfor sche cryed many tymes & oftyn whan sche met a semly man & wept & sobbyd ful sor in [th]e manhod of Crist as sche went in [th]e stretys at Rome [th]at [th]ei [th]at seyn hir wondryd ful mych on hir, for [th]ei knew not [th]e cawse (86).

What Kempe seeks is a physical substitute for her lover/husband/brother/son/lord Jesus. She uses everything at her disposal to access a pathway to the divine, while remaining aware of the impact—didactic, affective or otherwise—which she has on the audience who view her story unfolding, those who watch and "wondryd ful mych on hir." But her audience does not know what she is reacting to because they cannot see it, and thus at times like this her message is in fact lost. She is not always able to articulate what she wants her experience to "say," because she relies on her own behavior and her own interpretation of it—and so her story, as lived experience, often falls on deaf ears. This might in fact be the primary reason she believes Christ is so insistent that her story be at last given the privilege of the written, and thus divine, Word.

Affective piety structures how Kempe lives and responds to the world around her, and she in her own way masters the techniques of eliciting and experiencing affective response by so merging her devotional and daily lives that the two become inseparable. She often re-writes the Passion events in her mind with personal anecdotes which place her close to the action, and so re-tells it in her experience. Her most intense and affective meditations on the Passion occur while on pilgrimage in Jerusalem and around the Holy Land. Kempe the medieval pilgrim visits Mount Calvary, the tomb, the stone on which Jesus was laid after the deposition, the place where the "holy cros was berijd," the room where the apostles received the Holy Ghost, and even the place of Mary's burial. She was no doubt regaled with myriad stories and versions of the crucial events, stories which served to enhance her own devotional treasure-chest. When surrounded by the historical reality of her spiritual obsession, it makes sense that she would be overcome with emotion.

Kempe reacts to verbal, aural and visual stimuli, and her tears and sobbing seem to play the role of catapulting her into an emotional state of mind which further facilitates the visual imaging component of her devotion and turns the external manifestation of her devotion (her tears and behavior) into a didactic model. One vision she has on Calvary is especially rich with affective imagery, and the words themselves are meant to evoke the readers' own responses:

> Sche had so very contemplacyon in [th]e sygth of hir s[owle] as yf Crist had hangyn befor hir bodily eye in hys manhode. &, whan thorw dispensacyon of [th]e hy mercy of owyr Souereyn Savyowr Crist Ihesu it was grawntyd [th]is creatur to beholdyn so verily hys precyows tendyr body, alto-rent & toryn wyth scorgys, mor ful of wowndys [th]an euyr was duffehows of holys, hangyng vp-on [th]e cros wyth [th]e corown of thorn up-on hys heuyd, hys blysful handys, hys tendyr fete nayled to [th]e hard tre, [th]e reuerys of blood flowyng owt plentevowsly of euery membre, [th]e gresly & grevows wownde in hys precyows syde schedyng owt blood & watyr for hir lofe & hir saluacyon, [th]an sche fel down & cryed wyth lowde voys, wondyrfully turnyng & wrestyng hir body on euery syde, spredyng hir armys a-brode as-yf sche xulde a deyd, & not cowde kepyn hir fro crying,—and [th]ese bodily mevyngys for [th]e fyer of lofe [th]at brent so feruently in hir sowle wyth pur pyte & compassyon (70).

There is a definite verbal crescendo here. The spiritual eye sees things "as yf" they were real, reminding the reader how "real" this image is to Kempe. The text often uses multiple words to describe images which are especially powerful: the "precyows tendyr" body of Jesus, "alto-rent & toryn" with scourges; the "gresly & grevows" wound in his side. In addition, evocative adjectives are used to describe Jesus' limbs and the instrument of his crucifixion: "blysful handys," "tendyr fete," "hard tre," "precyows syde," building on the pain and suffering he experiences and bringing it into the realm of the reader.

By consciously or unconsciously "training" herself to respond to a wide range of affective triggers, Kempe guarantees herself continual access to a very personal and self-made form of devotional expression. She revels in such expression despite claiming at times that she wishes it was less intense; in "trewth," her "experiens" defines the "trewth" of who she is and comforts her as well as unsettles her.

Part of the problem in dealing with Margery Kempe lies in reconciling the disparate elements of a personality that, as portrayed in her own words, is at once profoundly self-referential, and profoundly self-deferential. She is obsessed with her own experience and its evolution, yet is self-negating and critical of her worthiness. Kempe's real text is an experiential one, well- removed indeed from the written words which record it, and removed yet further by the chronological gap which separates the events from their recording.

What then is the true nature of the spiritual exercise of Kempe's storytelling? Is the ultimate goal the path of re-creation or the finished product? To have two scribes copy and then rewrite an autobiography which began some twenty years before and is thus coloured by subsequent experience, emotion and the elusiveness of memory creates a hermeneutic nightmare for the reader, but if we are willing to see Kempe's life as the product, not the victim, of this literary shaping, the spiritual exercise for her becomes simply a refinement or re-writing of the past as a model for us, its future readers—and a way of ensuring that her story is not forgotten.

Notes

1. *The Book of Margery Kempe*, eds. Sanford Brown Meech and Hope Emily Allen, Oxford: Early English Text Society, 1940. 142. All references from the text are noted by page number in parentheses. ME "thorn" will be indicated in this paper by [th].
2. The full text is reproduced in *The Book of Margery Kempe*, 353-357. See also Sue Ellen Holbrook, "Margery Kempe and Wynkyn de Worde", in *The Medieval Mystical Tradition in England*: Exeter Symposium IV (Papers read at Dartington Hall, July 1987), ed. Marion Glasscoe. Cambridge, 1987. 27-46.
3. *Imitatio Christi* takes many forms in the Middle Ages, in secular, religious and mystical domains. The physicality of Christ's body forms the most intense point of focus. Nicholas Love's Mirror is a characteristic manifestation of this form of *imitatio Christi*. But *imitatio Christi* and the physical emulation it usually en-

tailed often took many forms for both men and women, including fasting, self-flagellation, and self-defilement. Other, involuntary forms of suffering included "bodily effusions and elongations, stigmata, tears, and seizures. Finally, a third kind of imitation, most familiarly demonstrated in the life of St. Francis, was subsumed by those interior models of devotion associated with Christ's Passion during the late Middle Ages", Karma Lochrie, *Margery Kempe and Translations of the Flesh*. Philadelphia, 1991. 15.

4. See for instance Valerie M. Lagorio, "Defensorium Contra Oblectratores: A 'Discerning' Assessment of Margery Kempe", in *Mysticism: Medieval & Modern*, ed. Valerie M. Lagorio, Elizabethan & Renaissance Studies, 92:20, Series Editor James Hogg (Austria, 1986) 29-48; Francoise Le Saux, "'Hir not lettyrd': Margery Kempe and Writing," in *Writing & Culture*, ed. Balz Engler (Tubingen, 1992) 53-68; John C. Hirsh, "Author and Scribe in The Book of Margery Kempe," *Medium Aevum* 44 (1975) 145-150.

The Complexity of Storytelling in Louise Erdrich's *Tracks*

Karen Wallace

In *The Sacred Hoop* Paula Gunn Allen writes, "How does one survive in the face of collective death? Bearing witness is one solution, but it is singularly tearing, for witnessing genocide—as with conversion—requires that someone listen and comprehend."[1] In this paper, I use Gunn Allen's assertion to analyze the juxtaposition of the main characters, Nanapush and Pauline in Louise Erdrich's *Tracks*. Their stories reveal the process of spiritual and cultural genocide which Native people must battle and the degrees of compromise they must make. As the local priest Father Damien tells Nanapush, "Your sin is not the wrong of witnessing, but of divulgence."[2] Survivors of the near decimation at Turtle Mountain, these characters narrate and reconstruct tribal identity. Erdrich's representation of the oral tradition reveals storytelling as an inherently complex and often dangerous endeavor, as evidenced by Father Damien's comment.

Nanapush and Pauline's experiences as storytellers, however, are radically different. Nanapush, far more self aware than Pauline, explains the conflict of adapting to modern circumstances that he feels: "I know what's fact, and have never been afraid of talking. Our trouble came from living, from liquor, and the dollar bill" (4). Part of the task Nanapush sets for himself is to record the history of change at Turtle Mountain to his granddaughter Lulu, the last Nanapush. The capacity for speech, and the power of the speaker, emerges as the crucial element for survival. Nanapush, one of the last Ojibway to live the old ways, whose first language is Anishnabe but who can read and write English, talks his way out of death. He tells Lulu, "I talked both languages in streams that ran alongside each other....The sound of my own voice convinced me I was alive" (7).

Nanapush is clearly the Ojibway trickster Nanabozho, infamous for his irreverence and excess. As Franchot Ballinger suggests,

> Rather than defining social limits, he deconstructs them; and instead of affirming the greater social order, his journeys continually threaten social disorder....In this role, Trickster represents not the creation of social reality but a comic cautionary social image of potentially dangerous human behavior.[3]

Nanapush assures the community's survival by questioning it, by disrupting people's complacency. As Gunn Allen explains, "[Trickster] is a metaphor for all the foolishness and the anger that have characterized American Indian life in the centuries since invasion...his irreverence for everything...even life itself [enables his survival]."[4]

Throughout *Tracks*, the threat of death, physical or cultural, is manifest as drowning. Pauline asserts early in the narrative that drowning is "the death a Chippewa cannot survive"(11). When Nanapush narrates the story of his survival following an epidemic at the reservation, he recalls finding Fleur, the last of the Pillager medicine clan, and saving her life. His story relies on images of drowning, particularly significant because Fleur cannot swim, yet survives death-by-drowning three times. Witnessing the deaths of her entire family has driven Fleur nearly insane. Out of danger finally, she and Nanapush sit silently in his house, trying to make sense of their loss. He tells Lulu later, "We felt the spirits of the dead so near that at length we just stopped talking. This made it worse. Their names grew within us, swelled to the brink of our lips...We were filled with the water of the drowned, cold and black, airless water that lapped against the seal of our tongues or leaked slowly from the corners of our eyes. Within us, like ice shards, their names bobbed and shifted" (6). Father Damien eventually comes to see if they've survived the consumption. Nanapush, surprised that life has continued despite his and Fleur's silence, makes the most of the moment: "My voice rasped at first when I tried to speak, but then...I was off and talking...I began to creak and roll. I gathered speed. I talked...in streams that ran alongside each other, over every rock, around every obstacle" (7).

Nanapush says, in trying to explain his own nearly incessant speech: "Talk is an old man's last vice...I shouldn't have been caused to live so long, shown so much of death, had to squeeze so many stories in the corners of my brain. They're all attached and once I start there is no end to telling...I saved myself by starting a story...I got well by talking. Death could not get a word in edgewise, grew discouraged and traveled on" (46). Gunn Allen suggests that "The oral tradition is more than a record of a people's culture. It is the creative source of their collective and individual selves. When that wellspring of identity is tampered with, the sense of self is also tampered with....The oral tradition is a living body...which enables it to accommodate itself to the real circumstances of a people's lives. That is its strength, but it is also its weakness."[5]

Pauline has trouble integrating new experiences and embodies this weakness. Frustration colors her narrative throughout the novel and explains her arrogance as well as her unreliability as a narrator. In *Native American Postcolonial Psychology*, Bonnie and Eduardo Duran explain the perception which Pauline signifies: "[following attempts at cultural genocide and with] the victim's complete loss of power comes despair...the psyche reacts by internalizing what appears to be genuine power...which is merely a caricature of the power actually taken from Native American people. At this point, the self-worth of the individual and/or group has sunk to a level of despair tantamount to self-hatred."[6] As Nanapush observes of Pauline, "She was born a liar, and sure to die one. The practice of deception was so constant with her that it got to be a kind of truth" (53). Pauline mimics those whom she believes have power. Pauline tries to assume a similar power from her status as an outsider, imagining that this gives her objectivity, to re-create in other people her own feelings of deprivation. Thus she recalls a story Nanapush had once told about witnessing the unprovoked slaughter of the buffalo: "...killed for their tongues and hides, the beasts that survived grew strange and unusual. They lost their minds....They tried their best to cripple one another, to fall or die. They tried suicide. They tried to do away with their young. They knew they were going, saw their terrible end"(140). Pauline sees Nanapush's story as a metaphor for her people's collective history as well as for her own personally.

Nanapush tries to identity the source of Pauline's hostility for Lulu: As he explains,

> You might not remember what people I'm talking about, the skinners, of whom Pauline was the only trace of those who died and scattered. She was different from the Puyats I remembered, who were always an uncertain people, shy, never leaders in our dances and cures. She was, to my mind, an unknown mixture of ingredients....We never knew what to call her, or where she fit or how to think when she was around. So we tried to ignore her, and that worked as long as she was quiet. But she was different once her mouth opened and started to wag...she was given to improving the truth....Pauline schemed to gain attention by telling odd tales that created damage (38-90).

Envisioning herself as a martyr, Pauline identifies with Christ and her bearing witness becomes a conversion narrative. She tells the story of her calling,

Christ's special interest in her and her attempts to remain pure: "at the Judgment, it would be my soul sacrificed, my poor body turned on the devil's wheel. And yet, despite that future, I was condemned to suffer in this life also... I felt all" (66). She attempts to destroy the Turtle Mountain community, taking great pleasure in, as she says, "escorting Death in." She assumes the right of re-creation through her voyeurism at the moment of death: "I was a midwife that [families] hailed down with both interest and dread. I was their own fate...[but] Death would pass me over, just like men did, and I would live a long strict life" (75). Earning a place in the community as the one to prepare the dead for burial, Pauline offers the antithesis of creation, she oversees the "birth" of the soul into death.

The first corpse she prepares is that of a young girl whom she watches die. Significantly, she accepts Mary's death as the turning point in her own life and describes the process as though she's witnessed a drowning: "[Mary] let [death] fill her like dark water and then...she began to pull away. But she was moored by her jaw, caught....She drifted. Her face loosened and her mouth shut" (67-68). Pauline believes that she has played an integral part in Mary's death, the image of silence emphasizing Pauline's own speech, and revels in the morbid position that sustains her throughout the novel. She sees herself in the image of Mary's death and often describes her own relationship to either Christ or her tribe in terms of drowning. In one instance, after she's left town to move to the convent and become a nun, she begins to starve herself as self-imposed penance, to prove the strength of her devotion, and Sister Saint Anne has to force her to eat: "I clenched my jaw and won a form of triumph as she lost her patience...I closed my eyes. In order not to breathe, I began to travel...I walked, unwilling, the old way to matchimanito Lake... I must have given voice to some dreadful note. At any rate, I must have opened my mouth. For I was swallowing a sudden rush of salty fish broth when I woke....You were so ill you did not know what you were saying, [Sister Anne] suggested" (193-4).

The contrast between Nanapush and Pauline's sense of bearing witness is a function of the rejection Pauline feels. The novel's title refers at times to the marks of a people's history, those things that confirm their existence. For Nanapush, though, tracks represent the telltale marks of lies: "You know how old chickens scratch and gabble. That's how the tales started, all the gossip...all the things people said without knowing and then believed, since they heard it with their own ears, from their own lips" (9). Like the chickens' scratches, Pauline's stories leave a distinct trail, one that reveals her deception.

As Nanapush explains, "There is a story to it the way there is a story to all, never visible while it is happening. Only after, when an old man sits dreaming and talking in his chair, the design springs clear" (34). Nanapush cautions Lulu and expresses doubt at Pauline's ability to identify the pattern that emerges from the web of stories. He reinforces the theme of multiplicity and the ambiguity inherent therein. Pauline's frustration as a witness, comes from the fact that tracks, whether they are footprints in the snow or words on a page, do not have a convenient linear structure leading one to a finite end. As Gunn Allen writes, "Reconciling the opposites of life and death, of celebration and grief, of laughter and rage, is no simple task, yet it is one worthy of our best understanding and our best effort."[7] In Nanapush we see the acceptance, if not resolution, of contradiction, but in Pauline we see only her burgeoning anger and incipient violence. Her ultimate rejection of Turtle Mountain is based on the birth of her daughter. It is in this critical, liminal space that Pauline decides that she has sinned beyond redemption, that her own contradictions must finally be resolved by choosing a direct and solitary path to God: "since I had already betrothed myself to God, I tried to force [the child] out of me, to punish, to drive it from my womb" (131). Once her daughter Marie has been literally pulled from her, Pauline feels free to talk herself into a new reality.

She returns to the reservation, undecided still as to how Indian she can be without sacrificing her newfound sense of control and sets herself in opposition to Fleur. As Nanapush comments, "There was no way we could have known, not until Pauline returned as well, of the terrible and strange things that had happened in that white town" (34). Referring specifically to violence Fleur has suffered, we also see the implications for Pauline as a victim of a violent assimilation.

From a family of mixed bloods, Pauline had always wanted to escape Indianness: "I wanted to be like my mother, who showed her half-white. I wanted to be like my grandfather, pure Canadian. That was because even as a child I saw that to hang back was to perish" (14). In Pauline, a vivid example of internalized racism and self-hatred, Erdrich demonstrates the process by which creates an illusion of power. In order to exert control over her environment in an attempt to externalize and therefore rid herself of self-hate, Pauline terrorizes other Indians, particularly Fleur. She tells a story intending to create a reality in which she dominates, in which, paradoxically, Fleur remains invulnerable. Though Fleur's compassion is what she desires most, Pauline explains, "[Fleur] was the one who closed the door or swung it open. Between the people and the gold-eyed creature in the lake....Fleur was the hinge. It was like that with Him too, Our Lord, who had obviously made the whites more shrewd, as they grew in number, all around... while the Indians receded and coughed to death and drank. It was clear that Indians were not protected by the thing in the lake or by the other Manitous who lived in trees...There would have to come a turning, a gathering, another door. And it would be Pauline who opened it...Not Fleur" (139). Pauline is caught between desiring intimacy and feeling disempowered by it. Her sense of competition with Fleur, Nanapush's favorite, compels Pauline to betray Fleur, nearly all her subsequent actions intended to deny that complicity.

Fearing the tension in her, Fleur and the others find they can no longer accept Pauline's lying. Pauline complains that "They treated me as they would a white. I was ignored most of the time. When they did address me they usually spoke English" (146). Finally, Pauline and Nanapush engage in an overt battle, each trying to outwit the other for control of the story. Unfortunately, Nanapush's skill, his ability to humiliate Pauline, only makes her that much more embittered and resentful and fuels her anger. "Some saints endured burning pitch or redhot tongs," she says. "...Predictable shapes, these martyrdoms. Mine took another form. Embarrassment" (152). The climax of the novel comes when Pauline determines to destroy Nanapush.

Pauline rows out into the middle of the lake, a pathetic and absurd figure in a leaky boat. She sees Fleur on the shore, observing that "Her heavy black clothes, her shawl, the way she held herself so rigid, suggested a door in the blackness. I stood before it and then she turned, so slowly I heard the hinges creak. A moment and I was inside where I could not breathe and water filled me, cold and black water of the drowned....I thought I would be shut there, but she turned again and off she walked, a black slot into the air, a passage into herself" (200). Pauline's boat is set adrift, the anchor severed, and she is forced to come ashore, throwing off her heavy robes as she does. Her nakedness signaling a metaphoric birth, she determines to find the Monster, Satan, and destroy him before he has another chance to defile her, to prevent her from becoming white and therefore invulnerable. "A light began to open in the sky and the thing grew a human shape, one that I recognized in gradual stages. Eventually, it took on the physical form of Napoleon Morrissey" (202-03). Marie's father, Napoleon, has passed out on the shore near where she emerges. Certain that she's right, that the devil has taken the form of this living man to fool her, she drags Napoleon's body into the weeds and strangles him with her rosary. Turning to walk home, "I realized I was still naked...I rolled in slough mud until my arms and breasts, every part of me was coated. I flung the beads high in a tangling arc toward the deepest bush. Then I stood. I was a poor and noble creature now, dressed in earth like Christ" (203). Her conversion is almost complete. The nuns care for her when she goes back, but finally send her away because even they recognize her instability. Pauline tries to explain her exile; "I asked for the grace to accept, to leave

Pauline behind, to remember that my name, any name, was no more than a crumbling skin. *Leopolda*. I tried out the unfamiliar syllables. They fit. They cracked in my ears like a fist through ice" (205). She is pulled from the freezing water of death by the sound of her own speech. She confirms Nanapush's assertion that speech is survival. Recalling Nanapush's introduction, we see how Pauline has become the inverse of what he represents. Talking about the presence of the dead, his and Fleur's need to move beyond their sorrow, illuminates Pauline's final words. Nanapush had said, "We felt the spirits of the dead so near...Their names grew within us, swelled to the brink of our lips...We were filled with the water of the drowned, that lapped against the seal of our tongues...Within us, like ice shards, their names bobbed and shifted" (9). The final narrative conflict occurs in Pauline's last abortive attempt to subsume Nanapush's story within her own. Failing, Pauline does, in effect, drown and Leopolda is born in her place. Gunn Allen concludes that "the oral tradition is vital; it heals itself and the tribal web by adapting to the flow of the present while never relinquishing its connection to the past."[8] This is most clear in Nanapush's narrative, recovering history by telling it to his granddaughter so that she can repeat it. As he tells her, "I talked on and on until you lost yourself inside the flow of it, until you entered the swell and ebb and did not sink but were sustained" (167). Lulu listens and comprehends. She emerges as the focal point of Erdrich's fourth novel *The Bingo Palace*, an old woman who carries the knowledge of her people with her so that, finally, we see in her the successful acculturation that so consistently eluded Pauline. *Tracks* bears witness to the experience of a besieged people, offering a solution to the reality of genocidal assault. As Gunn Allen emphasizes, it is one worthy of our best understanding and our best effort.

Endnotes

1. Paula Gunn Allen, *The Sacred Hoop: Recovering the Feminine in American Indian Traditions* (Boston: Beacon Press, 1986) 156.
2. Louise Erdrich, *Tracks* (New York: HarperCollins, 1988) 216. Further references to *Tracks* will appear in the text.
3. Franchot Ballinger, "Living Sideways: Social Themes and Social Relationships in Native American Trickster Tales," *American Indian Quarterly*, 13.1 (Winter 1989): 20.
4. Paula Gunn Allen, *The Sacred Hoop*, 158.
5. Ibid., 224.
6. Eduardo Duran and Bonnie Duran, *Native American Postcolonial Psychology* (Albany, NY: State University of New York Press, 1995) 29.
7. Gunn Allen, *The Sacred Hoop*, 45.
8. Ibid. 165.

Telling Stories: A Power Paradigm in Michael Ondaatje's *English Patient*

Afra Kavanagh

This paper has grown out of my increasing conviction that by inscribing distinctions between men and women in texts, writers, whether overtly or covertly, consciously or unconsciously, perpetuate traditional stereotypes of men and women and the relations between them. Such inscription can become a perceptual and behavioural model for men and women. Also, it entrenches a power structure that favours traditional masculinist values over emergent egalitarian ones. That is one of the two reasons I began to take a close look at Michael Ondaatje's representations of gender roles in his award winning novel, *The English Patient*. The other reason is that I am of the same opinion as Carolyn Heilbrun who says that "our future salvation lies in a movement away from sexual polarization and the prison of gender toward a world in which individual roles and the modes of personal behaviour can be freely chosen" (ix). The ideal of androgyny is surprisingly to be found in Ondaatje's work, alongside a more traditional portrayal of male and female roles.

In Ondaatje, I found a power paradigm suggested by the stories told, by who tells them, and by how they are told. In general, it can be said that we, individually or as audiences, admire the people who have a good story to tell and who tell it well, and let them dominate the discourse. Such dominance translates into greater influence–those who tell the great storie (by whatever definition) are followed, and remembered, and thus influence generations to come. By noting that in the novel, Ondaatje ascribes the better stories to the men, we understand that he is conferring on them a greater influence, and while this may be representative of recent and current reality, it stands in clear conflict with an opposite desire evident in Ondaatje's text which is to try and draw a new breed of males and females who are not restricted by the old codes.

In *The English Patient*, then, relations between the genders seem to be configured around the telling of and the listening to stories. The author assigns a higher value to telling, associating it with composing and controlling the narrative, in other words, writing, which he depicts as a manly art through several phallic symbols. The fictive cosmos of the male teller is portrayed as much larger than the female's, and his narrative strategies more complex—i.e. postmodern. These distinctions are to be found in the way the individuals themselves tell their stories, and also in the way the author tells their stories. Also significant, the English patient himself is allowed to narrate without the mediation of a narrator, and he sometimes subsumes the role of the omniscient author by narrating in the third person.

It is my contention that the feminist reader who is aware that "whoever controls the discourse controls the official version" (Bok 114), is able to resist the power structure inscribed in the novel and that is summed up in the reading lesson when the English patient corrects Hana's reading, as if she were his child or his student, and in her invitation to him to begin telling his story by asking, "How were you burnt?" Giving the power of telling to the English patient and assigning a traditional listening role to Hana may be expressive of a patriarchal ethic still evident in Ondaatje's writing despite his efforts elsewhere in the text to reject traditional masculinist values and outmoded power structures.

In the novel, we are told many stories; many of them are about men. Some are told by the omniscient- author/narrator, and some are told by the characters themselves. We are told and retold the story of Almasy's desert explorations and his disasterous love affair with Katharine Clifton, the wife of a British Intelligence man.This affair leads to the death of both Cliftons, to Almasy's involvement in the war as a spy for the Germans, and to the plane crash that caused his burns. In contrast, we are given only a brief account of Hana's loss of a father and a lover; her terminated pregnancy is merely mentioned, and her lover is never named.

For many of us, reading is closely associated with stories, and there is much about reading in the novel. There is specifically the scene mentioned earlier in which the English patient instructs Hana how to read Kipling: "Read him slowly, dear girl..." he says. This positioning of the older male as teacher and the female as student is in accordance with gendered stereotypes of these roles. The English patient is given the function of correcting Hana. This relationship of the "learned" to the learner is further highlighted by the English patient's calling Hana, "dear girl," a phrase of endearment which, it has been demonstrated, implies condescension by a speaker who does not care enough to call a woman by her name (As a matter of fact, Hana remains unnamed for several chapters. Similarly, in the story Katharine reads out, the queen, who is central to the action, is not named, while as her men, Gyges and Candaules, are). But in this narrative, the teacher is prostrate, confined to a bed, and completely dependent on his student for his well being, for his life even, so the "power" in the relatioship should be held by the nurse, the professional, the juicy and alive young woman. Yet, it is not. The question then arises: is Ondaatje, as the creator of these characters and their world, trying to write beyond the traditional restrictions of the images of the young and old, and of male and female, or is he caught, perhaps unconsciously, in the trap of gender stereotyping, letting the burnt-out-case yield so much power, including the power of knowing more than Hana (or any of the others), as well as the power of correcting her?

My analysis of the novel reveals that Ondaatje was both portraying the relationship between storyteller and listener as within the paradigm of power contained in patriarchal values, *and* attempting significant alterations to traditional representations of men and women and their interactions. For example, he focuses on Hana at the end of the novel as her own person, independent and admirable, qualities usually considered masculine, and he portrays Kip as sensitive and intuitive, qualities frequently ascribed to women. However, Ondaatje subordinates the women's stories to those of the males in the number of lines or pages devoted to each, in the type of story assigned to each, and in the way these stories are narrated. In the fictive cosmos created by Ondaatje, the power of the story is given to the English patient, and Hana is assigned the passive role of listener. So, there are no scenes where Hana tells her story to any of the other characters intra-diegetically, but there are many scenes of the English patient telling her his. Hana is depicted as a consumer of stories and we consequently perceive her as creatively inferior. She is someone who is seduced by the story in the books she reads, and by the oral telling of the English patient. The English patient himself is portrayed as an active reader, a writer at times and a storyteller. He is aware of the writing style and condition of, for example, Herodotus, whose *Histories* has become his (Almasy's) commonplace book. He also composes and controls the narrative which dominates the novel, and sometimes subsumes the role of the omniscient author as narrator in the third person. Hana is depicted as an encouraging listener, while the English patient chooses how long and on what topic to speak. These observations lead me to conclude that even though Ondaatje attempts to depict post-war men and women who are equal, he nevertheless portrays them as interacting in conventional ways.

Ondaatje introduces two kinds of stories in the novel, and both of them underrepresent females. First, there are the stories in books. *Kim, The Last of the Mohicans, The Red and the Black*, and *The Histories*. These are all written by males, and have male protagonists, which poses a problem for the female reader. Hana has no choice but to identify with male characters (She states: "I am Pico," and "I am the Mohican of Danforth Avenue.") primarily because of the absence of positive female role models in most literary fictions—for as feminist critics have pointed out, what reader, male or female, would desire the life or the end of Moll Flanders, Emma Bovary, or Anna Karenina? Secondly, among the oral self-representational stories, there is not one by Katharine. Katharine has a section named after her in the book, and is very important to the novel, but she never materializes as her own narrator. Instead, she is spoken for by Almasy. Ondaatje does not use her as a "seperate" character, or narrator. As a matter of fact, he delegates her to "the hell of being described by others." Her story is assumed to be "his" story as it gets told by the English patient. He has control over it and is allowed unmediated telling of it. He tells and retells without any checks on the "truth" of his version. Katharine is simply reported by Almasy, and while he continues to be an intriguing enigma, his identity undetermined, hers is fixed by him. He tells of her reading out the Gyges story and notes her emphasis, "Are you listening, Geoffry?" as she obviously addresses her husband, but then he proceeds to shape the story to portray himself as seduced by love into getting involved in the war, as if Katharine had invited him into her life, and not that he had (mis)read a role for himself into the tale. This last fact is made clear when the narrator says, "it seemed as if suddenly, a path opened for him..." as he listened to her and fell in love with her. What he subsequently develops and tells Hana, and the reader, is a story about him that he "heard" her tell, not the one she actually told about herself and her husband.

In *The English Patient*, Ondaatje depicts men and women as approaching texts differently. For example, in this novel, Hana, reads to escape. The English patient, in contrast, reads to understand both the historical past and his own involvement in the war. He is shown as having the intellectual ability to draw parallels and conclusions, and to visualize the big picture. Hana is shown to dwell over personal issues such as her father's death or her stepmother's character. This difference in approach to a story is significant. Hana is shown as regarding the book-stories as a substiute for life. She sinks into novels. She is satisfied by books, and needs to read. The novels for her, we are told, are a door out of her cell, and "half her life" (7). Books furnish her with something absent from her life. It is as if she, as well as the author, can not see her role in the war as an adventure, a puzzle, i.e. worthwhile writing material. She identifies with Robinson Crusoe, and other male protagonists in the novels she reads, not recognizing the gender heresy involved. She is what Judith Fetterly categorizes as the immasculated reader, the woman reader who accepts the universal appeal of the male writers' use of the masculine as the norm, as the inclusive gender, not even recognizing that she, as a woman, has been excluded from those texts. The stories are also a way of travel into spaces otherwise perhaps closed to her as a woman. "Take me somewhere," she thinks as the English patient launches into a narrative. For her, narrative presents an "other" world. Ondaatje, on the other hand, presents the English patient as travelling back in his narrative into his own past. The English patient is also presented as a superior reader because he seeks to complete the work in front of him. He cuts out and pastes into his copy of the *Histories* as he, in essense, produces his own version of the book. His power comes from the knowledge he has and that knowledge draws the others to him. He is then in a position to instruct "the girl," Hana. Also, when Hana reads outloud to the English patient, she selects which parts to read, and "the books, ...as he listened intently or not, had gaps of plot like sections of a road washed out by storms..." (7). She may select, but the English patient can listen "intently or not," thus demonstrating his power to accept or ignore her reading.

This difference in approach becomes even more significant when Ondaatje's text implies that writing is a gendered activity. Because of his condition, the English patient does not read to Hana. Instead he speaks his story to her, and is presented as the writer of his own history, as someone who has lived the narrative, and is now composing it. Creation and art are natural for him, because they are masculine activities, as the following phallic symbols used by Ondaatje confirm. Art is compared to a wand (no comment), and an Aladdin's lamp (i.e. you rub it and it releases a genie!).That Hana is not a writer is mentioned several times. She says, "If I were a writer, I'd write in bed," and then is shown climbing into bed like a child with "schoolbooks and pencils," and the reader infers that these are not the tools of a real writer. Hana is shown as unable to even write a letter to her stepmother in Canada. She also plays a traditional female role in conversation and asks the questions to begin the discourse. She climbs into the English patient's bed to warm him, and asks: "How were you burnt?" Then he, in male mode, takes over by deciding what to talk about, and for how long (Showalter 136). From then on, his voice seems to dominate the novel.

This listening role assigned to Hana is part of Ondaatje's narrative strategy wherein she is used as "an opening act." The novel begins with her at work in the garden, then lets her lead us into the villa, so that we may be introduced to the English patient, who is Christ-like and male. Later on she is similarly used to introduce the other male protagonist, Kip. She is a pretty girl, and as in the song, just like a melody used as a "prelude." The narrator describes a Gershwin song the characters listen to, and says that "the musician did not wish to leave the small parlour of the introduction and enter the song, kept wanting to remain here, where the story had not begun, as if enamoured by a maid in the prologue" (109). Hana is the maid (in both senses), her world the parlour and the prologue. Her story never really begins, even though they are all enamoured of her, and her ending is a fizzle. It is as if she is not at all a part of the war novel that Ondaatje has constructed, a novel that is part of a genre which, as Kip thinks, ends with the successful dismantling of a bomb, i.e. a heroic masculine act.

How the character's stories are told also differs. Hana's narrative is told simply in a straightforward chronology which is less challenging and interesting than the complex method used for telling the stories of Kip and the English patient. This difference in style suggests that her story is less important than theirs. Besides, her world itself is shown to be relatively less significant than theirs. Hana's world, that the narrator says she has created and is happy in, is judged as "miniature" and child-like. Her childishness is evident in the narrator's description of her late night game of hopscotch, and of the tag games she and Kip engage in. This suggestion that the woman's world is small, and therefore insignificant, is part of a stereotype that limits women to the space between the boudoir and the altar (Rhoethke quoted by Prose). Ondaatje too presents the woman's (i.e. Hana's) domain as the villa and the garden. And gardening, which is suffused with biblical resonance, is a kind of ghetto for women. It has been noted that gardens in literature have been presented as the only domain where women have control. And a garden made by a woman, Louise A. DeSalva says, maybe an act of creation and procreation, but it is also "the only terrain which a woman is allowed to conquer; the only battlefield upon which she can command regiments" (103).

In contrast, the author-narrator and the English patient, who are sometimes indistinguishable, set about to create a much bigger world than Hana's, a masculinist world of war and great causes. This tendency towards the grand scheme by male writers has been noted by some women writers and critics, such as Francine Prose. She writes that there is an existing premise that "Men write sweeping, phone-book-size sagas of the big city, of social class, of our national destiny, our technological past and future. They produce boldly experimental visionary fiction that periodically revives the moribund novel." She thinks that critics and readers eventually buy into this myth and assume that a book is important because it deals with war. This valorizing of a macro over a micro-cosm is evident in Ondaatje's own novel that scoops up everything in its sweep: world war, Renaissance art, colonial literature, ancient history, desert exploration, fading colonialism, etc. etc...

When a writer creates a fictive heterocosm, s/he tries to engage the reader. On the other hand, when a reader begins to read a book, s/he will only engage in the world created by the author if s/he can recognize or imagine that world. In the *English Patient*, the story of Hana is like many books that, as Ondaatje writes, "begin with an author's assurance of order. One slipped into their waters with a silent paddle" (93). But if the order the author assures the reader of is not recognizable (credible), the reader will resist its encoded ideology. Such a resisting reader rejects any inscription in the text of the status quo of the patriarchy, because such a reader is "conscious of the tradition of women's oppression in patriarchal culture, and is committed to breaking the patterns of that oppression by calling attention to to the way some texts can perpetuate it" (Fetterly 489). Thus a woman reading the *English Patient* who positions herself as a feminist reading the text, will become aware of the version of female subjectivity offered by the novel. Characterizations and plot in Ondaatje present women as stereotypes, and Hana is presented as a saint. By presenting her this way, Ondaatje does not have to deal with the problematics of the female self and its construction. Katharine is presented as the opposite stereotype, the adulteress. She is the seductress that causes the great man's fall. The men (the English patient, and Caravaggio), on the other hand, may be morally implicated, but they are also morally complex, therefore unique and intriguing.

The novel *The English Patient* permits the males to be the ones to hold forth, makes them owners of the voice, so the English patient is the only character allowed unmediated narrative. Furthermore, the English patient's story is like another type described by Ondaatje in the text. "Novels," he writes, "commenced with hesitation or chaos. Readers were never fully in balance. A door a lock a weir opened and they rushed through..."(93). Having assigned to Hana the watery grave of the novel that the reader immerses himself in and that requires nothing from him, Ondaatje uses postmodern strategies of disjointed and fragmented representation of experience and time to keep the reader unbalanced and at the same time engaged in the men's search for meaning.

In summing up, Ondaatje does try to present a new world order. He draws Kip as the new man, whose long hair, and hairless body suggest to Hana when she lies next to him in the tent, that she is embracing "an Indian Goddess." Kip himself tells Hana and the reader "That he had slept beside a statue of an angel, half male, half female that he had found beautiful...and for the first time during the war felt at peace" (90). Hana's portrait also transcends gender lines. The omniscient author sometimes disregards her gender and ascribes to her male roles and names. At the beginning of the novel, she is shown cutting her hair off, wearing a man's sneakers, and toiling in the garden like Adam. She is shown as able to lift and move the English patient single handedly, and is a Christ figure in the scene where she drags around the six-foot crucifix. Hana and Kip may be seen as Ondaatje's attempt to depict a new generation of androgynous men and women who have both male and female traits.

But the ending includes punishments and rewards that show a privileging of the males' stories, and thus their persons and their lives. The English patient may have blundered causing death and pain, but he is presented and received as a romantic sage worthy of Hana's devotion, who like Abishag, the handmaiden to King David, warms his bed. Kirpal may be making a mistake rejecting his friends along with Western racist politics, but he is given the last scene and the last save, and a full life as a doctor and a family man. But Hana who loved them all and was their family, and who was first to reject the violence of war ends up alone in Toronto, after Kirpal leaves her as if she were a part of the European dealmaking. In the final scene, Hana's story is absorbed into Kip's and she is placed on the same plane with Kip's daughter. Kip is depicted as the hero who in one swoop saves the objects let fall on two different continents (!) by each of them.

A feminist reader needs to be aware that the novelist controls the portrait of the world that he creates, and of the men and women in it. Putting these images in a book, as Herodotus, and the writer of the bible did, as Ondaatje does, creates a lasting official version that has the power to influence generations. The English patient walks out of the fire burnt to the skin, but makes sure to save his book. When the English patient dies, Kip predicts, the others will bury him, but his book will outlast him. A feminist reader must be able to resist these images of a man-produced, and man-preserved culture. She must also resist becoming immasculated by the values imbedded in this "epic," a war story even if it claims to be rejecting wars and epics.

In closing, a patriarchal ethic is still evident in Ondaatje's writing despite his efforts elsewhere in the text to reject traditional masculinist values, and to expose the conspiracy of the powerful who collaborated in the war that caused so much destruction. And while he attempts androgynous characters, he also depicts both Hana and Katharine as subservient to the males in the quality of their narrative. Also he deals those two heroic women characters harsh endings comparable to those of traditional novels, so that Katharine the transgressor dies while waiting for Almasy to return and Hana is abandoned by Kip. Furthermore, his own narrative provides to the men a larger sphere: a whole desert, or a whole section of Italy, while the women are restricted to the enclosures of house or hospital, camp or cave. The men's stories have a greater impact on readers because they are treated with greater respect, and we are exposed to them at greater length. Their narratives depicted in the *English Patient* have author-ity and complexity, while the women's stories are either simple or absent.

Bibliography

Bok, Christian."Destructive Creation: the Politicization of Violence in the Works of Michael Ondaatje." *Canadian Literature 132 (1992): 109-24.*

Culler, Jonathan. "Reading as a Woman." *Feminisms.* Eds. Warhol and Herndl. 509-524.

De Salvo, Louise A. "Every Woman an Island: Vita-Sackville West, the Image of the City, and the Pastoral Idyll." *Women Writers and the City*. ed. Susan Merrill Squire. Knoxville: University of Tennessee Press, 1984. 97-113.

Fetterly, Judith. "Introduction: On the Politics of Literature." *Feminisms.* Eds. Warhol and Herndl. 492-508.

Heilbrun, Carolyn. *Toward a Recognition of Androgyny*: New York: Harper Colophon Books, 1974.

Mills, Sara. *Gendering the Reader.* London and Toronto: Harvester Wheatsheaf, 1994.

Ondaatje, Michael. *The English Patient.* Toronto: McLelland and Stewart, 1992.

Prose, Francine. "The Scent of a Woman's Ink." *Harper's Magazine.* June 1998: 61-68.

Selden, Ramen. *Practicing Theory and Reading Literature.* University of Kentucky Press, 1989.

Showalter, Elaine. "Critical Cross-dressing; Male Feminists and the Woman of the Year." *Men in Feminism.* Eds. Alex Jardine and Paul Smith. New York: Methuen. 1987. 116-136.

Valdes, Mario, and Owen Miller. Eds. *Identity of the Literary Text.* Toronto: University of Toronto Press, 1985.

Van Herk, Aretha. "Booking the Lover." *A Mazing Place: Writing Canadian Women Writing.* Eds. Shirley Newman and Smaro Kamboureli. Edmonton: Longspoon/NeWest, 1986. 276-286.

Warhol, Robyn and Diane F. Herndl. Eds. *Feminisms: An Anthology of Literary Theory and Criticism.* New Brunswick, N.J.: Rutgers UP, c1997.

CONTRIBUTORS

Cheryl Bartlet , as she likes to say, plays hockey and teaches Biology at University College of Cape Breton (UCCB). However there are more dimensions to her than these two. She is a significant scholar in her field of parasitology, and an educational innovator who is interested in the study of mind and consciousness, and in a variety of approaches to teaching and approaching science.

Anne Butler is a professor of History at Utah State University, Logan, Utah, and the editor of *Western Historical Quarterly*. She is the author of *Daughters of Joy, Sisters of Misery: Prostitution the American West, 1865-1890* and *Gendered Justice in the American West: Women Prisoners in Men's Penitentiaries*. Butler has appeared in and acted as consultant for many nationally broadcasted television shows and series.

Kofi Campbell is a PhD candidate at the University of Western Ontario whose primary interest is the construction of sexualities and identities. He has presented several conference papers on this topic, including one to last summer's ACCUTE (Association of Canadian College and University Teachers of English) Annual Conference.

Cheryl Cowdy Crawford is a second-year PhD candidate at York University. She is currently exploring the meaning of the suburb as a literary landscape in post-war Canadian literature.

Pilar Cuder-Dominguez is an Associate Professor at the University of Huelva, Spain, and she received her PhD from the University of Seville, Spain. She has been a member of the Spanish Association for Canadian Studies since its creation in 1988, and the Director of the Women's Studies Centre at the University of Huelva. She is currently researching intersections of discourses of gender, empire and nation in early Canadian woman writers. Her latest publication is titled: "Negotiations of Gender and Nationhood in Early Canadian Literature" *(International Journal for Canadian Studies*, 1998). Pilar Cuder-Dominguez was a Visiting professor at McGill University in 1997 and a Visiting scholar at Dalhousie University from May-September 1999.

Mary Flanagan is a digital artist and media maker who concentrates on issues around women in cyberculture. Currently she is an assistant professor in media study at the State University of New York at Buffalo and co-editor of *Reload: Rethinking Women in Cyberculture* from MIT Press (2000).

Tomie Hahn is Assistant Professor of Music at Tufts University where she teaches ethnomusicology. She began studying nihon buyo (Japanese traditional performance) at the age of four and given the professional state title Samie Tachibana in 1989. She also teaches and performs the shakuhachi (Japanese bamboo flute). Tomie has lectured extensively throughout the United States at such places as the American Museum of Natural History, Japan Society, the Metropolitan Museum of Art, and numerous universities. She is currently collaborating with composer Curtis Bahn on an interactive performance piece utilizing physical data sensors.

Nina Jaffe is an author and storyteller who is known both nationally and abroad for her retellings of Jewish and world folklore. Recent titles include: *The Cow of no Color: Justice Tales From Around the World* (co-authored with Steve Zeitlin) and *The Mysterious Visitor: Stories of the Prophet Elijah*. Ms. Jaffe works in the graduate faculty of Bank Street College of Education where, this year, she is a recipient of the Bank Street Writer's Award. She lives in New York City with her husband and son.

Mumbi Jonson is the founder and director of Association of Art and Books for Children in Toronto (AABC). She teaches children about African culture with hands-on art and literature workshops in schools and in the community. Jonson is a graduate of University of Toronto where she obtained a degree in sociology. As a children's author, her main area of interest is cultural representation of African-Caribbean Canadian experience in children's literature. She lives and works in Toronto.

Afra Kavanagh teaches English literature and writing to first year students at University College of Cape Breton (UCCB). Her primary research interest is Marian Engel, a Canadian novelist from the 1970s and 80s. She is also the coordinator of the Annual UCCB Storytelling Symposium.

Laurelle LeVert grew up in Sydney, Nova Scotia, and completed an undergraduate degree at King's College in Halifax;. She has Master's degrees in both the Classics and in Medieval Studies. Last year she defended at the Centre for Medieval Studies at the University of Toronto her dissertation on

"The Rhetoric of Response: Affectivity and Didacticism in Middle English Devotional Experiences of the Passion."

For the last two years, LeVert has been Dean of Residence at Loretto College, and has also done some part time teaching at the University of Toronto.

Justin Jaron Lewis is a doctoral student in Jewish Studies at the University of Toronto who hopes to complete his dissertation by 2002. In addition to his work on Hasidic stories, he has transcribed and is translating an Old Yiddish manuscript from the year 1504 about the lives of women in the author's time and in Biblical history. Lewis will be publishing in The *Readers Guide to Judaism* and in the electronic journal *Women in Judaism*. He also teaches an adult education course on Jewish texts.

Zabe MacEachren is completing her PhD research on the ways we learn about the environment by making things. Hearing and telling tales that focus on crafts and what hand-made items mean in our lives is just one of her passions.

Elizabeth Mood taught during the 1980's and early 90's in primary and secondary schools in the North of England, developing an interest in children storytelling within education. While teaching at a Middle School in Northumberland, she began collecting data on children narrating their own and their family histories, as well as on fictional narratives by children. This developed into a doctoral research thesis on oral narrative. She now lectures in English language and narrative at St. Martin's College in Lancaster, England.

Petra Lena Orloff studies and teaches English at Wayne State University, in Michigan.

Ona Siporin, adjunct instructor at Utah State University and assistant editor and book review editor of the *Western Historical Quarterly*, is a member of the Utah Performing Arts Team. Her work has been aired on National Public Radio, and her radio essays are collected in the the book, *Stories to Gather All Those Lost*. She worked for seven years as a resource artist at Sundance Institute Playwrights Lab and has recently received a grant from the Mountain West Center for her novel-in-progress.

Karen Wallace is Assistant Professor of English at the University of Wisconsin, Oshkosh. Her area of research and instruction is native American literature.

Wendy Welch is a storyteller and folklorist, and the convenor of the American Folklore Society's Storytelling section. She writes a storytelling column published in the United States and presents a radio program in Scotland. Recent performances include the Ulster and Glasgow Storytelling festivals, and Festival at the Edge, England.

Diane Wolkstein is a gifted teacher and a distinguished storyteller. She is the author of more than twenty books, including *Inanna, Queen of Heaven and Earth*. She is interested in stories about courageous women, and women in the bible.

Dan Yashinsky is the founder of the Toronto Festival of Storytelling. He is the author of, among other books, *The Storyteller at Fault* and of the award winning *Ghostwise: A Book of Midnight Stories*. Last summer he travelled across Canada to meet and record storytellers for a radio programme that was broadcast by CBC (The Canadian Broadcasting Corporation).

Emma Zevik has led maypole dancing from Beijing to Boston. She collects maypoles stories and images from around the world. She is a composer, artist and teacher. Her works–masks, maypoles, music–have been presented in Europe, Asia, Egypt and throughout the United States, including a full-length concert of her original music at Carnegie Recital Hall. A Visiting Professor at the Conservatory of Music in China from 1995-97, Dr. Zevik earned her PhD in Creative Arts from The Union Institute where she wrote her dissertation on maypoles.